© Boris Vallejo 1977

"Golden Wings" by Boris Vallejo
FROM THE BOOKS OF

The Well-Tempered Angler

THE
Well-Tempered Angler

BY

ARNOLD GINGRICH

With decorative headpieces by
JOHN GROTH

NEW YORK : *Alfred · A · Knopf*

1973

L. C. catalog card number: 65–18755

THIS IS A BORZOI BOOK,
PUBLISHED BY ALFRED A. KNOPF, INC.

PUBLISHED OCTOBER 18, 1965
REPRINTED ONCE
THIRD PRINTING, APRIL 1973

Certain portions of this book have appeared, or will appear, in somewhat different form: specifically, Chapter 2 in the September 1965 issue of *Playboy*. Chapter 3 incorporates portions of an article "How to be a 20/20 Angler" which appeared in the December 1959 issue of *Field & Stream*, and Chapter 12 includes portions of an article "Trout by the Score" which appeared in the July 1960 issue of the same magazine. Chapters 13, 15, and 17 incorporate material written as entries under "Angling Literature," "Iceland," "Izaak Walton," "New Brunswick," and "Quebec," for *McClane's Standard Fishing Encyclopedia* (New York: Holt, Rinehart and Winston; 1965). Chapter 16 appeared in the September 1965 issue of *The Atlantic*.

FOR JANE,
in the thirtieth year
since we shared the stairs
of The Compleat Angler in Bimini

ACKNOWLEDGMENT

To Al and Lee and the Four Charlies,
for teaching me whatever I know about it,
and to Annie, Dorothy, and Florence,
for midwiving it into print

A Note about the Title

"I WILL WRITE a sort of a book of fishing," said William Scrope to his friend Lobworm, something over a hundred and twenty years ago. The result was *Days and Nights of Salmon Fishing in the Tweed,* and all true lovers of angling have been richer ever since.

"I should think you'd want to do some sort of book on the fishing life," said Alfred Knopf, one day in '63. So for a while this book was known, if only to him and to me, as *The Fishing Life.* There was even a day when I thought of calling it *The Fishing Death,* when I read in the London *Express,* on May 24, 1963, a story by Jack Hill headed "Angler dies in salmon fight." Here it is:

"Angling was the love of George Nicholls' life—and he died hanging grimly on to his rod in a battle to land a leaping 19 lb. salmon. The only spectator, his wife Gertrude, screamed as she watched her husband float down the river. Sixty-six-year-old Mr. Nicholls, of Holliesdrive, Wednesbury, Staffordshire, was fishing a friend's beat on the Wye at lonely Ballingham, near Hereford. His line tightened as he hooked the lively 19-pounder. For nine minutes he fought the fish, steadily tiring it—and himself. Victory was in sight and Mr. Nicholls shouted to his wife for the gaff. The fish made a last bid for freedom—and Mr. Nicholls slumped face down in the river. Police later recovered his body 300 yards away. "And the salmon was still firmly hooked."

I never knew George Nicholls, but that story tells me something about him. He was using a heavy rod, or he wouldn't have been ready to reach for a gaff after only nine minutes. Par for the course, the world over, is a minute per pound, so unless Mr. Nicholls had tackle stout enough to horse him in, he wouldn't have been ready to land for another ten minutes. Also, he was using a gaff. Well, fair enough, since he had no ghillie or guide to net or gaff the fish for him. And you must respect any angler who doesn't leave the end game to others to do for him. On the other hand, there are anglers who would as soon gaff their mothers as use a gaff on a salmon. These anglers use a tailer, which grabs the fish around the tail in a viselike grip of spring-released steel, or when possible they prefer to beach their fish, sometimes going great distances upstream or downstream to find a place where the angle of the riverbank is gentle enough to permit such a maneuver. These anglers can return their fish to the river, when they will, but a fish that is gaffed is a fish that is done for.

Such an angler was John MacCormac, the longtime Vienna correspondent of *The New York Times,* who died on the Laerdal in Norway, fast to a twenty-five-pound salmon. When I heard about it, I said: "Oh what a lovely death." The mutual friends who told me gave me a shocked look, but I know that if they had, instead, been telling him the same news about me, he'd have said exactly the same thing.

Death waits us all, but some of us would rather meet him that way than any other.

« X »

Contents

CHAPTER

1 · The Fair Rewards   3

2 · Horsing Them in with Hemingway   20

3 · The Larger Joy of Fishing Fine   28

4 · The Monster Rainbow of Mariazell   45

5 · Emergence of a Point of View   60

6 · Preston Jennings for President—or,
There Is a Royal Coachman   73

7 · Mr. Hewitt and His Water   92

8 · Paul Young and the Midge Rod   103

9 · A. J. McClane and the Double-line Haul   112

10 · The Turnwood Years   118

11 · The Four Charlies . . .   129

12 · Trout by the Score   139

13 · Iceland, the Angler's Ultima Thule   152

14 · Salmon in Connemara and in Devon   170

15 · Salmon in New Brunswick and Quebec   194

« xi »

16 · Lee Wulff and Light Tackle for Salmon   203

17 · The Angling Heritage   221

18 · The Boys Upstairs at Manny Wolf's   253

19 · The Earmarks of Aptitude   263

20 · Counting Tackle Instead of Sheep   276

21 · The Well-Tempered Angler   305

BIBLIOGRAPHY   317

A LIST OF PERTINENT ADDRESSES   324

INDEX   follows page 331

The Well-Tempered Angler

1 · The Fair Rewards

*I am conscious that the volume contains a number of
repetitions, but I have had to choose between making them
and crippling my argument by innumerable cross-references.
So I pray the forgiveness of my readers.*

G. E. M. Skues, in *Nymph
Fishing for Chalk Stream Trout*, 1939

I WAS BORN in Michigan, and at the right time too, but in
the wrong frame of mind. When I was born, at the end of
the century's fourth year, there were still a few grayling left

around Grayling, Michigan. But I was a backward child, if backward only in the sense implied in the colloquial term referring to getting things ass-backward, because I spent my boyhood and early youth sprawled in chairs with my nose in books, when I could have been up and into some of the best trout and grayling fishing there ever was.

It wasn't that nobody told me about it—as if you had to be told these things—but, worse, it was just that I wasn't interested. One of my most vivid memories today is of a snapshot my dad made, I would guess about 1909, of a trout clearing a falls, going upstream somewhere near Baldwin, Michigan. He made it with a Brownie box camera, no high-speed lens, no light meter, nothing. It was beautiful. I thought so then, and I know it now. That trout must have been the size of a grilse. But I admired it the way you admire a sunset, without wanting to possess it. It didn't make me want to go fishing.

He would have taken me. He used to fish up there often. But I didn't know what I was missing. I was too soon bookish, and too late outdoorsy.

There was an old song that began, "I was born in Michigan," and the next line was, "and I wish and wish again." Boy, I certainly do. But how was I to know that the books would keep and the grayling wouldn't?

The first two words I learned to read were "shipping" and "weight," because I taught myself to read, long before I got to kindergarten, out of the Sears, Roebuck catalogue. So when our first-grade teacher wrote on the blackboard, by way of introducing us to the mysteries that lay behind the first two of our three r's, these simple words:

Come away, come and play

I found them absurdly easy and intoned them in a loud soprano. She looked a bit disconcerted as she erased them and wrote:

Run with me, to the tree

and I promptly gave them the same viva voce treatment.

"Now *you* shut up," she said, most unteacherly, "I'm trying to teach these children to read, and you're spoiling it all."

How I wish, and wish again, that I could have met and played my first trout and my first grayling as early and as easily as those first two sentences. But whereas I read George Moore's *The Brook Kerith* at thirteen, when it first came out, I didn't discover *The Compleat Angler* until I was thirty. I've tried, within recent years, to reread *The Brook Kerith* and couldn't get beyond the first thirty pages, but I could reread *The Compleat Angler* every year and have, most years, ever since.

We are born with instincts, but a set of values is something we have to build as we go. That's as true of our fishing as it is of our reading.

Now fly-fishing for trout and salmon, the form of fishing to which we graduate, late or soon, is fortunate in one respect and unfortunate in another. It is blessed with the greatest body of literature ever devoted to one branch of a single sport, but it is cursed with the circumstance that almost all of it is classifiable under the heading of preachments to the converted. I suppose it has a mystique, though I hate the pretentious word, but if it has acquired one, over the years, what it still conspicuously lacks is a rationale.

There are some things, of course, that have always defied all forms of rationalization and probably always will. Love, for instance. And faith, maybe. There's a phrase in Hungarian, *nincs miert*, that means literally "there is no why." Perhaps it's as futile and as foolish, at this late date, to ask "why fly fishing?" as it is to ask "why jazz?" As Fats Waller said: "Lady, if you've got to ask, you'll never know."

But as with the mountain, as long as it's there the temptation is to attempt it. I probably won't come any closer to it than anyone else has yet come, though my angle of approach be different. But if, like the ancient mariner who stoppeth one of three, I try to convey some of what I feel about my particular brand of fly fishing for trout and salmon, which is stream fishing with the lightest of tackle for the sole and simple purpose of attempting to attain the highest scores, the chances are two out of three that I've stopped the wrong reader.

You may have "tried" fishing, as some have tried pipe smoking, and decided that for you there just wasn't enough in it to be worth all that bother. Or, on the other hand, *you* may be so contented with your kind of fishing that it's hopeless to try to get you to switch to any other kind, in which case I'm left with that not impossible he, and I'm out of luck if he isn't you, who may be susceptible to the fair rewards this form of fishing has to offer. So if I've lost you and you, you can take the book back to the library and I'm fairly sure it isn't the first time you've been disappointed; or even if you've bought it, perhaps at this point all is not yet lost if you've had the wit and the luck to keep this copy reasonably clean, so godspeed to the two of you, and that leaves you and me to appraise those rewards that I said were so fair. They'd better be, I realize, as I think ahead over the route we have to travel together, because it's long and may at times seem twisty and at other times rambling.

And in two respects this book suffers from that same disadvantage that has proverbially been attributed to the study of Latin, which is that the chief thing it fits you for is the study of more Latin. If you come with me all the way, it's only fair to let you know that you run a calculable risk of wanting to read some thirty-three other books, and of acquiring a considerable store of tackle, as a consequence. The journey that can be fraught with that much hazard, I am well aware, had better be well worth taking.

Well, it has its points. You'll meet, if not a better class of people, then certainly a better class of fish, if only because you'll meet them under circumstances that encourage them to be at their best, and in a degree of intimacy that very few fishers achieve. As for the people, only a few of them are famous, but none is infamous so far as I know, and a great many of them are dead. This is not surprising, for in this field of activity, which has been cultivated for untold hundreds of years, it stands to reason that in any age there can never be more than a very few of the living who can begin to teach you as much as the many who are dead and have gone, either lately or long, before you. It is to be hoped that in our progress through these pages we will miss very few in either category.

As for the places, there we have our one certainty in all

that has to do with this form of fishing: the places will be of great natural beauty, with water of gem clarity and the air so delicious you wish you could bottle it and take it home with you to drink. The places will, it is true, have a certain similarity, so that when after having seen one you come to another, you may greet it with an eerie sense of the *déjà vu*. If you've been around the Esopus, for instance, and you come to the Vorarlberg, or vice versa, you may well find that they remind you of each other. There are places on the Upper Beaverkill that are now interchangeable, in my mind's eye, with places on the Dorsetshire Frome. (Pronounced *Froom*, by the way, for the same lack of evident reason that Scrope is pronounced *Scroop*, which is the first sample of the kind of weighty learning you may expect to get from this book.) There are certain spots on the Risle in Normandy and on the Itchen in Hampshire and the Letort in Pennsylvania that, incredible as it may seem, are all of a piece, though the first two are chalk streams and the last is limestone. But paradoxically it would be no less true to say that no two trout streams are alike, any more than any two sets of fingerprints are exactly alike, though some pairs of identical twins are so similar as to be confusing even to their familiars. One thing is sure, though: places where trout and salmon are still abundant are by that very token places of pristine natural beauty. Of course I don't mean every place where trout are put in to be taken out, for that could embrace a motley of suburbs and exurbs and even the tanks at outdoor sports shows, flanked as they are by hot dog and soft-drink stands.

Wherever there is water that holds trout, I drink it happily and without the flicker of a thought for fluoridation, and have now for years, because I feel that if it's good enough for trout it's probably too good for me. In honesty I ought to add that I never drink water anywhere else, as I can't abide the stuff when I'm not on the stream, having no use for it except to fish in and to bathe in; I get my irreducible daily quota only through tea or espresso. But the point loses none of its validity for being thus candidly qualified.

As for the fish in this book, there are only two. There is the trout and there is the salmon. When I say the trout I mean, of course, all the trout, including the brookie, char though he be, but excluding that other char, the lake trout, because he's a low-lifer, dwelling way down where we couldn't reach him with this form of fishing even if we wanted to, so in his stead we adopt the grayling as an equal member of the trout family. And when I say salmon I include, of course, grilse and sea trout, meaning sea-run browns, brooks or salters, and rainbows or steelheads, but excluding Pacific salmon, which as far as this form of fishing is concerned is just something that comes in cans.

Comes now, and so quick, another paradox. As we go on, I say every so often, like a preacher who feels that he hasn't made a point in his sermon if he's said it fewer than nine times, that in this kind of fishing the fish is much less important than the act, or the art, if you will, of fishing. Well, true enough in its context, as you'll see, and I hope agree with, when we get there. But here, before we do get there, and out of that context, is as good a place as any to try to saddle and ride out this particular paradox.

While it's true that in the angler's progress toward the ultimate enjoyment of fishing, the point is soon reached and passed where the *killing and the keeping* of the fish is the object of the game, nevertheless the fish remains the star of the performance, because if the fish weren't there at all the game would be called for lack of any incentive to play it. For a fair if not a perfect parallel, take the argument that sex without affection—in other words, bought sex—is comparable to buying a fish in the market, as opposed to the sporting proposition of finding it and taking it by fair means. In sporting terms, then, sex without affection is zero. Good enough, as far as it goes. But when you turn it around, affection without sex is double zero. In other words, you can't win in that game in the long run, because unless some sex gets in there somewhere, pretty soon there aren't any more players. Same with this fishing. If in sporting terms fish without fishing is zero, that's all right. But fishing without fish is lunacy, from Simple Simon's day to ours. While it is perfectly possible that this book's argument may seem crazy in parts, sheer idiocy is not its object as a whole, though I can conceive of the eventuality that to some people the form of angling that it advocates could well appear to be The Fishing of the Absurd.

So here's where I have to hurry to assure you that I am no more anti-fish than I am anti-fishing, and the fish, in that sense, *is* the most important consideration, despite everything I may hereafter say to the contrary. End paradox.

But I've just announced this as a free election where trout come in first and salmon a close second, and after that, at least for a long time, comes nothing. And I'm as quick as you are to realize that this is one hell of a way to treat such a lordly creature as the smallmouth bass. I can only weasel out by saying one of two things. First, something as phony as that I love not smallmouth the less, loved I not trout and salmon the more. Or, second, I can break down and make the admission, tantamount to a big blot in the middle of the canvas that I've only started to paint, that the smallmouth *is* every bit as much fun, on this kind of tackle and fishing this way, as either trout or salmon.

So I've hobbled my argument before I've got started. If I don't rally fast, I sense that you will soon go off to join those two other guys that I lost virtually at the outset.

But the smallmouth really is the only exception, of course, because basically this is stream fishing with ultralight tackle and the essence of it is playing either powerful fish or fish that because of your tackle seem more powerful than they are and—oh God, I forgot the shad! On this tackle they seem like steelheads. Oh well, so that does make two exceptions, but otherwise only trout and salmon really qualify—

But it's true the little rod is very versatile, and you don't *have to* wade to use it. It's just that it's next to no good in a boat, so I think of it as for stream fishing, but from the bank of a pond, say—what, *bluegills?*

Well, now, I've nothing against bluegills. It's only that I thought we were going to confine this discussion to a higher level. But you take a good big bluegill, say about the size of a dessert plate, and you've got a very lively fish. In fact, now that I'm reminded of it, when I first got my first Midge rod, ten years ago, I was so afraid of it that I thought I'd better practice on some bluegills—sort of dress rehearsal, you might say—before risking it on some of the streams like the Esopus. So there were these bluegills in this pond—oh these were huge, for bluegills, they were dinner-plate size and you know what? On my Midge, they had me thinking, for a moment, that they had turned into tuna. And come to think of it, there were some pickerel in that pond, and on the Midge they behaved like chain lightning. But they *were* slimy.

All right, now that we've let bluegills in, let's forget we ever tried to start an exclusive club among fish—we'll let 'em all in. If all men are equal, then who am I to hold out for class distinctions between fish? If your fishing has to be where you find it, I suppose I can concede that this form of fishing probably can be more widely adopted, or even adapted, for other kinds of fish than those I talk about here. No, damn it, I've got to draw the line somewhere. So, positively *no eels allowed*, when fishing with the Midge or any near equivalent thereof. I've eaten them in Italy, though not knowingly anywhere else, and I just don't like their looks, besides which they remind me too vividly of the time I had to kill a water moccasin with a tire iron—General Randolph Pate had caught the snake inadvertently and it was dangling from the tip of his rod. He was looking around, hoping to see his aide, whom he had sent away somewhere on an errand. Instead he saw me watching him, wishing the snake would go away. It was quite possibly the only time in the long history of the Marine Corps, of which he had just been succeeded as Commandant, when after the Marines landed the situation got out of hand.

So with the sole exception of eels, I'll go along for any kind of fish anybody here wants to fish for. I've even gone crabbing, where there was no fishing to be had. But as long as we're talking about it, and I've agreed that no fishing is bad, then I'd rather stick to talk of trout and salmon.

Take the brookie first, because he's still the easiest trout to take. Have you ever watched one hitting at a Parma Belle streamer, hitting at it not once but anywhere from four to nine times, before impaling himself on it, to his own infinite surprise? God love them, they are still the most beautiful of all the trouts, and I never see the white edging along the rich maroon facing of that forward fin without a twinge of regret that these lovable creatures love not wisely but too well. They are the dumb blondes of this wonderful world of trout, proving all over again that it is a rare exception when the maximum in brains and beauty coincide. Sometimes when you're taking them onetwothreefourfive and justlikethat, you want to cry out to the rest of them: Hey clear out, can't you see what's happening? But no, they'll hang around, like housewives waiting to get into a shopping center, the day of a one-cent sale.

Pretty soon they'll be gone with the grayling, except for a sort of halfway survival through crossbreeding with the brown, in the form of the tiger. But the tiger is only faintly reminiscent of the brookie, chiefly in the similarity of the chain-like markings on the back, and while he has twice the stamina of the brook trout, somehow I can't give him either love or respect in utterly ungrudging measure. The brookie is "drenchingly beautiful," as Noel Coward said of somebody else, who happened to have almost equally delicate coloring. The vivid contrast of that dark green and almost milk white, accented by the surprise note of red, is somehow vulgarized and coarsened in the tiger's blend of green and yellow. Put him beside the brookie, and it's like looking for resemblances between a beautiful woman and her son the football player.

I suppose it has to be conceded that the rainbow is the most satisfactory, all round, of the various trout. He goes off like an alarm clock when you reach him on the edge of the foam, in the most agitated waters of the stream, and of course he does put on a pretty spectacular show, with all those jumps. But I find him, just the same, ever so slightly monotonous. I love to see him arc up and come down over a spider, but once he's done it, I find his subsequent performance a touch too predictable. It's just jump jump jump, as if he didn't know anything else to do, and I guess he doesn't. I love his looks, at a distance, when he seems black and white if he's of any size, but close up, well I don't know. Would you have picked quite that funny purple for the broad stripe along the sides, just supposing you could have ordered him like a custom body job?

Give me the brown, if you're giving me my druthers. Partly, I suppose, because I'm still flattered, even if it's the thousandth time, to think he'll have anything to do with me at all, when I know how choosy he can be. And then, every so often, he'll outjump the jumpingest rainbow you ever saw, but the best point of that is that you don't expect him to, as you do the rainbow, so added to the spectacular is the element of surprise. The brownie has everything. He can be as moody as the black bass, but as enthusiastic as a brookie when he finally makes up his mind, and he's more resourceful, after you've at last got him on, than any of them. I like best to get him on a nymph, just below the surface, to experience the thrill of what Skues called "that cunning brown wink under water," though I'd be more inclined to call it tawny than really brown. He has class, this fish, and the few times I've taken him at twenty-inch length on a size-twenty fly I've been ready to call it a day after his act, because I simply couldn't conceive of anything that wouldn't be anticlimactic as an encore. I know I'm at odds with most in thinking the brown is beautiful, as well as talented, and just naming off his colors sounds far from entrancing: cream and beige and brown and black and red. It sounds *ugh*, and it's the kind of combination that on anything less than a Rolls-Royce or a Bentley would be. Yet he not only can get away with it, but on him I find it vastly becoming.

Another kind of trout I think of with fondness is the *gebirgsforelle*, the mountain trout you find above the timberline in the Austrian Tyrol. I've never seen our Western cutthroats, but from color pictures of them I'd judge they are at least as closely related as kissing cousins, because the *gebirgsforellen* have that same red gash that gives our cutthroat its name. They behave like brookies, and are fun to pick up in the pockets of those narrower streams higher up in the mountains. As naturally follows, they tend to run considerably smaller than either the browns or the grayling that you find farther down.

Against the grayling's added attraction in that flag-size dorsal fin, which I love to see in the sunlight, there is the defect of that rather suckerlike soft mouth, which I will admit makes this otherwise gallant fish which I so much admire seem as incongruous as an outstanding athlete with a receding chin. He's as ready to bite as the brookie, and twice as flashy in performance when hooked. And then there is the unique added attribute of the grayling's exquisitely sweet smell of wild thyme, a fragrance far more aphrodisiac to my olfactory nerve than any perfume ever worn by any mere woman born of same. In my dreams I see them, always in sunlight, as a sort of dove gray, set off by the lavender of that enormous fin, and while gray and lavender is evocative of little old ladies, nevertheless on grayling I find it wildly exciting. In my dreams, however, although I am not deprived of the color, I can never recapture that unforgettable and unforgotten essence of thyme. I only wish that grayling were more get-at-able than they are for those of us on the East Coast, to whom even salmon are nearer neighbors. So grayling have to remain for me, except at very rare intervals, a sort of dream princess of this royal family of fish, and, most regrettably, a *princesse lointaine*.

What can you say of the Atlantic salmon, the king himself, except to bow or curtsey, as the case may be? Part of his awesome persona, I suppose, is the very fact that you can never get on really intimate terms with him. While I can't think of many old browns of whom I can honestly say that we are boonies by now, I've got an almost chummy acquaintance with at least three or four other members of the family of salmonids, and have had over the past decade with at least as many more, now alas of sainted memory, upon whom I could always drop in unexpectedly, take them out for a happy little chat and put them back, and I can honestly say that I liked them more and more on each successive occasion, as we got to know each other better and better. I have no way of telling, even if modesty prevented the report, whether the feeling was mutual.

But a salmon, no matter how long he may hang around a given pool, and you never know if he'll be staying even as long as overnight, will never ever get to be a friend. He'll snoot you every time but the last that you try for him, and even then the chances are overwhelmingly better than even that he will have the last laugh. I don't think it's a solecism to attribute a laugh to him. To me, he's the only member of the family with a sense of humor, perhaps because he's the only one who feels he can afford to have one. It isn't really a sense of humor, of course, but he can be a clown, and treat you in a crazily pixyish way that couldn't be any more weirdly funny if you knew as a matter of established scientific fact that it was deliberate. Try him with a spider or a big bushy bivisible or a palmered Pink Lady or a White Wulff or a Whiskers, and for one of them that he may at long last actually take, he will subject the others to a succession of bunts, tosses, and even burlesque slaps with his tail, that is as humiliating as it is frustrating.

I've known salmon to take on the more than hundredth cast, for no better or no other apparent reason than that this was the moment they had decided to take, a decision that they probably would have reached at that particular moment even without the hundred and some previous casts.

But even that isn't the most infuriating thing about them. If they won't be friends, you'd think they could at least pay you the common courtesy that is accorded you by the rest of the family, and regard you as an enemy, from whom they scamper at sight. But no, they won't even deign to do that. They see you, all right, but more often than not they just won't take the trouble to acknowledge your presence, so it's obvious that you are beneath their royal notice. There are times when they are as exasperating in this respect as alligators in a zoo, who also can't be bothered to let you know whether they are asleep or awake. That's why it so often happens, of course, that you can be in a position to see salmon clearly, and note their every move (or refusal to move) throughout the entire time you're fishing for them. You can throw your whole fly box at them, though naturally one fly at a time, and watch how the flies go by, above them, beside them, below them, and sometimes practically tickling them on the nose. Then after something like, or more than, a hundred such disdained offerings, you will toss in some one fly, say for instance a size 12 Jeannie, which perhaps is now being offered for the third or fourth time in an endless repetition of successive offerings that have so far been disdained, and then zing. Far from waiting, this time, for it to come anywhere near him, and before you're even sure that you've spotted it in the water yourself, he will launch himself toward it in a zany burst of locomotive speed, with a rush so madly insensate that if at that moment you were to come to such an unlikely conclusion as to withdraw it, you couldn't possibly make the move fast enough to get it out of his way.

After that, of course, anything can happen, and if you fish for them long enough, it does. Salmon are beyond anybody's prediction, either individually or in the aggregate. The ones you're sure you have on as tight as the bond of epoxy glue are suddenly and inexplicably gone, and the ones you're sure you've lost, when the line has gone suddenly slack after one or more jumps, reveal themselves to be just as inexplicably, and with twice as startling suddenness, still on there after you've disconsolately started to reel in.

No book yet written about them can even begin to tell more than a very few of the vast number of things there are to be known about them, though *The Salmon* by J. W. Jones, published by Collins (St. James's Place, London) in 1959, advances the knowledge line a little further into the realm of the previously unknown than any other book to date. But even if all the facts were known, you would still have to find out some truths for yourself, for they are of the kind that nobody can tell you, either by the printed or by the spoken word. For instance, you can almost always tell when he's about to make a jump, after the first one. You can't with any other fish, even one with the jump as a standard built-in feature, like the rainbow. How do you know when the hooked salmon is about to jump? You can feel it. How can you feel it? There words bog down.

There are people who claim to know when their partners are about to experience orgasm. They can't say how they know, but they know. They can't tell you, and they certainly can't show you. The foreknowledge that a salmon is about to make another jump is something like that. It can only be experienced.

For that matter, no book can tell you, or any picture show you, not even a color movie, the white flash that a trout makes, in the gloaming, as he takes a fly off the surface of the water. It's almost phosphorescent, but it isn't. It's white, but only in the very special manner that certain little flowers, like sweet alyssum, are white, in a most delicately lacy way. It's as fast as a flashbulb, or the shutter of a camera lens, or the bat of an eyelash. I always think of it as a sort of luminous wink. But while that's a way of thinking of it, it doesn't even begin to describe it. Until your own eyes have seen it, I don't know how you can say you've seen everything.

In fact, in my book, until you've seen that you can't say you've lived.

2 · Horsing Them in with Hemingway

"Gingrich is a pretty keen fisherman," I said.
"I started him," said Hemingway.

Robert Emmett Ginna, in a May 1958
interview with Ernest Hemingway

HE DIDN'T, and even if he had, the deep-sea fishing I did with
Ernest Hemingway would have been a false start, never leading to any real appreciation of the deepest satisfaction of

angling. We fished out of Key West and out of Bimini, first in '34 on the *Anita*, the boat that belonged to Josie Russell, and later in '35 and '36 on the *Pilar*, the boat Ernest bought when we advanced him the money he lacked to complete the deal. Most of that fishing was hard work, calling for a great deal of back-bending exertion, and though some of it was fun, none of it was what I later came to consider real angling.

Ernest was a meat fisherman. He cared more about the quantity than about the quality, and was more concerned with the capture of the quarry than with the means employed to do it. He was also—and this is what no true angler is—intensely competitive about his fishing, and a very poor sport. If the luck was out, then nobody around him could do any right, and he was ready to blame everybody in sight, ahead of himself. When things were going right, he was quick to promote everybody in his company to high rank as good fellows, and was jovially boastful about their every least accomplishment, as well as his own. But let a hook pull out and his attitude was never to praise the fish that managed to bend it, but only to blame the hookmaker.

In Bimini in June of '36, when the Atlantic record for marlin stood at 736 pounds, Ernest hooked a beautiful bright silver marlin, with the coloration of a young fish. It was big, and as it leapt again and again, with a long low trajectory like that of a horse going over steeplechase barriers, its faint lavender stripings glistened in the sun like the lights flashing off a diamond. Big fish, up in the 600- and 700-pound class, usually looked dark, of an all-over blue that almost verged on black. So Jane Kendall Mason, who had pioneered the Cuban marlin fishing with Hemingway some five years earlier, who had a boat of her own and at least as much big game fishing experience as he had, ventured the guess that the fish might go about 450 pounds.

The fish was still on, and still in sight—to me it looked about the size of a tank car—when she spoke. Hemingway bridled as if he'd been hit, turned his head to make an angry answer, and in that same instant felt the heavy line go slack. Back came the hook, a new one from Hardy, hand-forged and monstrous, looking as if it could do in a pinch as a spare anchor for the *Queen Mary* or the *Normandie*. It was pulled out to an angle of about 130 degrees, like a bent hairpin. Hemingway began shaking it in Jane Mason's face, so vigorously that he might well be about to claw her with it.

"Four hundred fifty, huh? Look at that hook—just look at it—fourteen hundred pounds if it was an ounce."

He was beside himself, shrieking about the marlin that Zane Grey had landed in Tahiti that went over a thousand pounds even though sharks had taken huge hunks out of its tail section, and insisting that this one would have surpassed that, not merely for a new Atlantic record but for a world record as well. His wife Pauline and her sister Virginia tried to calm him down. Pauline pressed a drink into his hand, to make him stop brandishing the bent hook, while Ginny wound up her Libertyphone to drown him out with *You're the Top*. I finally managed the diversion, like the successful one of three *banderilleros* trying to distract a goring bull, by at last getting him to hear me say that Jane hadn't made the slighting 450-pound estimate herself, but had only been echoing, in astonished disagreement, my own ignorant guess at the weight of the fish.

"She didn't say it was four fifty—I did, and what the hell do *I* know about it?" As a gambit, it compared to Peter Lorre's later line, in the film *Casablanca*: "But who am I to think?"

His wrath turned, in the instant, upon the Messrs. Hardy. They would certainly hear from him, and in certain colorfully specified terms.

He was more fun to fish with when there were fewer people aboard for him to show off for.

On its inaugural trip, there were just three of us fishing aboard the *Pilar*, because the fourth, who was supposed to have been F. Scott Fitzgerald, had refused to come, saying: "I can't face Ernest again, when he's so successful and I'm such a failure." The third man in the boat was John Dos Passos, who was even less of a fisherman than Scott Fitzgerald, but mixed a mean drink which he called a Gulf Stream Special. As I remember it, it was a poor country cousin to Pimm's Cup. Dos Passos mixed it in a zinc pail, to which he gave full marks for its contribution to the mixture's peculiar pungency.

The gin gave out at Dry Tortugas, where there were no facilities to acquire any more, so a search of the boat uncovered a case of John Jameson's Irish Whisky up in the bow, which somebody had thoughtfully put aboard as a christening present to the *Pilar*. It was over the Irish, that evening, that Ernest confided to Dos Passos and me his high opinion of Gary Cooper as Lieutenant Henry in the screen version of *A Farewell to Arms*, and his correspondingly low opinion of Helen Hayes as the choice to portray Catherine Barkley.

"Who would you have liked, Hem?" asked Dos Passos.

Expecting him to nominate somebody like Dietrich or Bergman, though neither was Scotch, I was utterly unprepared, at least by the book itself, for his answer that there couldn't possibly be any other logical choice, for Christ's sake, than a girl named Jean Harlow. Dos Passos, it seemed, had never heard of her, so Hemingway gave him an animated demonstration, worthy of the Hindu dancer Shan-Kar, of her salient points of personality.

On the run back from Dry Tortugas, in a most unlikely spot, we came upon a school of big barracuda, and Dos Passos, between his eyesight and the Irish, and coupled with his less than passionate addiction to fishing in the first place, seemed to Hemingway to be lousing up what might have proved an excellent chance to break the rod and reel record for barracuda, which back then, in early '35, stood only a few pounds above the record of 69 pounds and some ounces for muskellunge. Dos Passos and Hemingway were both into fish at the same time, but Dos appeared to be more the victim than the master of his, so Hemingway asked me to hand him a Colt Woodsman automatic pistol that was in the cabin. He shot both fish, to avert the threatened foul-up of the lines that might cause us to lose either or both of them, in getting them aboard. The more orthodox method would have been to brain them, once they were up over the stern, with a sawed-off baseball bat, but there were signs of so many other fish, any one of which might have broken the record, that he didn't want to waste another moment of fishing time. So Dos Passos was benched, and I was drafted to fill the other fishing chair, and admonished to for Christ's sake horse 'em in fast and not frig around like Dos, to see if we couldn't bring in enough of them that one might break the record. We managed to get some six

or seven more, before the school let out, but though all
weighed in high in the sixties, none went over the 70-pound
mark.

After the barracuda explosion, nothing else seemed to be
happening for a considerable interval, so as a dead soldier out
of the case of Irish went over the stern and bobbed away in
the wake where our filleted mullet baits were dragging, Ernest
passed me the Colt Woodsman and asked me if I shot. By the
time I figured out where the safety catch was and how it
worked, the bobbing bottle began to look as far away as a ship
on the horizon. But without raising the pistol to sight it—
shooting from the lap, as it were—I sheered off its neck with
the first tentative and diffident shot. Hemingway, jumping up
out of the fishing chair beside me, burbled excitedly that there
weren't a dozen men in the world who could make a shot
like that, and Jesus Christ if he'd known I shot that well we'd
have done some shooting at Dry Tortugas.

My enthusiasm for shooting being somewhat less than that
of Dos Passos for fishing, I tried to explain the shot away as a
lucky punch, but Hemingway, with the recent eyewitness
knowledge to the contrary, refused to believe my disclaimers,
so we had to turn around and go back to Dry Tortugas. There
our quarry was sandpipers on the shore, delicate tiny birds on
toothpick legs. It seemed to me, as a sporting proposition,
tantamount to attacking butterflies with a tank, but although
we blasted away at them until the ammunition was exhausted,
neither of us even nicked one. Hemingway was generally
credited with being an excellent shot with rifle and shotgun,
but a pistol is something else again.

In all the fishing I did with Hemingway over the three winter seasons of '34, '35, and '36, I never once tied into a marlin, which is, of course, the apex of deep-sea fishing, as salmon is of stream fishing. I would work hours on tuna, however, pumping and reeling to get one up for what seemed like forever, only to have the fish sound like an elevator when the cable breaks, and then pump and reel again until I could barely see, except for red and orange balloons at the corners where my sweat-congealed eyelids seemed to be coming unhinged, and my mouth began to taste of such a weird cocktail, compounded of all the elements of sheer fatigue, that I was ready to swear that part of what I was tasting must have been my own toe-jam.

Part of that fishing was fun, of course, because any fishing is more fun than no fishing, but most of it was the worst kind of work, the kind of work for which the worker is not in condition. I would fly down from Chicago to Key West or Bimini, in the days when night flights were slow and arduous, having had in the interim no more exercise than that involved in the waving of a pocket handkerchief, and would get back home utterly exhausted.

I won't say I didn't get anything out of it. One thing I got out of it, which is in itself beyond measure, is a wife, that same Jane Kendall Mason to whom Pauline Hemingway introduced me one June night in '36 on the stairs at The Compleat Angler in Bimini. But we didn't get married until two wives and two husbands later, in November of '55, so as a dividend of that fishing it was certainly deferred.

What I got out of it at the time was an abiding dislike for all boat fishing, and equally so for all bait fishing. It seemed to me that whatever skill was involved was almost entirely that of the skipper of the boat, and the work that was left for the fisher in the chair was largely the proverbial chore allotted to a strong back and a weak mind. There was no casting, just a letting out of line and subsequent trolling, and no element of hunting, either, except by the skipper. Even then, whatever attraction the lure exerted for the fish was more the skipper's doing than the angler's. The presentation of the bait was affected less by the manipulations of the angler's rod than by the actions of the boatman. Later on, with the development of faster and more maneuverable boats, and with the general adoption of outriggers, to release the trolled line to the fish at the moment of the strike, deep-sea fishing became even less dependent on either the skill or the strength of the angler in the fighting chair, and more than ever the province of the boatman.

I soon felt that I would prefer to concentrate on the kind of fishing in which the chief consideration was not how much, but how well, and the size of the quarry was less important than the degree of its elusiveness. It wasn't that I had in any sense lost my taste for fishing. I would still fish for perch off a pier, with pearl buttons for bait, if there were no other fishing to be had. But if there was a choice, I wanted the kind where the challenge was to the individual, rather than to a team.

I was to find it, though not right away, in stream fishing with a fly.

3 · The Larger Joy of Fishing Fine

Around the steel no tortur'd worm shall twine,
No blood of living insect stain my line;
Let me, less cruel, cast feather'd hook,
With pliant rod athwart the pebbled brook,
Silent along the mazy margin stray,
And with fur-wrought fly delude the prey.
John Gay, in *Rural Sports*, 1720

WHILE I NOW BELIEVE that the fishing is far more important than the fish, it wasn't always so, by any means. As E. R. Hewitt used to say, we all start out as fish hogs at heart, with the attitude of little boys who will go to any lengths to get as many fish, and as big, as they possibly can. It's only later on that they learn, if they ever do, to become selective, and discriminating as to the means employed, and at the last stage of the angler's development, to prize the means above the quarry.

My own development in this regard came late. For the twenty years I lived in Chicago, from the time I got out of school in Ann Arbor in 1925 until I moved to Switzerland in 1945, I caught so few fish, for the man-hours devoted to the effort, that any lectures on conservation would have been wasted on me. I counted that season a success in which I caught a fish that didn't get away. Weekend after weekend I used to take the Fisherman's Special out of Chicago's Northwestern Station, headed for Hayward, Wisconsin, and the Chippewa Flowage, a renowned muskellunge area. The only muskie I ever saw was mounted in the Hayward hardware store. Other weekends I used to drive from Chicago to a spot near Spring Lake, Michigan, a drive that in those days took five to six hours. That would bring me about midnight on a Friday night to a place known as the Jerusalem Bayou, where I had seen some monster bass. I had seen them by daylight, while rowing one of my kids around fishing for pan fish, and I reasoned that if I had seen them they had also seen me, and that my one hope of getting one of them would be by fishing for them at night. Night after night, that is both Friday night and Saturday night and weekend after weekend, I fished for those bass.

Just once, on a black July night in the dark of the moon, between one and two in the morning, I got one on. He hit a black plunker, a surface lure that made a sound like the clucking of the tongue on the roof of the mouth. He may have been on for no more than a minute to a minute and a half, though in the dark the battle seemed prolonged, before he contrived to wrap the line around an underwater snag and got away, plunker and all.

Other times I fished as far away from Chicago as Eveleth, Minnesota, or as near as Pistakee Bay, which is about halfway between Chicago and Lake Geneva, Wisconsin. Both those places I had the same thing happen—take a good-size bass, one four and the other five, the day before the opening of bass season, and under the watchful eye of a game warden hovering near, and dutifully sticking around long enough to make sure that he saw me putting it back.

Finally, after a dozen years of miserably poor fishing with a bait-casting rod and plugs and spoons, I found some ready-made fishing at a trout farm, near at hand, which offered fishing by the pound. This was in Dundee, near Elgin, Illinois, just west of Chicago, at the Fin 'n' Feather Club, which was not a club at all but a place that sold tinned pheasant and smoked trout along with a few other specialties, such as cheese.

I was introduced to it, in the spring of 1939, by a salesman named Felix Alter, who took me to a nearby sporting-goods store to help me pick out a fly rod, an item which I didn't own and which, except for hefting my father's in our house in Grand Rapids, Michigan, when I was a kid, I had never even seen. Up until then all the fishing I had done, aside from the deep-sea fishing with Hemingway, had been plug casting for bass, pickerel, and pike, though the latter always in the vain hope of meeting up with a musky. So I thought of fishing as something you do from a boat.

What I didn't know would fill a book, and I hope will. Like most people, I had started out thinking that the big thing in fishing was the fish, and that the fun was quantitative. I didn't realize, as the New English Dictionary (Oxford) could have told me, that fishing is "to catch, or *try to catch*, fish." So all the fishing I had done up to this point, whether trolling for bass in Pistakee Bay or for landlocked salmon in Lake Sebago or for big fish on the Blue Water, was alike in that its measurement of pleasure was purely quantitative and directly dependent upon the results.

Felix Alter started me out with what I would now regard as a beginner's outfit, a 9-foot Heddon three-piece bamboo rod weighing 5 ounces, with a Martin automatic reel and C-level line to which was attached a 7-foot leader that tapered to a tippet of no finer than 3X. The rod was a bass rod, with what used to be called wet-fly action, but I have acquired worse rods since, in the course of collecting the two-dozen-odd fly rods that I now regard as first-line equipment, as opposed to the half dozen or so that I may have kept but simply regard as mistakes. As fly-fishing equipment goes today, my first outfit lacked finesse, but compared to the 5- and 6-foot steel casting rods I had been using, it seemed a veritable fairy wand, and as the oiled silk went out, before and behind me, with never a thought of my old baiting-casting bugaboo, a nasty backlash, I began to enjoy the act of fishing, as distinguished from the act of catching fish, for the first time. I was graduating, if only from first to second grade, in the education of an angler, simply by passing from the casting rod to the fly rod.

Felix taught me to cast in the orthodox old-fashioned way, with my elbow held close to my body—"pretend you're holding a book under your right arm"—and with my forearm flexing back and forth in the motion of a rocking chair between an approximate eleven o'clock and one o'clock on an imaginary clock dial. Clumsy as I was at it, that first day, I still felt that the fly rod was in itself the most graceful instrument I had ever seen, and felt a joy in its manipulation that I had never felt before in fishing. The mere act of making that heavy line go back and forth in the air above and behind me, in order to propel a weightless fly in front of me, with a motion like that of a coachman's buggy whip, was in such delicate contrast to my previous baseball-like throwings of plugs and spoons—which all too often resulted in Gordian knots in the black-silk casting line that overran my so-called anti-backlash level wind casting reel—that it seemed as exhilarating as suddenly flying after a lifetime of walking.

As in the proverbial case of the idiots with the swimming pool, I was enjoying it so much that it was time to consider putting some water in it, and Felix took me to one of the Fin 'n' Feather rearing ponds to cast over a restless congregation of captive trout. After the first few casts, he handed me a pair of Polaroid glasses, saying: "Here, put these on and you'll have more fun." Fun indeed, it was sheer rapture—to see the individual trout rising out of a crowd of his fellows, to come swirling to the fly. If the mere use of the fly rod had made me feel as if I were flying, then this sudden ability to see beneath the surface of the water, and actually watch the fish seize the fly, was like acquiring, from one moment to the next, the knack of walking on water.

As angling, this was meat-fishing of the primary grade. Since the Fin 'n' Feather charged no rod fee, their rule was that you must keep any trout you hooked, and pay for your catch as you left at the rate of a dollar a pound.

But Felix Alter had a way around this. Motivated more by pecuniary than by sporting considerations, he pinched the barbs off the hooks of our size 12 flies with a pair of pliers, so it was easy to flip off any unwanted trout and thus prolong the fishing without acquiring an unmanageably big load of fish flesh when it came time to weigh and pay as we left.

Conservation never figured in, since this fishing was like hunting in a stockyards, where all the game was doomed, one way or another. These trout had nowhere to go but into somebody's stomach, whether sooner into ours, as whole fish broiled or pan-fried, or eventually into others', though no less certainly, after conversion into rainbow paté.

After the endless elusiveness of those moody bass in Jerusalem Bayou, these trout seemed ridiculously easy to take, as of course they were. I remember writing to Hemingway that trout, which I had always esteemed and admired ever since first reading *Big Two-Hearted River*, seemed upon this too-sudden intimacy to be "more of a cathouse proposition." He wrote back assuring me that they weren't, and that I would someday learn the difference between true trout in the wild and these liver-feds that I had found so easy to catch only because, in a sense, they were already in captivity. I was to find that he was right, of course, though only after I moved to Europe and was able to get in on the once-in-a-lifetime kind of fishing that prevailed in Austria and Germany right after the Second World War.

Even so, I had at this moment in '39 begun, when I at last got over trout with a fly rod in my hand, my education as an angler. Granted that the trout were next-to-tame, that the tackle was hardly fine, and that, as angling, this was just about the bottom rung of the ladder. Still, it was a step above the mere quantitative fishing I had done in the past, and a start toward qualitative angling and the realization of the extra fun that is to be derived from fishing fine.

It was another fifteen years after that kindergarten phase at the Fin 'n' Feather Club, or just about the length of time that we expect to spend in school, before I was to get to the postgraduate level, where all considerations of How Much are forgotten in the concentration upon the one main concern of How Well. Now, and for the past ten years, I hardly ever have occasion to use, out of my present battery of fly rods, anything longer than 6½ feet, or weighing appreciably more than 2 ounces. On such rods I have consistently taken salmon, though never yet larger than 14 pounds. As for trout, I now generally use, except on big rivers, a rod of 4 feet 4 inches in length, weighing exactly an ounce. On a rod like that, even an 8-incher can put up a very respectable fight, and anything bigger than that begins to take on proportions that are positively heroic. Correspondingly, the dimensions of the rest of my tackle have also shrunk, as I have learned that the increase in enjoyment, when you're fishing fine, is in direct proportion to the decrease in your size of tackle.

The object of the game, in this kind of fishing, is to try to become, and to be as often as possible, a 20/20 angler. This means, simply, getting a fish of twenty or more inches in length on a fly of size 20 or less. You're not likely to reach this kind of goal more than once or twice a season, but the thrill of it, when you do make it, is incomparably greater than that of hauling in a boatload of fish, by the old chuck-and-chance-it and troll-and-pray methods.

Of course, most places you go today, when you show up with a little rod and tiny flies you're still apt to come in for a lot of kidding about having stolen some kid's toy. This isn't as true today as it was ten years ago, when the original Midge rod, as made by the late Paul Young of Detroit, was an awesome novelty. Today a half-dozen rodmakers offer a midge rod, including Hardy, and the very name *midge* has become generic, like cellophane or victrola, to apply to a recognized category. Paul Young called it the Midge in the first place because he considered it useful only for delicate low-water fishing in the dog days, with tiny midges of size 20 or smaller. But today, thanks largely to Lee Wulff's pioneering, the midge rod is beginning to be seen on salmon rivers. While its use for salmon is still debated, on the grounds that it is, like the old Scotch definition of a golf club, "an instrument ill-adapted to the purpose," there can be no question that it is the only logical rod for "20/20" angling, or truly fishing fine.

The paradoxical part about this fishing with tiny flies is that while its most obvious justification is that it gets you more strikes in the overfished and overcrowded waters near our big cities, where most of us have to do most of our fishing nowadays, still it has an unexpected dividend, too, in that it is very apt to get you strikes from bigger fish than you would otherwise ever raise in such overcrowded and overfished waters. If this sounds contradictory, like sailing west to arrive east, then put it under that same perverse law of nature that makes it rain only on the days when you wear a freshly pressed suit. When you feel that you're least well equipped to cope with a big fish, why naturally that's when one of the creatures will take it into his head to strike.

Actually, it's not as mysterious as all that. Old saws about "big fish, big bait" to the contrary, it stands to reason that fish that have managed to survive to any real size in the face of the rising fishing pressures on our streams are bound to be too wary to strike at ordinary lures affixed to lines or leaders of conventional size. So there's where you come in for a great advantage when you start fishing fine. A small rod naturally calls for a fine line. It should be HEH or HDG. You'll get still more strikes, and from bigger fish, if it's IGI, or IEI, which means going back to the English number 1 or number 2 silk line, respectively, since none of our American line-makers has ever seen fit to put a true IGI or IEI on the market, though Gladding has of late been emphasizing true diameters, and most commendably, in their floating lines.

For the same reason that you must use a fine line, to avoid making a fish-scaring slap on the water, you must use a fine tippet on a long leader. The leader should be at least 10 feet long, and longer than that if you can manage it without "bird-nesting" it. At the butt end you can use .0185 or even .0197 if you find that you need more weight in the butt to get out its full length, and it should taper down to a tippet of .0059 for early season, .0047 for mid-May through June, and .0039 for the dog days after the Fourth of July, when the low water on sunny days makes the shadow of any leader look like that of a telephone trunk line.

It's axiomatic that the longer and finer the leader the more fish you'll move, but the axiom holds good only as long as you're laying that leader out to its full length and dropping it on the water quietly and in a straight line. If it lands in a tangled heap, you might as well move on to the next pool, because you'll have scared away every fish worth hooking. To help offset this, the most important single piece of your equipment, if you hope to fish fine, is a piece of rubber with which to rub your leader, several times over its full length, until you're sure it has no twists or curls or kinks. This should be done not only when you first start fishing, and before you make your first cast, but every time you add tippet to the leader's end or every time you see any vestiges of kink or curl coming back into your leader as it lies out on the water before you. I learned this long ago from Al McClane, the fishing editor of *Field & Stream*, and it has meant more to my own angling than any other single thing I ever learned. The rubber ring from a mason jar, or an old piece of an inner tube, or even an eraser or a big rubber band—anything will do, so long as it's rubber and you rub the leader with it long enough to get out every last and least curve or kink.

Except in very low water, the length of your casting distance doesn't seem to matter very much if you're fishing upstream and are being reasonably quiet and deliberate in your movements. Pausing for the length of time it takes to smoke a cigarette, once you've arrived in a spot where you intend to make a cast, is usually enough to make up for any slight disturbance you've caused in the course of your wading to that spot.

And now that you're there, what fly? Well, oddly enough, when you're fishing as fine as this, it doesn't seem to make a great deal of difference. If it's a size 20 or smaller, I honestly think it could be sky-blue-pink, and you'd still get a strike on it.

White, or black, or yellow, or blue, or gray—they all seem to produce. Also, flies this small are very tolerant of slight errors of presentation that might be fatal in the conventional sizes. Drag, for instance, which is supposed to be so terrible on an upstream cast with a dry fly, sometimes seems to serve as an added attraction to a midge that's floating on or in the surface film. When you see your fly starting to drag, give it an occasional six-inch twitch, and you're more likely than not to produce an answering explosion.

Then what? Chances are better than even that you'll lose him, but you'll have a picnic in the process. If he's a big rainbow or brown, over 18 inches in length, you'll probably find he's no longer with you after the second or third jump, assuming you have him on .0047 or .0039. But you'll be surprised how well even .0039 will hold, after you've lost your first few big fish. I've had .0039 hold on fish up to 3 pounds, .0047 up to 5 pounds, and .0059 up to 8 pounds. Your chances of holding onto the big ones get better all the time, as you become more aware, with each successive loss, of the limits of your equipment. Actually, it's only the fine leader that's working against you, since the little light rod is an advantage rather than a handicap, giving ground rather than allowing him something stiff to pull against. As long as you hold it up straight, with your arm extended full length, and even with or behind your head, you're giving him the maximum spring and you needn't fear breaking it. You might break it, just possibly, if you lower it too much and let it extend too far out in front of you, thus lending added credence to the old adage that fishermen often break rods, but fish almost never. And as for the leader, since the chances are that you wouldn't have got the strike at all on a heavier one, you can hardly resent the fact that you're bound to get a certain percentage of breakoffs. You'll soon learn, after the first few losses, to play the fish so gently that you're practically afraid to draw a breath while he's on, and once you've developed that attitude you'll find that each big fish is on longer than the one before, until finally, to your exquisite pleasure and surprise, you'll begin landing some of those lunkers.

If you're one of the many fishermen who long ago stopped using a landing net, your first experiences with trying to land fish of any size on these fine tippets may make you want to go back to using a net. But if you play the fish until he's belly-up, you can easily hold him head-up with your rod and grasp him gently from behind, to release the hook, without causing such panicky thrustings-about as to break off the fine tippet.

When you release him, you may think he's done for, but if you will hold him with his nose upstream in the current, with your right hand holding him right side up while you stroke his sides gently head to tail with your left hand, he will suddenly come alive and shoot forward like an arrow. It sometimes takes as much as five to ten minutes of this gentle massage before he comes out of shock—and that's a wonderful moment. This inert creature beneath your right hand, seemingly stone cold dead, will "wake up" as recognizably as a downed boxer coming out of it during the referee's count, and with a comic expression of "What am I doing *here?*" he will take off so suddenly and swiftly that you may well wonder whether you only dreamed that you just had him in hand.

Fishing fine is a relative thing. When the stream is up to your waist or higher, .0059 is plenty fine, and you can take fish readily on size 14 nymphs and size 12 streamers and buck-tails. And in this kind of water, you can fish with virtually equal success both downstream and up. In fact, the most consistent fun I have is with a size 14 hair-wing streamer called The Betsy—it's really only a hair-wing peacock-bodied wet Coachman—which I dress heavily with dry-fly oil, cast across stream, and let float down like a little sailboat. On the down float it often takes fish, but even when it doesn't it serves as a marvelous "locator," producing curiosity bursts and bunts. I then try to retrieve it back over those places where fish made passes at it on its downstream float, taking it in in quick short jerks that make it pull under and then bob up—and almost invariably one of the fish that poked at it on its way down will chase it frantically on its way back up—often seizing it within twenty or even fifteen feet of where I'm standing. They seem so engrossed in catching this bobbing little object that they fail to notice me and grab it almost at the moment I'm lifting the fly from the water for another cast. This happens again and again, not merely with the silly little jaspers under 9 inches long but with fish old enough to know better—big ones, at least by our standards in the East, where we have to measure our fish in inches rather than pounds.

When the water level is down to about knee-high, you'd better fine your tippet down to .0047. With this tippet you get a highly lifelike descent to the water on size 16 and 18 dry flies, particularly with spiders and hair-wings like the Quack Royal Coachman. It's only when the low water comes, and you're standing in water barely over your ankles, that you must go down to an .0039 tippet and stick to flies of size 20 or smaller. And it's really only then that you must limit yourself to upstream fishing. At such a time you must be fishing not only Fine, but Far Off too, or you'll move very few fish. If it doesn't make you feel too much of a fool, you'll be better off, when the time of low water comes, to crouch down out of sight as much as possible. If you won't go on your knees for any fish, your only alternative is to make a cast of better than forty-five feet upstream; otherwise you might just as well spare the strength of your casting arm.

To make a cast of better than forty-five feet, with the short light rod and fine gauge line, you must use the booster technique known as the double-line haul. The best way to learn it is from somebody who knows it. It has been adequately described in print, so you could learn it for yourself, only in *The Practical Fly Fisherman* by Al McClane.

The fair rewards of fishing fine are a soothing balm to the ego. Your greatest moment will come when you move into a pool that has just been abandoned by a couple of spin fishermen, after tossing several hundred pounds of assorted hardware through it between them, only to reach the disgusted conclusion that, just as they thought, it has been "all fished out." They may make some equally pejorative remarks about your toy tackle. But just watch their faces as you move fish in the very spots they've just finished going over with a fine-tooth comb, to no effect. Maybe it's because this has been happening lately that, as I understand it, some of the prominent manufacturers of spin tackle have now added fly tackle to their line.

Aside from such negligible triumphs, the biggest reward is a purely inner satisfaction when you find that your whole attitude toward angling is changing as you become more devoted to the question How Well as opposed to How Much. We all start out as fish-hogs at heart, as Mr. Hewitt said, but if we stick to it long enough we finally educate ourselves out of it. Fishing with light tackle becomes fun in and of itself. The satisfaction of making a long smooth quiet cast that settles on the water as softly as a fall of snow, and of watching the thistledown-way your tiny fly hovers down onto the water on that fine filament—why, you begin to enjoy even the casts that don't provoke strikes. Soon you find that you are playing at angling the same way you would play at golf, just to see if you can make a better score this time than last time.

You find yourself keeping score, rather than keeping fish. Oh sure, if you've promised somebody some fish, you'll keep as many as you feel you must to make good on the promise. But you'll also find that your enjoyment goes up the minute you realize that, having kept enough to fulfill the obligation, you *don't have to keep any more.* This feeling may well surprise you the first time it comes over you, but come over you sooner or later it certainly will. Because, as you've come within the charmed circle of dedicated angling, you've discovered that what really interests you now is the *fishing,* in and of itself, not the *fish.* You're no more concerned with what you take away from the stream with you than you would be over whether or not you could take home part of the golf course!

The ironical part of it all is that your headiest success as an angler begins when you start caring more about the fishing than the fish. I guess you could best compare this element of fishing luck to that of gambling, where they say "scared money never wins." Or maybe, in this, fish are like cats, who won't come to you if they know you like them but will swarm all over you if they know you don't. Or maybe that mysterious lateral line that seems to warn fish of unseen dangers works in reverse also and tells them when it's okay to bite. I only know that since I've been fishing fine I've taken more fish in a day, with water low or high, with weather wet or dry, than I used to take in a season in the days when I was heaving plugs with desperation.

Of course, I ought to warn you that going in for fine tackle is definitely doing it the hard way. You will get snarls, not only in your leader but even in the forepart of your line, and they will be pesky to pick loose because of the very fineness of your tackle. You must be temperamentally suited to getting a kick out of doing it the hard way, or this fishing is not for you. My wife says that a tape recording of me "enjoying myself" on the stream would strike fear into the hearts of a riot squad. Sure, the slightest unexpected trick of the wind or lapse in your own timing can make you goof into an unholy mess and you'll cuss yourself to high heaven. But when that little coil of oiled silk shoots out ahead of you the way it should, as it does about nineteen times out of twenty, fishing fine is an unexampled thrill.

Perhaps the best way to test yourself, before investing in a mess of light tackle, is to compare angling to driving. Automatic, no-shift gearshifts have been available to the motorist for just about the same length of time that spinning tackle has been available in this country to the fisherman. Both have been a boon to the guy who is only concerned with "getting there" in the easiest way possible. But there are those to whom a car, in and of itself, is more than a mere means of transportation. Of such dedicated motorists it has been written: "An accomplished motorist no more wants an automatic drive than an accomplished pianist wants an automatic piano." Shifting gears is getting there the hard way, too, but if you can understand the thrill of gunning a car through the gears, instead of leaving all that "work" to some mushomatic machinery, then you probably have the temperament to try becoming a 20/20 angler.

4 · The Monster Rainbow
of Mariazell

And ete the olde fisshe, and leve the yonge,
Though't they moore towgh be uppon the tonge.
Piers of Fulham, fifteenth century

FISHING is almost always either feast or famine, and either extreme can become equally boring. After the years of nearfishlessness when I was living in and near Chicago, I would never have believed that the day would come when I would find it boring to take too many fish. But the ready-made fishing at the Fin 'n' Feather, thrilling as it was at first, soon palled. I enjoyed the fly rod, and learning to use it was fun in itself, but fishing with it, at least in those artificial surroundings, seemed too easy to be worth doing. That was its "cathouse" aspect.

Charlie Ritz tells a story of the formidable fly fisherman who died and was conducted by an archangel to a dream river, told that it was his to fish alone, and promptly began pulling out enormous trout on every cast. After the fourth day in this fishing paradise, he complained that he was beginning to get a little tired of fishing, but was told by the archangel that it was his river and he was supposed to fish it. After another three days he complained to the archangel again, saying that he was getting very tired of taking a fish on every cast and that if this was his idea of Paradise . . .

"That's where you're wrong," said the archangel, "this is Hell."

Oddly, we had essentially the same story in *Esquire* once, only in that case it concerned a golfer who was doomed to go on endlessly making a hole in one.

I came to light tackle for precisely the opposite reason from the one which in today's suburban sprawl, where there seem to be more fishermen than fish, best justifies its use. In my case, I lightened my tackle because I again became bored with catching too many fish. But that was in another country and under circumstances most unlikely to recur. It was in Austria immediately after the war, when the trout and the grayling were both so abundant and so eager that they would rise to meet your fly on virtually every cast, shouldering one another like so many basketball players engaged in a wild scramble beneath the basket. There was a 10-inch keeper limit, but that was academic, as the winner in the scrimmage for your fly was almost invariably a fish of better than 18 inches. I'd begun fishing those wonderful Austrian streams, teeming with trout and apparently never fished, in April of 1946, when I borrowed some tackle from one of the officers at the British army press camp in Vienna and drove down to Styria, where I fished the Mürz, from Mürzzuschlag to Mürzsteg, taking trout virtually at will. It was my opinion then, as it is now, that the British, for all their near-monopoly on the traditions of the sporting life, are the most persistently and stubbornly stout-geared fishermen in the world. I would now amend that belief only to the extent of making a possible exception of the Icelanders.

The rod was a 10-foot Hardy, hefting a good 7 ounces, and the leader couldn't have been any finer than OX, though of this I can't be sure since I had no micrometer to gauge its size accurately. The flies were Sedges and Alexandras, though I think bare hooks, wrapped perhaps with the red strip of cellophane from around the top of a pack of cigarettes, would have served no less well. Waders were out of the question, so I waded wet, wearing *lederhosen* and tennis shoes, for though the bed of the Mürz is rocky, it isn't slippery, and there was no need of felts or chains for security of footing.

Fritz Steurer, formerly (and now again) an excellent tackle shop right behind the Parliament Building in the heart of Vienna, was fresh out of stock of almost everything, like most Viennese shops at the time. I managed to get some flies from him, but I had no hope of getting lighter tackle short of Switzerland. I had been living in Switzerland since the summer of 1945, so I returned the borrowed tackle and came back to the Mürz the next time with a 3-ounce rod and 6X leaders, both the lightest I could find in either Zurich or Lausanne. The result was that I now lost about a third more of the fish I hooked, but I found myself playing them for an average of about two thirds longer, and having twice as much fun. Also I'd remembered Felix Alter's trick, and had pinched the barbs off my flies, so there were more fish that either got off or could easily be let off the hook instead of being landed. Thus the paradise of fishing that Austria represented, that first summer after the war, was kept from turning into a hell of surfeit.

Each year thereafter the Austrian fishing slowed down somewhat, though still only slightly, and as late as the spring of 1948, in the course of a month when I fished all the Austrian provinces except the Burgenland with my youngest son, then a boy of twelve, you could take fish at any likely-looking spot, wherever you stopped the car. We fished from one of the earliest Volkswagens, delivered in Vienna in April of '47, in the pre-Nordhoff days, when the British Army of Occupation had just started up the Volkswagen plant. We'd keep our rods jointed and strung up, sticking out the car window, and wherever we went, up and down all the roads of Austria, we'd stop when we saw a weir, and we'd jump out and catch a half dozen trout in a half hour, and then drive on.

There were no restricted waters, and an AGO card and an ETO fishing license was all that was needed to fish anybody's water. My son's license had an asterisk after his name, and the notation that "the above-mentioned individual is twelve years old and will be fishing only in the company of his father." We had set out from Lutry, near Lausanne, where he was in school, and had provisioned ourselves for the long journey, with an abundance of Swiss francs, Austrian schillings, and American army currency, and plenty of cigarettes, which, even as late as '48, were still more welcome than money in most places in Austria. Our second day in Austria, however, we were reduced to living off our wits, our rods, and our cigarettes, as I leaned over too far, trying to free a fly that had been caught on the riprap bordering a mile-long waterfall down the Dead Mountain, south of Salzburg. I was wearing one of those waiter- or bus-boy-length Austrian jackets known as a *Joppe* (pronounced "Yawpuh" by their rightful wearers), and my breast-pocket wallet, with our hoard of assorted currencies, shot out into the stream. We watched it go down the cascading steps for a mile, ejecting banknotes at every step like a Bacchante throwing flowers in a Dionysian parade.

Fortunately we were carrying two Jerry cans of gasoline, enough to propel the Volkswagen all over Austria, and we could get overnight accommodations at the country inns for cigarettes. Our only problem was how to eat, and that was no problem at all, at that time in that place, because there's a trout stream beside every road in Austria, except for the Burgenland, where we weren't going anyway. And we knew that any Gasthof proprietor would be delighted to accept our catch in payment for cooking up that portion of it that we could eat ourselves, and pleased to give us black bread and boiled potatoes along with it.

For over two weeks, until our fixed rendezvous with the

rest of the family, when we could replenish our funds, we lived off the land, or at least off its waters. We worked our way down past Leoben and around through Carynthia and Styria, lingering longest on my old home stretch of the Mürz, and then we went up over the mountain beyond Mürzsteg, to come out on the other side, near Mariazell. From there, going off in three directions, we found some idyllic fishing spots. At one there was a statue of the old Kaiser Franz Josef right at the edge of the stream, and as we pulled out trout in his shadow, in the sun-dappled waters, there was nothing and nobody in sight to make us realize that we were not indeed enjoying his "good old days."

Nearby is the monastery of the Heiligen Kreuz, which the rest of the family, meaning chiefly my wife, accompanied by the other two boys, had wanted to visit, to see its glorious wealth of art objects. For this reason we had fixed upon Mariazell as the spot for the reunion of the fishing and non-fishing branches of the family. Having saved the spot nearest the inn in Mariazell to fish last, we had reached it just as dusk was gathering. It was a weir, with a little footbridge from the roadside to an embankment on which there was a small galvanized-iron shed about the size of a toolhouse and the shape of a Quonset hut, which presumably housed the machinery that worked the dam. Beside this there was a little patch of grass, and a concrete retaining wall, about the width of a sidewalk, on which one or even two could stand and easily fish the weir below.

I had taken the first couple of quick ones that we always pulled out almost immediately after wetting a line in any weir, nice fat fish of the prevailing size, 17 to 18 inches, and had just expressed the opinion that, with darkness coming on, we'd better not stay for one more, when my boy said that there was something big down there that kept making enormous swirls behind his fly.

He was fishing a long light rod that he had picked out for himself in Lausanne, a 10-foot magnesium derrick, stout enough and long enough to compensate for his own pre-teen stature, yet light enough that he could handle it with ease despite its giant size. On it he had rigged a fly reel and line, but with a short stout leader of not much over 4 feet, about comparable to the upper third of my own. To its terminal extremity, which you could hardly dignify by the designation of tippet, he generally attached a big bright bushy bucktail on a number 4 hook, usually altering the pattern only to the extent of trying a Parmachene Belle when a Mickey Finn didn't work immediately, or vice versa.

I had told him, when we started out, that such terminal tackle would probably repel any fish more sophisticated than a wilderness squaretail, but it had worked well from the start. He was usually quicker than I was to pull out a fish from any weir we stopped at, and in the first week, when he kept count of his fish by putting a pencil mark for each one on the wooden rim of his wicker creel, he had run out of space after making 198 marks. I couldn't argue with that success, and although I consistently stuck to flies no larger than size 12 myself, I soon decided to leave him to his own devices. One of them he had not yet tried, a fearsome engine he had picked up in Lausanne the same place we had bought his rod. Probably intended for trolling in Lake Geneva, it was a streamer of soft brown fur— he said he'd really bought it because he liked the feel of it—on a size 3/0 hook, with wire outriggers on each side to which were attached bright nickel spinners on brass ball-bearing swivels. I could only imagine that, in the water, it would look like a muskrat in distress. He had christened it the Whammy, but had not yet used it, and now he deemed that its time had come.

As I started packing up our gear, to go back across the footbridge and put our things in the car before darkness would make the trip too hazardous for my rod tip, he begged that I leave him on the dam just long enough to make one try with the Whammy. I said fine, if he could see well enough to tie it on, which I knew I wouldn't have been able to do myself.

As I reached the far side of the footbridge I thought I heard a short sharp soprano exclamation, a sound like "ow" or "ouch" or "ow-ee"—but I couldn't be sure against the noise of the waters rushing over the dam. On my return trip, as I neared the little toolhouse on the side of the dam, I thought I saw a sudden quick silver streak, making a short high arc through the now nearly total darkness; and then, beyond any doubt, I heard something hit the tin roof of the toolhouse. It was a loud plosive sound, just short of the shattering report of a grenade, and I actually wondered whether at this late date there might still be troops around who might be bombing for their suppers, as they had all too often been inclined to do in these Austrian streams the first year or so after the war.

I ran, as fast as the precarious sway of the footbridge would let me, to see my boy falling on something white that in the quick glimpse I had of it seemed very nearly his own size. Without a word, I threw myself on top of him, and felt him squirming beneath me. For what could only have been moments, but seemed minutes, there appeared some likelihood that our whole animated and agitated jam-pile might go over the edge of the dam.

When at last there was enough relative quiet underneath us that it seemed safe to do so, we unpeeled ourselves off the biggest fish that until that time I had ever seen outside of salt water. We were both gripping him anxiously, lest he regain the strength to throw himself off the parapet on which we were crouched. I couldn't even be sure, in the darkness, of what he might be, as I felt around his head for the leader, to try to take the hook out of his mouth. I groped and felt all around him, but couldn't find the leader, and I ran my fingers all the way around, making the grand tour of his mighty mouth. No feel of any part of line or leader, or of the Whammy.

"Try reeling your rod in," I suggested, "so we can see if he's foul-hooked somewhere, because I can't find a thing around his mouth."

I reasoned that he might have been stunned, if not actually brained, by the impact when he hit the corrugated, galvanized zinc or iron of the tin roof of the little toolhouse, and though he was now completely inert, I kept expecting him to revive. I asked the boy for his knife, having left my own in the car. I hoped I might make a deep thrust at the base of the brain without spoiling him as a trophy we would undoubtedly be wanting to get mounted back in Vienna. But the boy had only a pair of nail clippers that he had been using to cut off knots in changing flies.

When we reeled in, we felt the end of his leader, and there was no Whammy, just a smooth end of the nylon above the point where his knot had been. We felt all around the throw-rug-size patch of grass between the toolhouse and the concrete walk at the edge of the dam, but we couldn't make contact with any trace of leader end or lure. The Whammy was gone. Had it been ejected by the force of the slap on the toolhouse roof? Had it, against all probability, been ejected after the fish had left the water, so that the flight through the air had been sheer follow-through of a jerk exercised by a twelve-year-old? We were never to know. All we could do was get ourselves and rod and fish back over the footbridge in the complete darkness, in a slow groping and halting procession, sliding our feet as if on a slack wire, until we could get to the car and get the fish in the headlights. There we at last saw that it was a rainbow.

We had a De-Liar in the car, with which the boy had amused himself, weighing and measuring almost every fish we had taken, particularly on the first days of the trip, and particularly in the case of the fish we had returned to the water. But it extended to only 24 inches. That was all right: we could hold it carefully and measure again, beyond the length of its steel tape, to get an exact length. In this instance it turned out to be an even 30 inches. But we could only guess at the weight; the De-Liar registered only up to 8 pounds.

"You know," I said, "you could fish for thirty years and not get another 30-inch trout. This is the fish of a lifetime. Whether you grow up to amount to anything or not, you'll always be the guy that got the 30-inch rainbow at Mariazell."

"Gee," he said, "I thought he was pretty big."

But there is no way a twelve-year-old can be adequately impressed.

We hurried back to the inn, where we found the rest of the family more concerned about whether we had fallen in somewhere, and more inclined to discuss past and future comings and goings than the topic, which I considered of practically historic importance, of our trophy rainbow. Indeed, in the course of a lot of inconsequential small talk about our having lost all our money down a cascade and our having lived on our wits for two weeks, one of the help made off with the fish into the recesses of the inn's kitchen, and in the subsequent *va-et-vient* of having dinner and arranging when and where we would meet again after going our separate ways on the morrow, nobody thought about getting a picture of the fish, though one of the other boys had a camera with a flashbulb attachment, or even of telling anybody in the kitchen what care should be taken of the fish overnight.

I shouldn't have been as surprised as I was, the next morning, when the chef's treat, at our table for five, was revealed beneath the lifted cover of the biggest platter I had ever seen, one that I doubt had been used in the inn since the old Kaiser's time. It was, of course, our giant rainbow of the night before, baked whole, and artfully garnished with boiled potatoes and parsley. No trophy to be taken to a taxidermist in Vienna, no photograph, albeit by flashlight, not even a Whammy, which might at least have been mounted on a plaque, to serve as a souvenir.

That fish was the high point of even the heyday of the Austrian fishing in the immediate postwar years. No other trout, even in the glut of the spring of '46, when the fishing was still virtually virginal, had gone beyond 24 inches, and although fish of 17 and 18 inches were common in those first years, even then trout beyond 20 inches in length were exceptional.

The next year, with currency reform and the Pulmotor effect of the Marshall Plan upon the Austrian economy, you could no longer pay your way all over Austria with a few cartons of cigarettes, and it was not long after that before the private rights of preserved and posted waters were restored. You could no longer expect that the *förster*, come to see who was fishing the Herr Baron's waters, would back away in confusion at the first glimpse of an AGO card or an ETO fishing license. And after the spring of '55, when the country's sovereignty was fully restored, fishing rights were difficult to come by.

I managed to get a beat to fish, in the late summer of that year, that belonged to the Municipality of Vienna, and the same boy and I fished it for two days, all we could get. It was superb fishing, by the standards then prevailing and by present standards in the Eastern United States, but it was a far cry from the teeming trout waters of those first years after the war. We both succeeded in taking a few that ran over 14 inches, and he took one that measured 17, though none on the slaphappy big bucktails he had formerly employed. This time they would touch nothing larger than a size 14, or a leader any coarser than 5X. I did manage, twice, to take doubles, by bifurcating an 8X leader to make a tandem float of two Cahill bivisible spiders, size 16, twitching them across the slow late summer stream in "skates" of six inches at a time. And that's a feat I would hardly expect to accomplish today on the Beaverkill or the Willowemoc without the accompaniment of a brass band and dancing in the streets of Roscoe or Livingston Manor.

But oh for the days, in '46 and '47, when I would pick up that same boy, then ten and eleven, after his last class in Lutry on Saturday afternoons, drive across Switzerland and through the Vorarlberg, letting him sleep in the back seat as we went over the Arlberg Pass (once in a blizzard on the Fourth of July), to arrive at St. Martin just after dawn, about four in the morning. There we would wander over meadows in the shadow of the church steeples, fishing little streams that even he could jump across and that I could nearly straddle, pulling out trout as long as your forearm, trout that could see you because you could see them, seemingly almost as close as behind glass in an aquarium. We would keep enough to last us through Saturday's and Sunday's meals at the Gasthof, alternating between broiled and blue to avoid monotony. Then back over the Arlberg again, after fishing until the last rays went over the backdrop of the mountains, to slide him back into his room at school in time for the first cry of *Debout, les douches!* which was supposed to awaken him at seven o'clock on Monday morning.

Those were the days when you could fish where you liked, and almost as you liked, because the trout were so eager you could almost do no wrong. Even the zones didn't matter and you could fish them all, American, British, French, and even the Russian, where all you needed to pass any control point was a Texaco credit card, or any typed piece of paper on which you had pasted a red star, in those days of jeeps and uniforms and the interzonal currency of cigarettes and chocolate bars. After the first months, when you could go native and drive your own car, you might be held up at a checkpoint, particularly at American ones, until you opened your mouth and let them know that under the *gemsbart* and the *joppe* and the *lederhosen* was something as American as Mom's apple pie. You could, that is, most times. Occasionally there'd be a GI who wouldn't wave you on in spite of your profane inquiry as to when he had last picked his earwax.

"Can't you tell I'm an American, for Christ's sake, the minute I open my big bazoo?"

"Nawsir," he would drawl, "we git a lotta them Owstrians speaks English lot better'n yew dew."

You could take a jeep and run down to Mürzzuschlag and in the course of a morning fill one of those *viviers*, the water-filled wooden casks with shoulder straps that European fishers use, and give Herr Lehner something new to wake up the guests with at the Weisser Hahn, the little hotel on the Josefstätterstrasse that served as the American press center the first years. When, as very seldom happened, there were fresh eggs instead of powdered, he would excitedly telephone every room and yell: "Hey, vake up, ja? gives today frische eier!" So for a change you could be the occasion of his changing his glad alarm to "gives today frische forellen—vunderful trouts."

And if none of the trout, before or after, was ever as wonderful as that 30-incher from Mariazell, I was to learn why much later. I never found out what became of the Whammy, but I did find out what became of the 30-inch rainbows. In '55, when I was flying to Vienna after fishing in Iceland, I happened to sit beside an Austrian who had been a game warden in, of all places, the area around Mariazell. When I told him about it, he said: "Oh *ja*, that was an Isonzo *forelle*—our boys in the First World War, they used to bring them back when they came home on leave from the Italian front." Shades of me and my *vivier*, jeeping back with live fish from the Mürz to the Weisser Hahn.

"They were most terrible cannibals," he added. "We used to shoot them when we saw them. There wouldn't be any left today. I don't think so."

5 · Emergence of a Point of View

La pêche doit rester un sport et un plaisir, faute de quoi elle devient pire que le travail. Charles Ritz, in an interview with Bill Higgins

ONE BAD THING about the wonderful fishing in Europe was that it spoiled you for the kind of hard fishing you'd be likely to encounter most places you'd go in the overfished and over-

populated places around our big Eastern cities. It was as hard
to readjust as it was to readjust to American cigarettes.

When I stepped off the plane, after a mere four years of
smoking Colonials (Maryland caporals) in Switzerland, Gaul-
oises in France, Nazionale in Italy, Munkacz in Hungary,
and Woodbines in England, I naturally asked for the cigarettes I'd been smoking for more than twenty years before
I went away. My first drag set in train a series of self-cocking
automatic coughs that kept up as long as I puffed. I had to get
weaned from the harsh workmen's cigarettes to which my taste
had become accustomed, a course of treatment that led me
through Picayunes to Home Runs to Sweet Caporals to Pied-
monts before I could finally settle on to something as univer-
sally available as Camels, a brand which I had not smoked
before but which at that stage was the only popular American
one I could smoke without coughing.

Much the same thing happened with my fishing. I found
that I had acquired habits, in the course of dealing with the
too-permissive Austrian trout, that might possibly have been
persisted in with impunity in some of our Western fishing,
but could not possibly escape penalty in the East. An added
difficulty was that everywhere I went with a fly rod I found myself lost in an army of hardware-heavers armed with spinning
rods. In the early fifties a lot of people who really should have
known better, along with a lot more who had never known
how to use anything else, had suddenly discovered spinning,
and few and far between were the trout waters that hadn't
been literally scoured with spinning lures. I was to find it almost impossible to raise a trout to a surface fly or a nymph,
right after somebody had just bombarded him with brass lures

and silver spoons. The trout were huddled on the bottom and nothing I could do would lure them out.

In desperation, after a few futile tries I began to look around for a New York equivalent of my old Fin 'n' Feather ready-made fishing of Chicago days. In the company of my second wife, who loved fishing but had the patience of a wounded she-grizzly, I thought I'd better find a place where we could go fishing and get some fish.

I was to find nothing comparable to the Fin 'n' Feather, but I did learn of a place, just seventy miles from Manhattan and only in its second season, which now offered fly fishing on a daily rod-fee basis. It had been converted from a century-old fishing club on the Carmans River on Long Island, where Daniel Webster had according to legend once landed a 40-pound trout. It offered, as indeed it still does, three miles of the Carmans River, a slow-moving stream, much like one of the Hampshire or Normandy chalk streams, weed-filled but with a good sand-and-gravel bottom and crystalline water. The two and a quarter miles could easily be waded, even in hip boots, while the lower three quarters of a mile deepened into a fifty-acre lake. The club had actually ceased to function as a club in 1923, when one of its members, Anson W. Hard, had taken over its original 600 acres as his own estate and then enlarged it to its present 1,300-acre size. Upon his death, his son Kenneth, who had been studying forestry, intending to go into conservation, decided to convert the estate for his mother's benefit into a hunting and fishing preserve. The residence, a rambling shingle-sided dwelling with attached stables, of an impressive manorlike sprawl, was adapted to house guests in a style more baronial than any of them could possibly have known at home. And the one-time Suffolk Club became The Suffolk Lodge Game Preserve.

When my new wife and I went there for a weekend, back in '52, we had the feeling of going to visit some Lord and Lady Algy, somewhere in Hampshire. We were met at the Brookhaven stop on the Long Island Railroad in a station wagon driven by Bud, one of the gamekeepers, and driven to the parklike grounds. On the way, my wife wondered whether Bud had any other name.

"Yes, ma'am," he answered, "Stuyvesant Van Veen."

If he'd said "Henry Van Dyke," I couldn't have been more surprised—or even "Washington Irving," because everything about Bud, and indeed about the establishment as a whole, was as shaggily friendly as a sheep-dog pup, but it all seemed old, old, old New York, and very Long Island.

Ken Hard and his wife Lee, looking like prototypes for the illustrations of an Abercrombie & Fitch catalogue, met us at the porticoed front door, which gave onto a large courtyard where you expected to see carriages drive up. He was dark and clean-cut in a way somehow reminiscent of the late Richard Barthelmess, and she, blonde and outdoorsy, tall and scrubbed to a bright burnish. They both wore shooting clothes of most casual elegance, and both looked absurdly young, as if they were playing house while the elders were out, and not really running a place as impressive as this. But run it they did (and Ken and his second wife still do; Lee subsequently married Bud), and in those early days they pampered their guests ineffably. We were driven through the preserve's then-narrow sand trails to and from the various beats on the stream in a shooting brake, and brought Lucullan lunches onstream in wicker hampers, with the sparkle of the glassware only exceeded by the gleam of the silver, with hot dishes covered in stiffly immaculate napery.

The wading is easy, no more than mid-thigh deep, even for a woman of junior size, and the current gentle. In most places the stream meanders through green thickets, companionably narrow, permitting two people just enough room to fish it downstream with wet flies, side by side. Here and there are V dams where the stream is hollowed and widened enough to create good holding water for the trout, making it a near certainty to get at least one strike in the vicinity of each V dam. Other hot spots for fish action were created by long smooth glides where the stream whispers along beneath overhanging trees. Throughout the more than two miles of stream, divided into three beats, or sections, there is nothing in sight, beyond the several stream-side duck blinds and one power line, to remind you that you are within a thousand miles of anything but wilderness, save for an occasional weathered sign tacked to a tree and a couple of abandoned cabins dating from the long ago days of the Suffolk Club.

Places where you can clamber out of the stream, to answer a call of nature, are mercifully frequent, though never less than a long city block or so apart. In most sections, once you're in, you're in, the margins of weed and shrubs and assorted undergrowth and overgrowth making both sides virtually bankless. So complete is the sense of seclusion that we felt free to answer a mutual call of nature, still in our hip boots, on a mossy promontory that formed a dappled bower too delectable to resist. This advantage of hip boots over chest-high waders, nowhere to my knowledge stressed in the notoriously discursive wanderings of angling literature, and certainly not in the catalogues, was possibly then first, though probably not last, enjoyed as one of the unadvertised attractions of this primitive but hauntingly beautiful preserve on the tangled banks of the Carmans River.

The fishing was fine—Ken stocked the stream weekly with fat and coony browns and bright and sassy rainbows, from 11 to 12 inches long. There was even the admixture of some perky little native brookies, averaging 8 inches, diminished but unabashed descendants of the undoubtedly seagoing whopper with which legend credits Daniel Webster. It was because of these denizens of the stream that Ken made sure that everybody who fished his water, private and stocked and restricted though it might be, had a New York State fishing license in addition to Ken's permission, implicit in the daily rod fee. Ken set the daily creel limit at five fish, just half of that permitted by the state on its public streams, and at first tried to enforce the rule that any fish landed must be kept. Since the fishing was limited to the use of flies only, except on the lake, where all forms of artificial lures were allowed, the rule seemed actually to be counter to his own interests, and when he was finally convinced that the individual fisherman had sense enough to handle his catch carefully, so that the fish was returned to the water no worse for the experience, and possibly somewhat wiser after being caught, Ken was willing to relax the regulation. Actually in most cases this consideration was academic, as the fishing at Suffolk Lodge was not a snap, as it had been at the Fin 'n' Feather. For most anglers, especially those fishing the stream for the first time, the limit of five fish became a goal rather than a restriction. Certain anglers, such as three priests from St. Patrick's in New York who had season rods and fished every Friday and Saturday—Sunday being their busy day and they working, as one of them put it, for a very stern Boss—came to be so expert in placing a Grey Ghost in known sure-fire places in the South Section that they undoubtedly could and did reach multiples of the limit, but they were the exception.

Why then, since the fishing was ideal in that, though the fish were abundant, they were not too easy to catch, was I not altogether happy with that first season at Suffolk Lodge? The company was congenial, the meals were superb, the bedrooms and baths were par for every comfort and convenience, Ken and Lee were the best of hosts, anticipating your least wish and yet leaving your privacy intact, and the nights were as much your own, to do what you liked, as were the days. The answer was not in the fishing, or in Suffolk Lodge; there wasn't, or isn't today, anything wrong with the Lodge. I have gone back there, again and again over a decade, and have always found it delightful. The fault, as Brutus was told, was in each other. We weren't happy with each other's fishing, and if you're not happy with each other's fishing, it will not be long before you're not happy with each other. We used to leave our gear at Suffolk Lodge through the week, to avoid having to cart it back and forth to the city, but before the next season came around I had to make a solitary trip out there, to separate his from hers and see that hers got back to her.

Eight months for a marriage, *aller et retour*, is short even by today's standards. And it would be an oversimplification to say that, but for fishing, that marriage might have lasted longer. Still, it might not be too wide of the mark to apply here the words with which General Sarnoff has been credited: "Competition brings out the best in products and the worst in people." I keep hearing about happy fishing couples, like the Lou Hartmans who catch all those muskies, and the Chauncey K. Livelys who not only fish together but keep talking about meeting other people who do too. I can only conclude either that one member of the happy couple must be a liar or, if not, that they must have in equal parts the disposition of angels and the patience of saints.

Charlie Ritz is on record, rather wistfully I feel, to the effect that fishing is a sport and a pastime and not a competition, and that it ought to remain a sport and a pleasure, because otherwise it's worse than work. Charles Ritz is one of the happiest fishermen I know, and the one who without entirely turning professional has with evident impunity permitted fishing to take up a measurable portion of his waking time. But it's a long time since he's been married.

We would get out on the stream at Suffolk Lodge and I'd take a fish. Mistake. I should have had sense enough to wait until she'd taken the first fish. So the next time out, I'd try to be more thoughtful. But fish are like cats, in that the only time that you can be sure they'll come to you is when you don't want them. And a fish is even harder to shoo away, once you've hooked it, than a cat. Almost any fish will get off the hook if you're scared enough that he will, but no fish will ever get off a hook if you're afraid he won't. And it was the same with every fish thereafter. I couldn't be one ahead at any time. Or, if we were even, then it was impolitic to have mine even a fraction of an inch larger than hers. Or if her fish, whether first or last or current, happened to be a rainbow, then mine had better be a rainbow, too. It didn't dare turn out to be a brown, because even if it were considerably smaller it would still outrank the rainbow, since browns had a scarcity value in the average fishing at Suffolk Lodge; there might be anywhere from three to six rainbows for each brown. On the other hand, it had better not be a brookie either, no matter how small, because the browns were stocked and the brookies were wild, so status was involved there, too.

The only thing to do, under the circumstances, was to try to fish ineptly, but that has its drawbacks, too, when you're fishing side by side. You don't dare make a fish-scaring slap with a deliberately bad cast, because in a narrow stream it will scare all the fish, not just those on your side. So you try making as unlikely motions as possible with your line hand on the retrieve. This has its dangers because sometimes all it takes to make a reluctant fish decide to take is some unorthodox jerking of the fly to vary the monotony of the too-steady retrieve. Another expedient is to leave a bit of moss or grass trailing from the hook point, but that will be noticed, no less by her than by the fish, and after a time it gets you classified as stupid. Still another gambit is to try a larger size than the fly on which they took last. This is good, but still risky, on the "big bait, big fish" premise. It is safer to try some utterly unlikely fly. If they've been taking a dark Cahill wet, size 14, then try a big gaudy Parmachene Belle, size 10 or even 8 if you've got one. But that's catnip to brookies, and the smaller they are the bigger size fly they'll take. The only safe device is to spend as much time as possible getting hung up in the trees or shrubs. But not on the forward cast, for God's sake, because then you're likely to louse up the patch of stream ahead of you where she's fishing. Of course, you can always be a gentleman and offer to wait, before trying to get your fly down off the branches, until she's finished working this spot and is ready to move on downstream. But then you're rushing her, and you know how she hates to be rushed. Safer to get hung up on your back cast, where you can dawdle around upstream getting it freed, although if you spend too much time at it you earn icy contempt for the lack of coordination which is obviously adding an insuperable handicap to your innate stupidity. Still it's the best choice, because the one time you can't catch a fish is when your fly is nowhere near the water.

The one time the charge of lack of coordination may have been well founded, we were fishing in a section which, while still manageable in chest waders, was too deep for our hip boots, and Ken had given us a small aluminum pram to use. This diminutive square-ended skiff, about the size and shape of a cement mixer, could be poled or paddled about the stream, which is considerably wider in this section, and because of its platform-like bottom was considered safe to stand up in. It was close quarters, even if we stayed as far apart as possible, for two of us to fish from at the same time. As we drifted into sight of an abandoned cabin set back in the woods some fifty yards from the left bank of the stream, she became curious about it, wanted to see it, and even wondered if it might be possible to fix it up enough so that Ken might let us stay in it. I poled us over toward the left bank, started to get out on the vestigial remains of a one-time pier or dock, and only realized as I jumped onto an old rafter that the rest of it was resting under the pram, which was catapulted over neatly, unfortunately with her still in it, by the leverage exerted by the rest of the board as soon as my weight hit its other end.

The pram didn't sink, but she did. I had tried to correct my mistake by attempting to jump back away from the rafter as soon as I sensed its motion, but of course I missed the pram and landed in the water hardly more than a few seconds after she did. Each of us looked funny enough to the other when we had both scrambled to our feet and stood, respectively, waist and chest deep in the river that involuntary laughter was the first reaction. But though we visited the abandoned cabin as planned, it was to wring out our wet clothes, and not another word was said, then or ever, about fixing it up as a place to stay.

I had long before decided that I didn't like any form of fishing from any sort of boat, but the pram may have helped to reinforce that decision. What I had also long thought, but now knew for certain, was that competition takes all the fun out of fishing, and makes it, as Charlie Ritz says, worse than work. As for women and fishing, while I know that superstition and tradition are against them, as was pointed out by William Radcliffe in *Fishing from the Earliest Times*, still I have no feeling against it. Some of my best friends are women. I'm married to an ex-fisher now.

One of Radcliffe's citations has a certain interest, however: "Women seem usually fatal to good catches; as one instance out of many we read in Hollinshed's *Scottish Chronicle* that if a woman wade through the one fresh river in the Lewis, there shall no salmon be seen there for a twelvemonth after." On the other hand, some great fishermen have fished with women, as I've mentioned, and there are many more. Al and

Patti McClane fish together. But I throw that out. Al Mc-
Clane can fish with anybody. And Patti McClane can fish
with me, and often has and I hope will again.

The sainted Theodore Gordon himself fished with at least
one woman, and I've been in love with her picture for a decade. You will find it in John McDonald's volume of the notes
and letters of Gordon, *The Complete Fly Fisherman*, published by Scribner's in 1947. There they stand together, in
the Neversink in a spot that I believe I recognize as his
favorite pool in Mr. Hewitt's old stretch, with Gordon looking pale and wan and delicate, and she looking tall and stately
as Tennyson's Maud, her long skirts in, but somehow none-
theless disdainful of, the flowing waters. And a lovelier sight
I never saw.

Women fishing is one thing, and watching women fishing
is another. But women watching fishing—well, in my experience, women who watch fishermen, at least stream fishermen,
almost invariably remind me of a dog watching television.
They have no capacity of sustained attention, no concentration whatsoever, and an eye only for the extraneous and inconsequential. Still, there is a fairly general feeling that for
some reason fishing should be a shared experience. There's
industry propaganda to the effect of Take a Boy Fishing. I've
taken boys fishing, and on two of them out of three it didn't
take. As for just taking any boy fishing, well, why? Bless Dave
Bascom of San Francisco, who edits that hilarious fishing
paper, *The Wretched Mess*, and is to my mind the funniest
man on feet since W. C. Fields went horizontal. "Yes," says
Dave Bascom, "Take a Boy Fishing—and throw the little
bastard in."

I've known men who said they didn't go fishing any more,

since their old buddy died, or moved away, or whatever. And
they didn't mean their wives. I wonder if these men really
ever did go fishing. Maybe they just went on what used to be
called "outings," presumably because they let you out of the
house. I'm all for friendship, and partnership has been a good
idea since Damon and Pythias, I suppose; but if what you're
setting out to do is to come, by the most permissive of
definitions, within the pale of angling, then you don't need a
partner. Your partner, your one true old buddy, if you could
only get it through his minimal brain, is the fish. In its deepest self, fishing is the most solitary sport, for at its best it's
all between you and the fish.

6 · Preston Jennings for President —or, There *Is* a Royal Coachman

Ever since fishing rods were first used, fixed ideas have been responsible for blank days.   W. F. R. Reynolds,
                                                                          in *Fly and Minnow*

THEY SAY THAT NATURE has mercifully rigged our memory mechanisms in such a way that our pleasures are magnified in recollection and our pains minimized. You forget the thousands of fruitless casts you made, in any one spot where you've fished, and remember it only at the breathless moment when one of those casts produced. Maybe that particular spot is one where you were often snagged, or hung up on branches beyond reach, or where treacherous currents, either of wind or of water, made an exasperating mess of your leader tippet. Maybe it's even a spot where insidiously slippery rocks, working in league with the current, contrived to give you an ignominious ass-over-appetite spill, resulting at best in total immersion and at worst in some nasty contusions. But unless you broke either an important bone or a prized rod in the process, even the recollection of that disaster can be glossed over, in your subsequent memory-image of that spot, by a later instance of success. In the palimpsest of memory the darkest layers, painted there by pain and discomfort and frustration, are quickly washed over and submerged beneath the gloriously roseate hues, flamboyant as those of Turner's skies, that can be superimposed by one heady moment of success.

This no doubt accounts for the fact that angling books, almost without exception, tend to be happier documents than they have any right to be, if memory had some way of keeping a truly honest scorecard. I have searched, Diogenes-like, through shelves and stacks of fishing books, looking for one honest account, adequately conveying the ring of the awful truth that almost all of the time spent on stream is devoted to the enjoyment of being miserable. It's like the vulgar appraisal of the supreme joy of motherhood: "One moment of pleasure and nine months of pain."

I've found only one book that gives me any sense of the

exquisite discomfort that is endemic to most of the time
spent in the pesky sport of stream fishing with a fly. The rest
of the angling authors, from Dame Juliana on down to Al
McClane, all seem to me to be guilty, though in enormously
varying degree, of some gilding of this lily. (As for Hewitt,
and his wondering whether it would be safe to impart the
secret of his nymphs, for fear that our streams might be
emptied by them—mine own eyes have seen Hewitt skunked,
using his own nymphs, and on his own water, at that.) The
one honest book I've found that gives off the reek of undeo-
dorized authenticity is a thin volume published by Putnam
in London in 1960, written by John Inglis Hall and called
How to Fish a Highland Stream (The Truim).

Summarized, its message is, for all but the hardiest of souls,
simply: Don't. The duckings, the snaggings and the snarls, the
bedevilments of the winds, the vagaries of the currents,
the endless frustrations building up to a beside-yourself pressure of mindless rage, all the demonic perversities of this
"wretched little burn" are caught here as Cromwell wanted
to be, warts and all. A nonfisherman reading it would put it
down as the meaningless ravings of an idiot. But it makes
any addicted angler itch to try the Truim.

To date, it's the one fishing book I know in which the
author never tends, like an absentminded fishmonger, to
weigh his finger with the fish. But there might be another,
if Paul O'Neil, who wrote a piece about the Esopus in the
May 8, 1964 issue of *Life*, ever takes time off to do a book
about it. The article was called "In Praise of Trout
—and Also Me," and was subtitled: An Unregenerate Angler
Reviews the Fish in His Life. The truth is in him, too, and if

he ever lets it all out, then there will be two books with which to start what might some day become a five-inch shelf of angling works that, for a change, really give stream fishing the works.

The Esopus was called a most murderous stream by Theodore Gordon, but that was before 1912, when the Ashokan Dam was built, to create a reservoir for New York City, and before the Portal was put in, at Shandaken, to connect it with another reservoir, making the intervening stretch of stream into a sort of cosmic dipper for the slaking of New York's thirst. Filled from the Portal as desired and drawn on by the Ashokan Reservoir as needed, the Esopus is kept at a heavier, if less predictable, flow than other New York streams. It is ironical that it is called a creek and not a river. As a wading stream, where it was once most murderous perhaps it would now be charged with being merely manslaughtering.

On it I spent the two most miserably happy years of my fishing life. For it was to the Esopus and its tributaries that I turned when chivalry suggested that I do my fishing thereafter in another direction from Manhattan than that of Suffolk Lodge. Gordon Dean, who ran the Sportsmen's Information Desk at Abercrombie & Fitch, directed me to Rainbow Lodge at Mt. Tremper, which Dick and Blanche Kahil had recently set up as an anglers' haven. They had previously had a similar place on the Mongaup. The Kahils took over an old frame structure, typical of the Catskill boardinghouse of the first years of the century. It was a dump, but it had a sort of Edwardian charm and a shabby-genteel vestige of tone, run down though it was.

Within a couple of years fire was to dispose of it, but meanwhile the Kahils were exploiting its every disadvantage as an element of its peculiar charm, and making us all like it.

Rainbow Lodge fronted on one of the lesser tributaries of the Esopus, a tiny stream that joined the Big Creek at Mt. Tremper, a mile to the south, and bordered the road toward Woodstock almost halfway to that Greenwich Village of the Catskills. This stream was called the Little Beaverkill, but when I tried to look it up on a map I was confused by the fact that there were half a dozen Catskill streams so designated, none of which seemed to pass anywhere near Mt. Tremper. It was easily fishable when the Esopus itself was in roaring spate, and while most of it was pocket water, it featured occasional small pools that were stuffed with small trout.

I was still confused in my judgment of trout sizes by the average size of the Austrian trout, and hardly less so by the general run of the browns and rainbows that Ken Hard stocked at Suffolk Lodge, all of which were above 11 inches. Dick and Blanche would often ask me to go out and get some pan-size trout for breakfast, to serve to those guests who might like them, reminding me that they had to be at least 7 inches long to be legal keepers under New York State law at the time, but still hoping that they would not go too much over the limit, as the smaller the better. I measured all the little trout against the span of my hand, which I assumed to be 7 inches. I kept throwing them back, one after another, as they seemed to measure, with maddening uniformity, between 6¾ and 6⅞ inches. No matter how I would hold them against the palm of my right hand, they invariably missed bridging the span of my extended fingers by from an eighth to a quarter of an inch. I would keep trying the easy first pool above the lodge, returning empty-handed and dejected every time. Infuriatingly, it was the only truly easy pool on the whole stretch. All you had to do was to cast almost any small dark wet fly across to the edge of the foam where a spillway fed the pool, let the fly swing with the current past an enormous rock that formed one wall of the pool, where the trout congregated in the cool shade, and you'd get some sort of action almost every time. There was nowhere else in the area where you could count on any sort of touch or bunt even on every hundredth cast.

Because of my consistent failure to bring back trout from this pool, Dick encouraged a growing habit among the habitués of Rainbow Lodge of referring to it as Frustration Pool, and it was so identified in some of his subsequent promotional literature. It was only after the better part of the season had elapsed that it occurred to him one night, when I had again demonstrated on my outstretched fingers by how narrowly the trout I'd caught had failed to qualify as keepers, to measure the span of my hand. It turned out to be just over 8⅛ inches. All those trout I had put back had run 8 inches or just under, when I had thought they were so narrowly missing 7.

There were many other places, on the Esopus and its tributaries, where the trout would school up by the hundreds, lying motionless in the current, but nothing I could throw at them would attract their attention. This sometimes included stones, when I would become convinced that they were all sound asleep. But even stoning the pool made no difference, except to get them to scamper while you were actually doing it.

Afterwards they would all resume their positions, like students in a classroom after recess, and remain as torpidly inattentive as before. It was only in Frustration Pool that they would queue up, waiting for the arrival of your fly as patiently and obligingly as if it were a bus. Ironically, it was the only pool for miles around that I *didn't* find frustrating.

I would go out at the dim edge of dawn and stay out, except for hurriedly snatched meals, until after dark, but there were many more days when I didn't take fish than there were days when I did. One time I would try the Chichester, a pleasant little stream that flows into the Esopus right across the main street of Phoenicia. Above its straight stretch, which comes into the town under an avenue of trees, it had some beguiling twists and turns that led to pools that were filled with fishermen and trout, it seemed in equal numbers, throughout the first weeks of the season. But I hardly ever caught a fish in any of them.

The next time I might try the Woodland Valley or Stony Clove. In the first I never caught a trout, though there were many to be seen, and in the second, while I caught quite a few, they were all stunted, baby-sized but prognathous, looking like little old men. In general, I did better in the big creek than in its tributaries, and though I fished it in all kinds of weather and at all times of the season, from the reservoir itself throughout its upper reaches as far as Big Indian, I never took trout with any semblance of consistency except in the lower waters, from the Five Arch Bridge, at Boiceville, down to the Chimney Hole. In the mile below the Five Arch Bridge I could almost invariably count on one fish. There was no other part of the stream that I could approach with that much confidence. The fish were larger, too, and though I never caught anything bigger down there than a 16-inch brown, most of the trout hooked in that stretch ran over 10 inches, and every so often I would play and lose, after one or two jumps, rainbows that were the size of grilse, 22 to 25 inches long, which would snap my tippet as contemptuously as if they were brushing aside a cobweb.

There were bass, too, in the lower river below Boiceville, and after the trout season, since bass could be taken until the end of November, I would go on blithely fishing below the Five Arch Bridge, wading the stream in stocking-cap weather, ready to assure any inquiring warden that I was intent only upon bass. They never asked me, though several of them asked Dick Kahil about that lunatic they'd spotted below the bridge, but he assured them all that I was harmless.

Harmless, yes, though not necessarily safe from all harm. One November day—when the date was the 22nd and the temperature was 22—I stepped into the stream in the lee of the Five Arch Bridge, standing in line with one of its arches as I paid out line for a first tentative cast. Perhaps I was thinking about the new rod I held in my hands, which I had acquired a couple of months before from Fritz Steurer in Vienna. Certainly I wasn't thinking of the fact that the river, after the fall rains, would be just as swollen in November as it would be in April, when any fool would know that its current can be murderous. So I absentmindedly essayed a half step forward, past the line of my alignment with the stone arch of the bridge, instead of taking a step backward, before turning to get around a big rock that I had to pass to start wading downstream. I might as well have put one foot

out into the path of a subway train. The current caught at
my extended boot foot and literally snatched me out of the
protective patch of relatively calm water in which I had been
standing about waist deep in the lee of the bridge, picked
me up bodily and began rolling me downstream in the torrent,
handling me as if I were a small piece of gravel. I must have
been upended and turned completely over somewhere
between twelve and twenty times in the course of being
tossed and carried downstream about the length of a football
field, before I was finally plastered onto a large rock and held
there, by the force of the current, like the Shakespearian
"alligarter on a wall."

After a few minutes of coughing and sputtering, I cleared
my head and regained my breath, enough to notice for the
first time that I was still clutching my new two-piece rod,
but that it was now neatly strung out along its line in seven
splintered pieces. After prying myself off the rock, I still had
a nasty piece of water to cross, which I negotiated with
elaborate care, and two more spills, before regaining the
calm edge of the stream. When I got back to the car for a
change of clothes, I noticed that my watch had stopped at
twenty after six, and the car clock read twenty of seven. I
felt that I must have aged at least twenty years in those twenty
minutes, but except for an involuntary tendency of my teeth
to chatter, I didn't feel too uncomfortably cold in my soaked
clothes. The temperature of the water, by my stream ther-
mometer, was 43 degrees, as against the 22 degrees of the air,
and my body heat had evidently added considerably to the
warmth of the water.

I had other rod cases on the back seat of the car, but my

fishing clothes were all in the trunk. And the trunk lock was frozen, and my soaked lighter wouldn't function to permit an attempt to thaw it. The sun was not yet in sight, but I could see from the look of the sky in the east that it soon would be, so I drove the car over to a little promontory and turned it so that the lock of its trunk would catch the first rays. Meanwhile, since there was another rod to be had, the logical thing to do to keep warm was to go fishing. I emptied the water out of the feet of my chest waders, put them back on, strung up another rod, and went back to the stream. By the time the sun had been out long enough to make it likely that the lock of the car trunk might function, the wind had so well dried off my outer clothing that it hardly seemed worthwhile to go back to the car. I had laid my lighter on a rock, where the sun and the wind had soon dried the wick and the flint enough to let them work, so I went on fishing, feeling with Robert Musil that "life is a terrible thing, made tolerable chiefly by smoking."

About nine-thirty, John Groth showed up on the stream, having driven up that same morning from town, and his horror at my admission that I had not yet changed my clothes made it seem somehow a point of pride not to change them, so I didn't until that night, back at the Rainbow Lodge. I pointed out that while I'd caught many colds from activities I had indulged in when I might better have been fishing, I had never yet caught cold from fishing. I was nearing fifty then and I'm sixty now, but it's still true.

Somebody asked me once what fly to use on the Esopus, and I said it was "basically a Light Cahill stream." It was a stupid thing to say, because no stream can be, at all seasons, a one-fly stream, and of the Esopus it might better have been said, at least for the first month of the season, that it's a no-fly stream. Certainly up to mid-May those of us who persisted in sticking to flies were hideously outfished by the yokels with minnows and worms and the slickers with spinning lures. But what I should have said, and probably meant, was that I took fish on the Esopus more consistently on the Light Cahill than on any other fly. It mattered less than not at all, except to me, because the man who asked my advice probably didn't bother to follow it, but was only making conversation. So it was even more stupid of me, having said it, to start believing it, and to practice what I had only preached because I had been asked.

But from then on I used only a Light Cahill, size 14, and dry at that. It seemed to match what I saw in the air, better than the wet. It made astonishingly little difference, by the day or the week or the month. I still got skunked on days when it was apparently written in the stars that I was meant to be, and I lost just as many rainbows every bit as big, and I managed to hang onto just about as many fish. I didn't get anything over 14 inches, whereas I had taken the 16-inch brown previously mentioned, on a size 14 *Dark* Cahill, wet. (I remember that fish especially well. I took it on a Sunday afternoon just before I had to leave to go back to the city, and gave it to Benny Goodman, who was staying overnight to fish the next day, because he was his own boss, as I wasn't, for his Monday morning breakfast. I also remember it for another reason: Jimmy Deren was fishing the same stretch, halfway down between the Five Arch Bridge and the Chimney Hole, and he saw me beach it. This is exceptional only in that Jimmy Deren is an expert, and when experts are watching, except Al McClane, I never seem to catch anything but my fly on the back of my jacket.)

Probably what made me stick to the one little dry fly, good luck or bad, was that sense of ultimate exasperation that all of us get, one time or another, who fish for trout. The hell with 'em. If they won't touch one fly more than another, after I've used up yards of tippets changing scores of flies to try to find out what might tickle their finicky appetites, then I might just as well leave one fly on for them to ignore, since the more I change, the less they seem to notice. I've often felt the same way while trying to get a family cat to eat. The hell with him, too. Starve, if you won't touch that, for all of me.

When trout are hitting, you get the feeling that it doesn't much matter what you toss at them, and when they aren't, after so many hours of patient experimentation trying to determine the exact thing they're after, you finally get the same feeling. So my one-fly policy wasn't so much a matter of purism, of preferring to get skunked on a dry-fly rather than stoop to fishing wet, as so many men used to profess in my father's time, though fewer in mine. It was rather a case of nihilism, of indifferentism, of so-whatness. This creeping malaise, the cumulative consequence of so many hours of frustration, of too intent concentration upon the tremendous trifles of what my wife condemns as "a niggling, piggling pastime," at one point began to affect my attitude toward the rest of the tackle as well. I went so far as to buy a $3 rod at an army surplus store, possibly with the thought at the back of my mind that I might want to use it sometime for display purposes, when I could conceivably wish to have a rod to break across my knees in an access of ultimate impatience and annoyance, but rather more, I believe, so I could show those little finny bastards what I really thought of them. Too good for them, by God, at half the price. The true trout addict, I should think, doesn't breathe who has not felt about his sport, at some time, as so many men have felt about their wives. If I didn't love her, I couldn't stand her.

My own one-fly phase came to an abrupt end, one August evening in 1953, when I came back into the Rainbow Lodge after having fished the stretch below the Five Arch Bridge for twelve straight hours, since early morning, without a strike.

"Dare I ask how you did?" said Dick Kahil as I sat down in the dining room to wait for my dinner.

"No hits, no run, total error," was probably my answer, if not something even more banal.

"What were you using?" asked a thin florid white-haired man at the next table, who was sitting with a woman who had kind eyes.

"He always uses a Light Cahill," Dick answered for me. "I'm touched, because while I can't get him to admit it, I'm sure it's only out of loyalty to me."

"Yes, I do it to advertise Kahil's Rainbow Lodge," I said, figuring I might better go along with it.

"Well, I see you're going out again," said the man, in tactful cognizance of my cloddish habit of eating with my waders on, "so if it's all the same to you, I wish you'd try this." He reached into his pocket, and from a little plastic fly box passed me a dark red nymph, gold-ribbed, with grubby whiskers, on a size 10 hook.

"I never have much luck with nymphs," I temporized, not

wanting to say that I thought it was much too big, and less attractive than an unmade bed.

"Fish it like a wet fly," the man said, "because it's the only nymph that swims." He added that he had tied it himself, though I would have thought that was obvious.

"It's called *Isonychia bicolor*," he said, getting up to leave, by way of acknowledgment of my mumbled thanks, "and it's the nymph phase of the Royal Coachman."

Well, hell, he was an older man and I don't go around trying to pick fights, but it was obvious now that he was pulling my leg. I may not know much, but I simply had to let this old joker know that I knew that there isn't any natural fly known as a Royal Coachman for this thing to be the nymph phase of, or any other phase.

"It's sort of like the Admiral of the Swiss Navy then," I said.

"Something like that," he said, smiling, as he walked off after his friendly-looking wife, who had gone on ahead.

But even if it was a joke, it was a joke that could be passed on to the recalcitrant trout below the Five Arch Bridge. I could offer it to them, after all my day-long devotions, as a final raspberry. So I took it back down on the stream and tried it, feeling just as glad that there were no other fly fishermen around to see what a huge hook it had. Size 10, indeed, and in August at that, when even a 14 seems ungainly. Plop it went into the water with a splash that made me cringe, after the thistledown delivery I'd been giving my little Light Cahill all the livelong day. But bang came the answer, almost immediately, from a 14-inch brown.

In the next forty minutes, it took eleven more trout, six of them rainbows, with four more browns and only one brookie, and all of them, except the brookie, over 11 inches. A dozen trout, averaging as many inches, in not much more than a half hour, when in the previous twelve hours I hadn't raised a fish. And this in the dog days, on a stream where even in June I seldom took that many fish in an entire weekend. I went stuttering back to Dick Kahil with the news. Who, I wanted to know, was this old guy, if not St. Peter himself, the patron saint of all fishers.

"Why I thought you knew," said Dick. "You read all those books all the time. Well, he wrote one of 'em. That was Preston Jennings. He wrote *A Book of Trout Flies*. There used to be a copy of it around here, but I guess somebody must have made off with it."

"Preston Jennings for President," I yelled. "What this country needs is more guys like him and fewer like Ike."

He wrote the book, all right, and I was ready to take from him for life. I couldn't wait to lay hands on the book, as soon as I got back to town, but it wasn't easy, as it had been issued in limited numbers in 1935 and was now out of print. I finally succeeded in borrowing a copy (a reprint by Crown has since become available) and went through it avidly, looking for any mention of "the one nymph that swims" and anything it might say about whether there actually was such a thing as a Royal Coachman. By now I was ready to believe anything he said. I found no mention of the swimming nymph, though. I had forgotten the name, *Isonychia bicolor* —I had never had a head for botanical names or any of the rest of the scientific Latin tags—but I thought I remembered it correctly and would recognize it in the book. But I still saw nothing that resembled the ugly dark red nymph that he had given me. As for the Royal Coachman, the one reference to it that I found in the book was negative, to the effect that it was representative of no particular fly, just as I had always thought, and just as all the other books I'd ever seen had said.

I learned from Dick Kahil that Preston Jennings lived nearby, in Woodstock, so on my next trip up to the Esopus I made it a point to look him up, to tell him of the spectacular success his nymph had brought me and to try to find out whether he had been kidding me when he said it was "the nymph phase" of the Royal Coachman. Not at all, it turned out, or if he was kidding, he was kidding on the square. There *was a* Royal Coachman, he insisted, and this was its nymph, he said, getting out a half dozen more and giving them to me. The reason for its peculiar effectiveness, he explained, was twofold, first in that the natural swimming motion of this nymph more nearly resembles the action the average fisherman gives it on his leader than that of any other nymph, and second, that fish are much more sensitive to the red side of the spectrum than we are. He became very scientific about this point, losing me throughout most of his explanation, although one example he cited, to show how much more sensitive we humans are to the blue side of the spectrum, stays with me after a dozen years. He said that when the French tricolor flag was first devised, all the Frenchmen who saw it insisted that it was lopsided, that there was more blue than red, although the bands of blue, white, and red were absolutely equal. The flag had to be corrected, he said, by making the red band larger and the blue smaller until they appeared to be equal.

He explained the lack of any reference in his book to the existence of a natural of the Royal Coachman by the fact that he had learned a lot of things in the nearly two decades since the book was first published. He had learned, for instance, that because of the peculiar sensitivity of fish to the red side of the spectrum, you really didn't need a fine leader tippet to fool them. All you needed was a color that would fool them. He said a 2X tippet dyed with purple Tintex dye would be just as effective as 6X, or perhaps even as effective as the 8X on which I prided myself.

I made a note to get some purple Tintex at the first opportunity, but meanwhile I felt that the rest of the world should know these things, and offered him the pages of *Esquire* in which to make them known. He said he would be delighted, and a couple of years later he did write it up, under the title "There IS a Royal Coachman" and it was published in the July 1956 issue of *Esquire*. In the article he explained that the Royal Coachman family is represented in nature by a group of May flies consisting of some twenty-five slightly varying species, under a generic name of *Isonychia*. The word means "two pads of equal size," a characteristic of four of the six feet of the nymph. The Eastern is known as *Isonychia bicolor*, although it has recently been designated *albomanicata*, as if *Isonychia* weren't hard enough; the Western is known as *Isonychia velma*. So the California Coachman, too, has its counterpart in nature.

Preston Jennings said that the reason hardly anybody ever sees the natural fly is that it is usually present over streams just at dark and it is such a strong flier that few fishermen ever even see it, let alone get a chance to collect it for examination. The only way he managed to get one, for the photograph of the natural to compare with the photographs of his flies in the article, was by determined and pertinacious use of a butterfly net and a bottle of quick-killing cyanide.

The nymph is free swimming, he said; it is the only one of its type that is in our trout streams, and it could be found there almost from opening day on, throughout the entire trout season into October. The point of fishing it like a wet fly, as he had made clear when he first gave me his copy of the nymph, was that, in order to simulate its natural motion, it could not be allowed to drift free in the current, but should be retrieved, slowly but steadily, by gradually weaving in the line with the fingers of the left hand, from the moment of its cast toward the middle of the stream. Thus it would follow the course of the natural, swimming toward the bank, whereas if it were allowed to drift, fish would pass it by as an empty shuck in the current, instead of nailing it, as they certainly had done for me, as a living swimming nymph.

Needless to say, the nymph never worked that well again for me, but then nothing ever does. I suppose the fellow who invented DDT must feel much the same way about it, and I'm sure that Mr. Hewitt's nymphs, when he first tried them on the Neversink, must have worked almost as well as he said they did, though I saw them failing to work for him on the same water later. As for the Tintex, though there are kitchen sinks which must still bear traces of that purple, deep in their cracks, this dozen years later, I long ago gave it up. I faithfully dunked all my different sizes of leader material in the mess, from .030 down to .0031, but the time inevitably came when I said the hell with it. I tried for a long time to test out, between dyed and undyed tippets, the difference in fishing effectiveness. I found, as I might have expected, that when the trout were hitting they hit them both with what appeared to be equal avidity, and when they weren't they sneered no less loftily at the dyed than at the undyed.

Poor Preston! no truer devotee of angling ever lived, but still he didn't live long enough to acquire that ultimate degree of wisdom that was once expressed by Hart Stilwell: the only safe theory to hold about angling is that there is no safe theory to hold about angling.

7 · Mr. Hewitt and His Water

"Charlie, what about that fellow you were hoping to rope
in for this year—the one whose wife died?"

"Well, that is—uh—Mr. Hewitt, this is—well, this is
Mr. Gingrich."

"Oh. Sorry. I don't seem to catch names very well any
more."   Edward Ringwood Hewitt, at
dinner at the Kerlees', on the
Neversink, April 1955

HE WAS PUSHING EIGHTY-NINE, that first time I met him, and
though he could still thread a fly without glasses, he didn't

hear everything you thought he heard. I was fishing at the Big Bend Fishing Club, which held a lease on Mr. Hewitt's water on the Neversink, as the guest of Charles Kerlee. It was the second time I'd fished there, Charlie having had me up once before as his guest during the previous season, when we'd had wonderful fishing and he had suggested that I might join the club if I wanted to. It hadn't worked out that year, but circumstances had changed and Charlie had renewed the invitation. So we had fished the stream again today, this time without a strike, and had come in, skunked, and sat down for dinner at the cabin that the Kerlees had built on the Neversink's bank just above the spot known as Theodore Gordon's favorite pool.

Vivian Kerlee had said what a shame it was that we hadn't had a fish between us, and I'd said that it couldn't matter less, and what a thrill it was for me just to be on Hewitt's water and to be sitting in sight of Gordon's pool, when there was a sliding rattling noise outside. It sounded like a minor avalanche.

"That must be Mr. Hewitt," said Vivian.

And it was. At last I was to see him plain.

He had come down off the mountain, like Zeus from Olympus, and at something of the speed and noise of a thunderbolt in his antique high-sprung sedan with holes bored in the top to poke rods through. Incredibly small and ancient, he and his car alike, but they were equally spry for their years, and he looked as perky as one of the seven dwarfs. He had come down from his home up above to bring a reel he had made the previous winter to give Charlie as a present. On it he had graven Charlie's name, and his own, and the date.

(I have since seen one other like it which he made for Ellis Newman, and I would give all but two of the twenty best reels I own to have either of them.)

They asked him to sit down to dinner, after the reel had been sufficiently praised and admired, and he did. He couldn't believe that we hadn't moved a fish. That is, he could well believe that I hadn't, because he didn't know me from the nearest rhododendron, but he couldn't believe that Charlie, whom he obviously respected and admired as an angler, could have failed to cause a fish to stir on this fabled water.

"Did you try the iron blue dun?"

"Yes, we did, Mr. Hewitt."

"Did you try one of my nymphs?"

"Yes, we did."

"The one with the dirty white belly?"

"Yes, and the yellow one, too."

"But was it size 14?"

"Yes, and we tried the 10 and the 12, too."

"Did you fish 'em upstream, and let 'em bump?"

"Yes, we did, Mr. Hewitt. And downstream, too."

"Ah, but you didn't wrap those little bits of lead fuse wire around your leader!"

"But we did, Mr. Hewitt."

And we had, much as I had disliked the idea at the time.

"Well, did you let 'em dead-drift, too? You never can tell, you know."

"Yes, we tried 'em every which way."

"Hmm. Well, I never fish this water before May tenth, myself."

He was very positive in all his pronouncements, and he

tended to make a pronouncement out of almost everything he said. But sometimes he'd forget a name, and other times you could only assume that he might not have heard correctly. Talking about flies, he tried to remember the name of "that fellow out west."

"Could it have been Dan Bailey?" I suggested.

"Yes, I believe that's the fellow."

But when we were talking about the known tendency of big browns to be cannibalistic, he said: "I've never known one to be." That was directly contrary to what he had written more than once in more than one of his books, including the last, where revised versions of *Telling on the Trout* and *Secrets of the Salmon* had been incorporated into *A Trout and Salmon Fisherman for Seventy-five Years*. But Charlie Kerlee, who knew him much better than I—who had only just met him and whose name he didn't catch—seemed disinclined to argue, so I contented myself with telling them about the two dead rainbows I had found on the Esopus, one stuck halfway inside the other, which I had carefully pried apart and measured. A 10-incher had tried to swallow an 8-incher, and had halfway made it before dying in the attempt. Again, Mr. Hewitt professed never to have seen the like, in eighty years of fishing, man and boy. But I couldn't be sure whether he hadn't fully heard me or was just trying to be polite.

Though I did join the club that year, and fished the Hewitt water at least once a week that season and the next, I wasn't to meet him again. But I did see him again on the stream. He was fishing in its upper reaches, with Herman Christian, who for years played Sancho Panza to his own Quixote, and instead of going on to another spot I shamelessly stayed behind some bushes, to eavesdrop and eyedrop. After all, he had turned ninety by then, and I can always have the dubious pleasure of my own company wherever there's water for me to fish, but how many times more might I have the privilege of watching one of the sport's acknowledged masters?

The only thing I heard him say was that Herman Christian ought to be using a nymph, as he was. Christian was too far away for me to see, even if I had had binoculars—exactly what he was using—but even from twice the distance I could have deduced that he was fishing a "ladder" of three flies. When he made his lazy cast it was as casual as—and indeed that's what it resembled—the motion of a farmer tossing aside a rake or even a pitchfork. He jerked his rod constantly, and more often than my eyes could credit he would give a sudden upward hoist, as he set one of the flies in a fish. I must have seen him peel off a dozen trout in the course of a hundred yards as he stomped and splashed downstream. His every motion seemed awkward, and I would have thought that the manner of his wading, high-stepping and as forthright as the goosestep of troops passing in review, would have been enough to scare away all the trout and most of the suckers, but he seemed to be attracting them like the Pied Piper.

Mr. Hewitt, meanwhile, appeared to be working on one fish. He cast with elaborate caution, peering ahead and crouching, as if casing the water like a burglar. Working upstream, he rarely moved, and then barely, while Christian crashed on downstream like a brass band on parade. But though I watched for better than half an hour, I never saw

Mr. Hewitt get a strike, whereas whenever I looked at Christian, as long as he was in sight, he was prying a hook out of the
mouth of another trout. I wish I could report that Hewitt
seemed the picture of grace, that the movements of his rod
were poetry in motion. They weren't. But then what kind
of figure would you cut when you're ninety?

The one thing I got out of two years' membership in the
Big Bend Club, aside from the privilege of being able to say
that I had fished Mr. Hewitt's water and that I had seen him
fishing it himself, was my first acquaintance with the Midge
rod, and though membership in the club was not cheap, it
would have been cheap at many times the price if I might
not otherwise have met the rod that entirely transformed
my fishing life. Charlie had got one from Paul Young in
Detroit, where he often went in his work as a professional
photographer, and had bought it with no intention of using
it himself, as he is over six foot, with the build of a tackle.
But Vivian is small, and he wanted a light little rod that she
could use without arm fatigue.

The morning after the night that Hewitt came to dinner,
Vivian let me try it, and the very first cast was a revelation.
I had been using an Edwards, 8 feet and 4¼ ounces, and
liked it. I still have it, and it's all right in its way, as such
rods go. But the Midge, at 6 feet 3 inches and weighing just
1.73 ounces, made a bum out of it, and giving it back was
like giving back a piece of my arm. I wrote a check for one
that same day. They cost only $65 at that time, but I'd have
paid five times as much, if that had been the price. I never
wanted anything more avidly in my life.

Once I got it, I used no other rod, except another one like

it, and then another and still another, until finally I had acquired a dozen in the same general category. But more about that later on.

The Neversink trout were wary, and they grew to impressive size. But with Mr. Hewitt fishing fairly infrequently, and with only a half dozen members in the Big Bend Club, they were less often fished over than those at Suffolk Lodge, and hardly at all, compared to those in the Esopus. The other members had built cottages along the upper half of the Hewitt water, and while I was entitled to do the same it never worked out for me to do it, so I kept on going to Kahil's Rainbow Lodge on Friday nights, fishing the Esopus through Saturday. Then, getting up early Sunday morning, I would drive on the back road over the mountain from Big Indian, coming down at Claryville, which was hardly more than a minute or so from the covered bridge that led to the rudimentary road, facing a schoolhouse, which curved around to the Hewitt water in the Neversink Valley. Thus I would get one full day on the Neversink each week. And I would leave after dark on Sunday nights to head back for my work week in New York.

Mr. Hewitt was always experimenting with the stocking and the feeding of fish on his water. He had even tried bringing over salmon from Scotland. The construction of the big dam had made the lower mile of his three-mile stretch too deep to permit wading any more, completely obliterating the place where his own old camp had been, and the creation of this little ocean at the foot of his water led him to attempt to introduce into it all sorts of seagoing specimens. He kept U. S. Customs in New York in an uproar, those last years of his life. They never knew what live thing, short of the Loch Ness monster itself, he might be trying to import.

Once, peering down into the sun-illumined waters at the big bend in the river from which the club took its name, I saw or thought I saw something hugely white, looking almost man-size, even after making due allowance for the magnifying effect of the water. What it was I'll never know, nor do I think any of the other members ever found out, but of an evening, from the porch of the nearest cottage, we occasionally heard splashes exceeding anything that could have been caused by a 200-pound policeman taking a bellywhopper.

The Atlantic-salmon experiment was a fizzle, so far as I know, but Charlie Kerlee more than once pulled out landlocks, and some of the 24- and 25-inch rainbows he consistently raised on a Quack Coachman and returned to the water were kissing cousins for steelheads. Charles Kerlee was one of the two fishermen I've ever known whose lives I truly envied. The other one, of course, is Al McClane, but perhaps that should be thrown out because he's a professional, one of the rare types who succeed in merging their work and their fun. When he shows up in his office they say: "Why aren't you out fishing?" so about three hundred days a year he is. Why couldn't I, with about a fifteen-year head start on him, ever find an office like that? Charles Kerlee never fished for a living, or ever studied ichthyology and all that, as McClane did, to prepare for a career in any aspect of fishing. But with a cabin on the Neversink, and another on the Southwest Miramichi, and still another in the Bahamas, he can legitimately be at ease with himself and in the bosom of his family, fearing and beholden to nobody, in the right place at the right time, very nearly all around the calendar.

There is the consideration that he's one hell of a photographer, and those fellows are notoriously well paid, while I never got beyond a 2A box Brownie, and can't even master a Polaroid. There is the further consideration that he is now avowedly at least semi-retired, but even when I was wholly retired, as I was for the last three of my four years in Switzerland, I never had sense enough to arrange myself a setup like that. There is the one additional consideration that he has a wife who not only loves to have him fish but loves to fish herself, and is actually a member of something that is known, in what my own experience would have branded a contradiction in terms, as The Ladies' Fly Fishers.

There, perhaps, is the rub. Still, I too had a wife—for eight months—who loved to fish, and my angling life was never more wretched.

My first wife, whom I had married twice in youth and who was the mother of my three sons, had before she died become my third wife, or fourth, depending on whether those first two weddings are counted as one or as two. She was the eldest of four children whose father was an avid fisherman and a rabid hunter. He was the kind who wants "a little pal," and God help the little pal if he's a she. He made her fish and shoot and ride before he could have been any too sure she could walk, with the perhaps not entirely surprising result that a more vigorously anti-sports-minded female never grew up. When she went to girls' camp in Maine, she begged to be allowed to curry the horses, if only she could be excused from riding any of them. As for rods and guns, she'd seen enough of them to last her a lifetime before she was able to read *Elsie Dinsmore* or the Oz books.

My present wife, on the other hand, whom I hesitate to identify as fifth except that she has herself been married four times and a man must try any way he can to assert rank, was riding and showing horses in Madison Square Garden before she was knee-high to them, and had shot elephants and rhino in Tanganyika and Kenya with Philip Percival before Hemingway had ever heard of him, and had her own boat on the blue water, from which Ernest helped her pioneer the Cuban big game fishing, before he did. She could well have been one of those whom Scott Fitzgerald had in mind when he said that Ernest was always ready to lend a helping hand to the one on the rung above him. She shot two elephants so big that their tusks comprise the posts of a monumental four-poster bed, and a rhinocerous that was the biggest of its year, and while she never held any big game fishing record, she has insisted that every trout I ever caught was smaller than something she had once used for bait, and it is a matter of record that while fishing with her second husband she tried to throw back a 9-pound smallmouth as an object that nobody could conceivably want to keep. With a sporting background, but one devoted to the cult of bigness, she can no more understand my passion for trout than if I were, instead, to develop a mania for collecting broken milk bottles. Or just possibly she might understand it if I were to get completely hipped on collecting mushrooms, because I suspect that the only form of the chase that she really respects is one where the quarry has something like an even chance of getting back at you.

Though these two women, in their attitude toward sports, were alike only in the way the extremes of hot and cold are alike, both being equally painful to the touch, it was only between the death of one and my marriage to the other that I managed to sneak in two seasons of membership in the Big Bend Club, after which I had to explain to Charlie Kerlee why I could no longer be a member, and never hope to have a cabin, like his, on the Neversink. I told him I envied him his freedom to fish when and where he liked, but I consoled myself with the recollection of that passage in D. H. Lawrence's *Studies in Classic American Literature*, which reads—when looked up, for I had only recalled its gist: "Men are not free when they are doing just what they like. The moment you can do just what you like, there is nothing you care about doing. Men are only free when they are doing what the deepest self likes."

8·Paul Young and the Midge Rod

"Well, yes, light tackle—well, all right, but that—ça alors, c'est vicieux!"   Charles Ritz, on the Risle in Normandy, upon first hefting a Midge rod

PERFECTIONISTS are not necessarily inventive, nor was Stradivari the first to make a Cremona violin. And the late Paul Young of Detroit was not the first to make the light rod as we know it today, when the name Midge that he first gave it has become a generic adjective used to categorize all split-cane rods with light mountings, measuring under seven feet and weighing two ounces or less. But Paul Young was certainly the one who took the midge rod out of the toy or novelty class and made it the versatile rod it has become. Midges are now widely used on everything from bluegills and bass on through all the salmonids, including Atlantic salmon.

Probably nobody made the small rod any earlier than Leonard. I remember when I first fished at Suffolk Lodge in '52, Ken Hard's mother had already had for some time a Leonard rod that was the lightest in their Baby Catskill class. It was a two-piece, 6-foot stick weighing 15/16 of an ounce. Wm. Mills & Son, Inc., New York's (and the world's) oldest and largest house dealing exclusively in fishing tackle, who long ago took over the manufacture of the H. L. Leonard rod, advertised it as the lightest rod made. It was a conversation piece, but it wasn't much more. Compared to the Midge, as Paul Young first made it and as Hardy, Orvis, Payne, Winston (and Leonard themselves) now make it, that first Baby Leonard was as limp as a noodle. Mills must have had complaints on it. Before very long they had raised the weight on it to an ounce. They were still able, as of then, to call it the lightest rod made.

Today, only a decade later, 1-ounce rods at 4-foot 4-inch length are another recognized category. Hardy and Orvis both make them. They are now considered the bantam class, and are used on small streams with tiny flies, as Paul Young first intended his Midge to be used. He was as surprised as anybody when the first reports came back that the Midge was an Atlantic salmon killer. He himself had never thought of the rod as suited to any line stouter than HEH or HDG, or to any flies larger than size 14. But Paul Young, as so often happens, built better than he knew. I remember in '56 and '57, when he first began getting orders from people who had written in after I had started touting the Midge in print, he wrote me in some panic, hoping to God that these weren't a lot of greenhorns who wouldn't know how to use a delicate rod like the Midge after they got it. If any of them were, they had at least sense enough to blame themselves and not him or me, because I never got any letters from people who took up the Midge on my say-so which were not expressions of delight, and I assume he never did either.

Paul Young died in the spring of '60, too soon to realize the full extent of the vogue for light tackle which he started and on which he never really capitalized. He will be remembered, by knowing anglers, both for the Midge rod and for the strawman nymph. But already, a scant lustrum after his death, I find myself running into fishermen all the time who have midge rods and have either used or at least heard of the strawman nymph, yet are completely blank at the mention of Paul Young's name.

The rods were his hobby, and even before he died they were the small end of the business the Paul H. Young Company was doing. With the postwar boating boom, Paul Jr. was making more money in a week on boats and motors than Paul could hope to clear in a year on his rods. For one thing, he never charged enough for them, as his prices were always from twenty to forty percent lower than the range of prices charged by his peers, from Orvis to Payne. And he spent more in tinkering with new machines of his own devising than he could ever hope to clear, short of going in for the kind of mass production that alone would have justified his machines. But the music of his mitering machine, when it was set to its finest slicings for the Midge, its cutters shaping the slender sticks down to tolerances of a thousandth of an inch, was all he really cared about hearing. He said he would rather have fun than make money, and the most fun he had was making Midges. The rest of the family indulged him, particularly after his first heart attack. He knew that Paul Jr. was much more interested in motors than in rods, but he felt that his other son, Jack, "had bamboo in his blood." He has, and I've had rods from him, since Paul's death, every bit as good as those I got when his father was alive. (Still, I was glad that I had got two more Midges and a Martha Marie, as a Christmas 1959 present from my wife, just a few months before he died.)

The proliferation of Detroit's expressways caused the Young's location to be changed twice within a couple of years after his death, and the last time I was out there the machines that were his pride and joy were still under tarpaulin. Paul had made rods since 1914, when he first set up shop in Duluth, Minnesota, having moved there from Arkansas, where he was born. According to Jack van Coevering, he was completely self-taught, and made his first rod with the aid of a book on amateur rodmaking. His first store, in Detroit in 1921, was devoted chiefly to taxidermy.

Somewhere along the line, whether in the perfection of his tapers or in his own ingeniously devised method of heat treatment and impregnation of the bamboo, Paul Young found a paradoxical combination of attributes with which he endowed his light rods, and particularly the Midge, which I continue to find astonishing each time I pick one up, even after a decade of constant use. The rod seems an equal blend of what you naturally think of as opposite qualities, delicacy and power. How such a slender wand, glued together from six strips of bamboo, themselves thinner than matchsticks, can withstand the shocks it gets and still spring back to its original shape is far beyond my understanding. When you wave it back and forth in the air, it seems as springy as a fencing foil, but when you hold it aloft as it makes a full arc against the pull of 14-pound salmon (I've never had the luck to hook into anything bigger with it), it feels as tensely solid as a cable of the Brooklyn Bridge.

I can't say I've never broken one, but I can say that a fish never has, thereby bearing out what Paul always said, that fishermen break rods often, but fish almost never. I hadn't had my first Midge two seasons before I'd broken both its tips, one in a car door and the other against a concrete culvert when I stumbled. Paul made me two new ones, and repaired the two that had snapped by re-tipping them, giving me two rods of the original 6-foot, 3-inch length, and two of 5 foot 9. The latter make a rod of just 1½ ounces, but extremely powerful, with a thicker "ankle," as it were, having lost the slenderest part of the bamboo in the 6 inches that were broken off at the tip.

The only three other small rods that I have that are as powerful as this shortened version of the Midge are an Orvis Superfine, a one-piece, 6-foot stick weighing 1⅞ ounces, a Hardy of the now discontinued old Casting Club de France short model, weighing 2⅓ ounces, and a Pezon et Michel, weighing about the same, that Charlie Ritz had made up for me by way of giving me his answer to my "vicious" Midge. I like them all for salmon, but none has the Midge's delicacy in laying down a dry fly for trout.

If I knew more about the dynamics of rodmaking, I could probably give you a better explanation of the magic of the Midge. I could never get it out of Paul Young himself, as he always at least affected to be as surprised as anybody else at each new account of the exploits of his mighty little rod. So, as always when I'm stuck to understand anything about fishing, I asked Al McClane, and here's his answer:

"The secret of the Midge is that it has a built-in delay (as does the Perfectionist, but at 7½ feet instead of the Midge's 6¼) and does nothing to hinder the flight of the line. The best that can be said of a fly rod is that it gives the line momentum, then velocity, then has the common sense to get out of the way. If the rod is too fast, or too slow, there is no harmony, and you break up the flow of the line as it unrolls. Once the line loop is formed, which is almost instantaneous, all the pushing you may do does not add one flea power to the cast. In fact, the harder you try, the worse it gets. The virtue of any good rod is that it 'waits' for the line to unroll, without vibrating excessively, and harmonically does nothing to destroy its flow—providing speed without causing the line to deviate from a straight path. The Midge will pick up and give velocity to a 118 to 125 grain line (IFI or HEH), 'leaning back' with it, then recoiling at a rate that does not exceed the capacity of the line."

I'm sure that if Paul Young were within reach he would confirm this diagnosis of the nature of the inherent characteristic with which he endowed both his Midge and his Perfectionist, even though he never did manage to express it himself in so many words. Paul was complaining, in the last letter I had from him, just weeks before he died, about how hard it was becoming to find workmen who had any feeling at all for the qualities and characteristics of bamboo. He seemed to sense that he and his kind were a dwindling breed, and he speculated ruefully on which would outlast the other, the supplies of the essential Tonkin cane, which comes from Red China, or the supply of people who can be taught to work the cane if you can get it. Much as I love his little rods, and to me he was the Stradivari of the light rod, I couldn't stand his heavy ones.

Before going to Iceland, I had him make up a couple of salmon rods. Knowing nothing about it beforehand, I assumed that for that fishing I would need a stout rod and I ordered two 9-footers, of a model called the Bobby Doerr, weighing about 6 ounces. He threw in a third rod, with the compliments of the house, which he called the Iceland Special but which was known in his line as the Texas General—8½ feet and 5⅓ ounces—saying he thought it might be prudent to have it along, in case the lady of the party might grow arm-weary after casting the 9-footer any appreciable length of time. Well might he have been apprehensive on that account. The lady, or the gent, could never manage to flex either of those Bobby Doerrs, even with GAF lines. She wound up using her Orvis 8-foot trout rod, weighing 4¼ ounces, and although I felt bound, if only by gratitude for Paul's thoughtfulness, to use the Iceland Special, after the first few days I found myself neglecting it, almost entirely, for my Midge.

We finally gave the two Bobby Doerrs away to Icelanders, in whose eyes a 6-ounce rod is practically a toy. A stiffer, more stubbornly clublike and unyielding stick I never tried to wield, but then, I never tried to use one of the 14-foot, 23- to 25-ounce rods that are virtually standard equipment on every one of Iceland's sixty salmon rivers. Maybe if I had, I too would have welcomed a shillelagh like the Bobby Doerr with a blissful sense of relief. In Charles Cotton's time, when a rod for trout and grayling in a clear stream was expected to be from 6 to 8 *yards* long, a mere 9-footer would have seemed smaller than a midge or even a bantam now seems to us. But in those days, before reels made the use of long lines possible, there was no other way to fish "fine and far off" than by dint of using a rod long enough to permit you to keep your desired distance from the fish. Rod sizes, like so many things, are relative, and maybe the best thing about the current craze for the bantam size is that by contrast it makes the midge seem big.

Oddly enough, while the bantam rods have been on the market only in the sixties, Al McClane anticipated them by a good five years. He made me a 4-foot rod by inserting a 3-foot tip section of a conventional fly rod into the 1-foot grip handle of a spinning rod, on the hunch—perfectly valid, too, as it turned out—that I could do a lot more with my Midge if I got used to practicing with something even smaller. It worked like a charm, suddenly making my Midge seem, by contrast, a normally "big" rod. I am quite sure, now that I look back on it, that I might never have ventured to get any distance out of the Midge, or tried to use it on big water for big fish, if I hadn't had this psychological breakthrough afforded by the short practice rod. I would have gone on using the Midge, only with the light line and the small flies, for short casts on small streams, where distance was never a factor.

I know I started out that way with it. I found it so delightful to use, the first time on the Neversink when I tried out Vivian

Kerlee's, that it never occurred to me to use it any other way
than with the easy, graceful, elbow-hugging-the-side, traditional cast, the way all of us were once taught. When I got
my own Midge, I went to Wm. Mills & Son for the smallest
reel, the Fairy reel that they make for use with their Baby
Leonard rods. This is a hard rubber and Duralumin reel, made
in the old raised-pillar style, with a diameter of only 2¼
inches and weighing 2¾ ounces. On it I put their HFH Im-
perial silk line, which filled the little reel with only a modicum
of backing. Paul Young had specified HEH line but I thought
I'd play safe by going one size smaller. I used number 20
nymphs and midges, with an 18-foot leader tapering from .023
to .0031 or 8X. With this setup, I was getting casts of 35 to
40 feet, and feeling pretty chesty in the process. I was also
raising, quite suddenly, a lot more fish than I'd ever dreamed
were there to raise, in the same waters where I had fished before with larger tackle.

That was simply because I was fishing finer, with a lighter
line and a longer taper on the leader, and smaller flies, than I
had been using before. And while I credited the little rod with
my enhanced success, probably the rod had very little to do
with it, except in a negative way. Because I was still half
afraid of it, it kept me from fishing as vigorously as I might
otherwise have done, if I'd felt more familiar with it, and thus
it kept me from scaring away just that many more fish. But
what I was doing, I later realized, was comparable to the kind
of pat-ball *la-de-da* tennis they used to play back in the early
days of the game, before Maurice McLoughlin revolutionized
it with the introduction of the big serve. That same break-
through was made, in casting terms, by the double-line haul.

9 · A. J. McClane and the Double-line Haul

There is such a tremendous lot to know about trout fishing that men who are keen on it can discuss theories by the hour. Stephen Leacock,
in Here Are My Lectures, 1936

As LONG AS I CONFINED my use of the little rod to conventional casting methods, I was really indulging, without realizing it, in a sort of miniature angling which is to the real thing what miniature golf is to that game. It takes the double-line haul to take full advantage of the marvelous advantages of the light rod. I'd heard of it, and even read about it, but until I learned it I didn't know what I was missing.

I learned it from Al McClane and Ellis Newman, and I suppose the best way to learn it is still to get somebody to teach you who knows it himself. Still, it has been written up in books, best of all to my way of thinking by A. J. McClane himself, in *The Practical Fly Fisherman,* published in 1953 by Prentice-Hall. But if you can't lay hands on that, he has written about it again in the July 1964 issue of *Field & Stream.* Two other good treatments of the subject are contained in *Advanced Fly Fishing,* by Eugene Burns, published by Stackpole in 1953, and *The Atlantic Salmon* by Lee Wulff, published by A. S. Barnes in 1958. The Wulff book, especially, is valuable in that it goes beyond the mere mechanics of the double-line haul, to light up the whole mystique of the light rod. Probably the simplest explanation of it is contained in Norm Thompson's *Angler's Guide,* which you can get for a dollar from Norm Thompson, 1805 N.W. Thurman, Portland, Oregon. But while it does give a workable explanation, you must look sharp in reading it, because it doesn't call it "the double-line haul" as such, but only tells you, very simply, what to do with your left hand.

Titles and labels are sometimes too frightening, and perhaps the worst mental hazard of the double-line haul is the fact that so much has been made of it that, like double-clutching in driving a sports car, the average guy is afraid to try it for fear of gumming up the works. After all, it's only a rhythmic trick, as easy as the one kids learn, of patting the head while circularly rubbing the stomach. If you can do that, you're a cinch to do the double-line haul. The head-patting hand, the right, is the one that moves the rod back and forth, while the tummy-rubbing one, the left, works the line up and down.

First heresy in the use of the small rod, to the old-school fly-rodder who was traditionally made to hold a book between his elbow and his ribs while learning to cast, is that the whole arm is brought into the casting motion, and not just the forearm, as he was so carefully taught. The fulcrum of the cast, which he was constantly admonished to confine to his wrist— "keep your arm out of it and let the rod do all the work"— was formerly at a point about opposite the right shoulder, where the wrist flexed the rod while the right elbow remained dutifully down, figuratively still squeezing that imaginary book between body and arm. Now the fulcrum of the cast is raised some 2½ to 3 feet upward, and some 18 inches to 2 feet rearward, as the extended arm gets up and back, well over and back of the head, in thrusting the little rod up for the beginning of the back cast.

The old-timer, on hearing this described, or even on seeing it in action, feels that it is tantamount to throwing the rod away. In a sense he's right, and that's just what it is, at least in a relative degree, as compared to the old method of putting all the pressure of the line's successively lengthening false casts onto the spring of the rod. The new way uses the rod itself only as a direction changer, between forward and backward false casts, keeping the major part of the strain off the rod and leaving to the angler's left hand the greatest part of the work of building up the mounting velocity of the line, through successive quick tugs of the line with the left hand, as it goes back and forth through the air fast enough to assure a long forward "shoot" to the desired distance when the cast is finally let go.

Good casters of the new school have frequently demonstrated this principle of casting at the various outdoor shows around the country, and they can do it just as well with the upper tip section of a fly rod as with the whole jointed rod. A. J. McClane, when instructing a beginner, is apt to say: "The fish are way up there in the trees behind you," to get that thrown-back, extended motion of the right arm on the first back cast. His stance, utterly unlike that of the old-style elbow-down purist, is much more like that of a tennis player about to come forward with the racket at the start of a powerhouse serve. Ellis Newman goes even further. He carries the "throw the rod away" thought to the point of doing it literally, and lays out the entire 35-yard length of a torpedo-tapered fly line without any rod at all. Al McClane can do that, too, but it's primarily a sports-show stunt rather than a technique of value to the ordinary fisherman.

There are two techniques that do help to acquire the new style of casting more quickly than any others. Put your index finger on the back of the rod and keep it there, just as if you were admonishing somebody, throughout the casting. You will thus be blocking any tendency you may have to work your wrist, as the upraised forefinger effectively keeps your wrist out of it, and helps you acquire the feeling that the rod is now just an extension of your forearm. Leave to the bickerings of the opposed experts whether or not this helps or hinders in the ultimate push for distance. Until the day you're ready to enter a tournament yourself, this final consideration, affecting only the ultimate stretch of the cast to get the last possible inch of distance out of it, couldn't affect you less. Unless of course, you are a caster of tournament caliber, in which case you aren't bothering with this anyway.

The other trick is to do all your practicing with the top section of your rod only. Put the reel in your pocket, and try pretending that you are casting the line without any rod at all. The little tip is next thing to no rod, after all, and you can't very well fall back into the old habit of throwing all the work onto the rod if there's hardly any rod there.

After the first few miserable fumbles, when the tangle of the line has you impersonating Laocoön, you'll finally begin getting the line out high up and back of you. Turn your head back, and watch where it goes. Until it goes up and stays up there, without falling dejectedly onto the lawn behind you, it's a good idea to look back, with each back cast, to see where it goes, before turning your head forward with the forward cast. The whole knack is to get the line up and keep it up, while the quick tugs that you make with the left hand impart, much more than the changing motion of the rod itself, the speed to the line as you throw it back and forth in the air.

You know the whistling sound, *whee-whee-ew,* that is vulgarly known as a wolf call, the two sibilants that are made by the boys lounging around the corner cigar or candy store when a commendably built babe goes by? Well, that's the exact sound the line makes, once you've caught the rhythmic trick of shooting it back and forth in the double-line haul. It may help you, in fact, to catch and maintain that rhythm if you make those two sounds yourself, as you give the line the quick little tugs with the left hand, fore and aft and fore, *whee* and *whee-ew*, as you build up the speed and distance of the lengthening false casts in the air above you.

Captain Tommy Edwards and E. Horsfall Turner, the English tournament casters, in their book *The Angler's Cast*, pooh-pooh all the emphasis we Americans give the double-line haul, saying it's only, after all, the left-hand "boost" that every tournament caster gives his line, and it isn't worth making all the fuss over it that we do. Their attitude is a healthily corrective one at that. Most fishing is done within 30 or at most 35 feet ahead of you in the stream, and you don't really need the two tugs of the line that are involved in the technique of the double-line haul until you have to reach out more than 60 feet. Also, it's much less likely that you'll actually hook and hang onto that fish you see rising more than 60 feet away from you than it is that you'll get the fish you're likely to encounter at just half that distance. And in actual fishing, once you have mastered the double-line haul, you'll find that most of the time you're only using half of it anyway, getting all the extra boost your cast actually needs just by giving a single tug with your left hand, without resorting to the rhythmic one-two that works on both the forward and the back cast. It's like speaking prose: once you've learned it, you are not actually aware of doing it. But without it, your use of the small rod will perforce remain confined to short casts of small flies, sizes 14 to 20—for which Paul Young originally intended it— whereas once you learn to "cast the line and not the rod," then you can safely fish it with salmon flies, at least up to size 4 or with streamers or even bass bugs.

10 · The Turnwood Years

When one has fished a water season after season for five years, then is its friendship a great and living thing. These things are a possession that nothing can distract so long as memory serves.   William Caine,
                              in An Angler at Large, 1911

FOR FIVE SEASONS, from '56 through '60, I fished with Al Mc-Clane and Ellis Newman on the Marks water, a mile of the Upper Beaverkill beyond Turnwood, above the Salmo Fontinalis and below the Balsam Lake clubs. Margaret, the widow of Arthur Marks, lived in the big house, a château-like struc-

ture in Norman style, and on the property, which extended
on up to include Forest Lake, there were a large farmhouse
and a number of small cottages. Ellis, who had been a protégé
of Arthur Marks virtually from childhood, had a small studio
workshop in the courtyard behind the big house, and in addition to being Margaret's faithful and constant companion in
her last years, acted as general factotum, giving casting and
shooting lessons to the guests, and at the same time serving as
troubleshooter for the farmhouse and the cottages.

One of the cottages, Jay Gould's old fishing lodge, was on
an island reached on foot by crossing a steel-wire suspension
bridge and by jeep through a shallow ford in the river a few
yards below the bridge. Here Al and Patti McClane spent their
summers—and we were more or less their constant guests.
This lodge was fronted by a large open porch racked with rods
and festooned with boots and waders, and inside it had one big
low room with a huge fireplace, a bath, and two small bedrooms. The big room had sofas that could be used as bunks
when needed. The cooking and dining facilities were in a
separate building, a small pavilion across the lawn, one end of
which was a screened and glassed-in dining porch overlooking
a kitchen pond, part of a series of interconnected ponds and
pools that debouched off the other branch of the river, which
formed the other side of the island. In this pool Al kept fish
that were to be stocked in the river as needed and some that
were being held there largely for observation and study, as
they were the results of crossbreeding experiments he had been
engaged in with a number of different hatcheries. Guests, and
the McClane's small daughter Suzy, amused themselves tossing bits of cheese to the milling trout.

It was in this kitchen pond, for photographic purposes, that Al had placed the first tiger trout, hoping to get a good enough picture of it to make a cover for *Field & Stream*. He placed me on the bank, across from the kitchen, against a setting so sylvan that you would never have guessed it bordered a pond, much less a pond adjoining a kitchen. Taking off the bottom half of the leader on my Midge, leaving a tippet of about OX, he tied on a huge orange feather streamer that he had brought back from the Argentine.

"This will do fine," Al said. "Since he's never been fished for, I'm sure he'll hit anything you toss him, and I just want to be sure you get him on a big enough hook that you can hold him, no matter what he does, until I can get a good color picture."

The tiger, a mammoth hybrid of brook and brown weighing some 9 pounds, lay glaring at us, enjoying the splendid isolation his size assured him. The 15- and 16-inch fish with which he shared the pond were all giving him a wide berth. I crouched at the edge of the bank, half hidden by the tall grass and bushes that bordered the pond, waiting for Al to signal that he was ready with his camera. Al kept urging me to creep a little farther forward, and each time I did, he asked for a little more.

"This has got to be right," he said. "After all, you're making history with the first tiger trout ever taken anywhere."

The tangled thicket of greenery, so effective as a pastoral setting for the picture, made it difficult to determine the exact point of the bank's edge, and the third time Al urged me forward, I took a header into the pond. Its bottom was pure mud, so a recess of a couple of hours had to be declared until, after a complete change of costume, we could try again. This time the picture was snapped hurriedly. By the time we could charm the tiger into taking a favorable position again, the light was no longer ideal, and the cameraman feared the consequences of any further delay for reasons of artistic exigence. I tossed the big orange streamer, feeling as self-conscious as a politician throwing out the season's first baseball, and raised the little rod high as the tiger cooperated with a slashing lunge.

The picture never made the cover of *Field & Stream*, and I had forgotten all about it when, some three and a half years later, I saw a copy of the American edition of Charlie Ritz's book, *A Fly Fisher's Life*, and was struck by a sense of vague familiarity about the color picture on the dust jacket. I hadn't seen Charlie for a couple of years, but I couldn't accept that a short time would have transformed him so completely from the personification of elegance that he always appeared to be on the stream.

"Charlie's getting to be pretty slobby-looking," I thought, still wondering why the background looked so familiar. It couldn't be the Risle, or any Norman stream; in fact, it looked more like the Catskills—and it dawned on me that it was the Catskills, but it wasn't Charlie. It was me. My wife and Al always agreed that when I set forth, accoutered like the White Knight, every pocket bulging with fly boxes rampant, I looked more like the fashion editor of *The Hobo News* than anybody employed, even in a janitorial capacity, by a magazine like *Esquire*.

If Al carried fly boxes, they were discreetly stowed away in the kangaroo-like pouch inside his waders, so you were never aware of them. His example shamed me into streamlining my own peripatetic inventory, with the result that I reduced the portable stock in my Tac-L-Pak to a mere 342 flies. He always looked coolly unencumbered, and maddeningly efficient, whenever he approached the stream. Yet it was he who always made all the fly changes, until he found just what they were taking. I on the other hand, laden with flies like an old-time railway lunch counter, always went on slap-happily skittering and skating my Cahill bivisible spider, which my wife calls a bicuspid, until it would finally occur to me that Al was taking five or six fish to my every one, and I would ask him what they were taking, and finally make the change.

The fishing on that stretch of the Upper Beaverkill was so good, for all five of those seasons I fished it, that if I were condemned to go utterly fishless from here on out until I pass ninety, I would still figure that I was ahead on points. There were days when I would take and release better than forty fish, fishing from early morning until night; Al, fishing only a couple of hours between sessions at his typewriter, would take even more. One day even my wife, whose patience-quotient at any one time on any stream is well under an hour, took fourteen before she got bored. There were five dams in that one mile, and above and below each of them it was almost a certainty that you would get at least one fish. Needless to say, my wife's were taken in the Home Pool, reached by stepping some twenty paces off the front porch of the lodge.

The upper two thirds of the water featured long narrow fast runs, alternating with deep pools, but the lower third, where the river widened, was comprised, except for the vicinity of one dam, of long stretches of what at first glimpse you'd have written off as flat dead water. But along its slightly undercut banks, on either side, lurked the best fish of the whole beat. Up above there were rainbows, often running to 18 inches, but here would be canny old browns that might even touch 20. They were very cagey, holding aloof from all but the tiniest flies.

It was in this stretch that I learned, almost by accident, to be a 20/20 angler. There was no other way to move most of those big browns. In fact, in this long flat stretch it virtually became necessary, as the season wore on, to add another "20" to the formula—a 20-foot leader to which to attach the number 20 fly.

Most anglers have an undue timidity about trying long leaders. A good way to get over it is to do what Al McClane does, when he's tying leaders up for his own use. He casts them —not on a rod, just by hand, holding the butt as you would grip a rod handle. It's not half as hard as it looks. Also it teaches you, faster than you will ever find it out by trial and error during the course of an actual day's fishing on the stream, to correct what's wrong with the leader's balance, before you even begin using it.

An essential first step—before you can lay out a fresh tied-up leader in a cast to see if it will cast satisfactorily—is to rub all the coil and curve out of it, which you do with any handy piece of rubber, as previously mentioned. Try casting one of the ready-mades, of the 7½- or 9-foot lengths, until you get the knack of laying it out across the living-room floor, before you try to graduate to casting longer ones. Leaders that are ready-made are much better nowadays, in that they are more likely to have satisfactorily heavy butts, than they were even as recently as five or six years ago. Then it was unusual to find a store-bought leader of more than .016 or .017 at the butt end. Now they generally run .021 or .023. Since your line end is, or should be, .025 for a true H and .022 for an I, my own feeling is that the .021 butt is all right for the I line-end and the .023 for the H.

Al disagrees, and always tries to get me to reduce the leader butt by at least a couple of points, feeling that otherwise there's too much tendency to slap the water at the point where line and leader join. But he's a perfectionist, and I doubt that my own presentation will ever be fine enough that such a nuance can make a difference. The saving grace is in the leader length. If that critical juncture point is eighteen to twenty feet away from the fish, I think it's unlikely, assuming that the fly itself has been brought down onto the water without a resounding splash or slap, that a secondary slight disturbance that far away is going to make an appreciable difference. Which is why, probably, he consistently outfishes me.

Most anglers have now come around to the use of the knotless leader for at least the upper seven and a half to nine feet, next to the line, adding their own lengths of leader material below it to complete their taper. It makes sense, because on a 7-foot rod, or shorter, you will probably at all times be using a leader at least twice as long as your rod, so the upper half of it, at least, is likely to be drawn back through the guides whenever you bring a fish in close enough to net or grasp. Then's when you're glad you don't have a lot of knots to risk getting caught in the guides, beyond the one knot at the join of the line and the leader butt.

Mr. Hewitt held out against knotless leaders to the last, saying that they were wrong in principle, that the knots of the leader were needed to slow it up in the current and keep it from outracing the fly at its end. But then Mr. Hewitt insisted to the last that his silver-nitrate stain was the only thing that made a leader sufficiently dull and low in visibility to make it consistently take fish, and while Mills still stocks his stained leaders for the few diehards who feel the same way, most have come to the conclusion, after staining up enough kitchen sinks, that the color of the leader doesn't make enough difference to worry about.

What does make a crucial difference, however, if you're using a long leader on a short rod, is that all-important join between leader and line. I use the wedge knot, which is formed by passing the line end through the leader loop, then three times around it, and then through it again, crossing under and over the portion of the line that was first put through the loop, before pulling it taut. This has the effect of tightening the leader loop when the knot is pulled taut, and makes a neat small knot that will pass easily through any rod's guides. Al devised an even better knot, and for a long time I used it on the join of all my lines and leaders, until one day I had it pull out on me when I was fast to a 20-pounder, and I promptly converted them all back to the wedge knot. Al's knot, which he discovered one night while toying with bits of leader material on the dining-room porch at the lodge on the Upper Beaverkill as we were sitting late over the Chianti, was formed without making an actual loop at the leader end, but merely laying the end back against itself, then passing the line around it and back on itself. It seemed to combine safety and simplicity—until my version of it failed me by pulling out on the tug of a 20-pounder. I had probably not tied it just as he had originally taught me to do it. But I have noticed of late that Al himself seems to have gone over to the nail knot, which he described and photographed in the July 1964 issue of *Field & Stream*, so maybe his failed on a 50-pounder. I have duly tried the nail knot and both pictures and instructions seemed clear and simple enough. But then, I have ten thumbs, and although Al said it could easily be done on any nail or ice pick or cocktail swizzle stick, I've tried it on everything up to a broom handle and haven't been able to make it work.

The best thing about Al McClane, as a fisherman's fisherman, is that he is always open to something new and maybe better, and is never inclined to sit back and take the attitude that he wrote the book, as Mr. Hewitt was so prone to do, at least in his last years, and regard his last word as the last that could be spoken. Unique among the experts I've known, he takes it easy, seems to be fishing only because fishing is fun, and is suitably impressed with every least and last fish that anybody else takes. He will stop on the stream and ask you what fly you're using, and you tell him, forgetting that this is like Toscanini stopping to get the advice of an organ grinder.

He's fun to fish with, as many experts aren't, because his enormous learning sits on him so lightly that you forget he's a scientist in this field in which you are dabbling, and think of him as still the farm kid from Margaretville, atingle with excitement at such a rare lark as being down on the river, playing hooky from his chores. But I've seen him approach a strange river, when we were away on trips together, and find fish before the locals could. In any party it's an odds-on bet that he will be the first to be into a fish, just as it's a near certainty that I will be the last. Yet I've seen days, and nights too, when he was as ingloriously skunked as I was. The best part was that he seemed no more surprised at the one phenomenon than at the other. For, as I have often heard him say: "It is only in the eyes of the salmonids that all men are indeed equal."

Once I was on the Little Southwest Miramichi fishing for three weeks—and feeling very set up over averaging a fish a day including grilse. I came into Silliker's, up the road from Red Bank, to pick up a carton of Sweet Caporals they'd ordered for me, and couldn't get anybody's attention. The whole place was buzzing about McClane. Seemed he'd hit the river for two hours, the day before, and hung up three salmon, all over 20 pounds. One 20-pounder is worth a week's conversation in July on the Little Southwest Miramichi. The guides were all as agog as if the river had been visited by a magician.

Later I asked him if he'd been to a place called Silliker's, on the Little Southwest Miramichi, on or about that given day in July, and at first he wasn't even sure he had been, because he'd been so many places, spending no more than a couple of hours at each one.

"You must have been," I said. "I heard about nothing else for a week. They all said you took three salmon, all over 20 pounds."

Even that didn't identify the place for him. (My God, I can draw you a topographical map of every spot I've even *lost* one.) It wasn't until I described the pool that his memory focused.

"Oh, there," he said. "Oh yes, I was ridiculously lucky there.

And I thought of you at the time, because you know what I took them on? One of your Cahill bivisible spiders."

I had practically mowed over that water with my spider, at least five times in the previous ten days, without so much as raising a grilse. If we are indeed all equal in their eyes, why do they notice some of us so much more readily than others? But I would never begrudge a salmon to Al McClane, for I would always remember that it was he who said of them: "Every time you hook one, you feel like tipping your hat to him." He deserves all he catches. After hundreds of salmon and countless thousands of lesser fish, he still reacts with as much awe and appreciation as if he'd never caught one before.

I've seen him come back from Norway, after weeks of playing really big fish, and act just as excited over a 12-inch brown on the Upper Beaverkill as if he'd never seen one. It's a faculty as rare as it's happy, this ability to keep the sense of wonder honed to a razor edge, long after earning the right to act jaded. Maybe it's as much a tribute to the fish as it is to the fisherman.

11·The Four Charlies . . .

When fish are well fed is the time to say who is, and who
is not, an angler. About ninety in one hundred fancy themselves anglers. About one in one hundred is an angler.
Lt. Col. Peter Hawker,
in Instructions to Young Sportsmen, 1814

CHARLES COINER, the long-time art director of N. W. Ayer in
Philadelphia, now retired, was for many years as avid an angler
for trout as anybody you could name. But then the salmon

bug bit him, and he's never been the same. He sits above the river, at a place he built for himself on the Miramichi above Blackville, in Buddha-like contemplation of the pools in sight of his cabin, and if you try to talk to him about trout it's as if he were asked about a classmate he's forgotten. I suppose this ought to be applauded, on the ground that in view of the relative fishing pressures, there's more room for anglers for salmon than there is for anglers for trout. But in comparative angling terms, I think it's a shame. The salmon is only a tourist, in whatever pool you may encounter him, whereas an old brown trout is practically a pillar of local society. The salmon is only pausing for a relatively brief interval, and his real interests lie elsewhere, as he's headed upriver with nature's business on his mind, whereas the trout is installed, has a home he's ready to defend from all encroachments, either of your kind or of his own, and it's a much greater feat to get him to leave his lair under that old snag, which he knows as well as you know the back of your own hand, than it is to persuade the salmon to quit his after all very provisional lie.

To vary the figure, the wiles you must exercise to seduce a salmon are only tantamount to picking up an out-of-town buyer during market week, while luring a brown trout is like getting a demure colleague in the Sunday-school teaching staff of your church to pack up and run away with you. Granted, the salmon averages ten times the size of the trout, but if all you're after is size, why aren't you out on the blue water where you really belong? To most of us, salmon are, and should remain, the occasional bender, to be anticipated and to be remembered, but they shouldn't spoil our taste for the nightly cocktail before dinner.

To these arguments, Charlie Coiner turns an ear that seems to go up or down in its decibel-quotient at will. He is one of those who, having once "tasted blood," as it were, by taking salmon, can never again be tamed down to be happy with trout. Speaking of Charlie Coiner's variable hearing, it's like a thing Dorothy Parker *did* say, although she said very few of the many dicta which legend has attributed to her. I was going on one night, as fatuous as you can get, about being "just a country boy from Michigan," when she brought me down like a punctured balloon by muttering, in that ineffable, velvet-pawed voice: "When convenient."

But what I started to say about Charlie Coiner, until he crossed me up with the wrong answer about fidelity to trout, is that it strikes me as odd that four of the best fishermen I know are all called Charlie. And as far as I know, no two of them ever laid eyes on any other two of them. There's Charlie Coiner the aforesaid; and Charles Kerlee, of Mr. Hewitt's water on the Neversink, who transformed my fishing life with the Midge rod; and the one and only Charlie Ritz, of course; and then there's the redoubtable Charles K. Fox, the master of the Letort, and a real angler if ever one breathed.

Isn't it odd, all these Charlies? Charlie De Feo's another— the list must be endless. What affinity is there, do you suppose, between fish and boys named Charles? It's not that it's any new thing, either. Think back, and there's Charlie Cotton, Walton's alter ego, in whose towering shadow we all aspire to stand. Coming on down, there's Charles Bowlker, and Charles Hallock, and "John Bickerdyke," behind whose pseudonym was still another Charles. And while we'll get back to all of them later on, there must be many others who don't come immediately to mind. If you don't want your boy to be an angler, don't name him Charles.

But to get back to the Charlies nearer at hand, there's something that I cherish, in my make-up as an angler, which I owe to each of them. Without Charlie Coiner, I might never have known much of the lure and lore of the mighty Miramichi; and without Charlie Kerlee—well, but for the Midge I might by now have taken up tatting. But he's something of a disappointment, too, in that he seems to have been enlisted as another recruit to that insidious cult of bigness. The last time I saw him, I asked him about his Midge, like trying to exchange the secret grip of a knowing fraternity, and got a blank look. "Oh yes, the Midge," he said, placing it at last. "Well, I guess Vivian's still using hers." And then he got really enthusiastic, talking about the fiberglass rods he was getting from Russ Peak, out on the Coast. And after that, the next I heard he was taking tarpon on a glass fly rod 9 feet long, off Islamorada, down in Florida, with Jimmy Albright. Well, good for Charlie, and far be it from the likes of me to sniff at a glass rod in the hands of Charlie Kerlee when there's a 90-pound tarpon at the other end of the line. Knowing from the Neversink days how well Charlie Kerlee fishes, and remembering that he was teethed on steelheads when he lived on the Coast, I could get some idea of the difficulty of this wild chase when I heard that of the first fourteen he hooked he managed to hang onto just two, of 65 and 90 pounds, and that he used a new GAF line for every third fish played. The fish would tow the two of them in their skiff, out into the blue, until at last they either broke off or were boated. I can well estimate that I might have hung onto just two out of the first two hundred.

But who wants to play Captain Ahab, and if you've got to do it from a boat, why not go all the way and use a harpoon? Still, Lee Wulff does it too, and I know he loves trout, as much as anybody. But I excuse his going in for stunts like that, on the grounds that he had to do it for a feature for television, just as I condone any amount of spinning and plug-casting that Al McClane may be obliged to do in the course of the broad range of his professional duties. I know they both have their hearts in the right places, after years of demonstrated devotion to trout. But what does Charlie Kerlee have to stray off like that for, in search of madder pastimes and of stronger kicks, when he has a place of his own on the Neversink, and another on the Miramichi?

Charlie Fox, now there's another story. He has a place on the Miramichi, too, but there are years when he doesn't even get to it, because his home in Carlisle is on the Letort. He's one fisherman who need never worry about whether or not he'll go to the anglers' heaven. He can say, as the Parisian says about travel: Why bother? I'm already there. The Letort, as much for the men who fish it as for its fish, is our cis-Atlantic version of the Test. The men who fish it are the naturalist-anglers of our day, who have made contributions as great if not greater than were made in their day by Captain Marryat and Halford on the Test. Ernie Schwiebert feels, and I agree with him, that the regulars of the Letort, and most notably Vincent Marinaro and Charles K. Fox, will in the future perspectives down the aisles of angling's hall of fame loom every bit as large as the Marryats and Halfords, and also as the Hewitts and the La Branches, of the past. Paul Young told me that he had made more examples of his Midge rod for fishermen on the Letort and the Yellow Breeches, in the general small area around Harrisburg and Carlisle, than for all the rest of the trout areas of the country put together.

Special respect is due these anglers—Charlie Fox and Vince Marinaro and Ed Koch, and probably Bus Grove and a few others whose names I don't know—because they attack the problem from the opposite direction. The rest of us get rod-happy and reel-hipped, and worry a lot about our lines and leaders, and then, as the last consideration, put on the flies that everybody else uses and always has, and when the fish don't take, we shrug fatalistically and console ourselves with a thousand equivalents of the one about being able to drive a horse to water but not being able to make him drink.

These fellows devise flies that haven't been used before, and come up with tiny terrestrials made to simulate the infinitesimal bits and globs and smudges found on a handkerchief if you have the wit to hold it in the current to pick up some of the little specks of nothing that we always suspected the trout were taking when we saw them "tailing" and "dimpling," working at something in the water. These men, whom I think of as naturalists first and anglers second, had the sense to approach the angling problem from the fish's side of the affair, instead of from the fisherman's, which is how the rest of us would do it. They made unconventional flies and experimented endlessly in the process, when the rest of us would simply have said tomorrow is another day, and left to come back again when the fish were in a taking mood. That's where, as anglers, naturalists like these make mere rod-carriers out of the rest of us.

The whole story is told, in two parts over a span of more

than a decade, and much too modestly in both instances, in Vincent Marinaro's *A Modern Dry Fly Code*, published by Putnam's in 1950, and Charles K. Fox's *This Wonderful World of Trout*, which Charlie had published himself (at Foxcrest 1, Carlisle, Pennsylvania), in 1963. Out of their efforts came such marvelous flies for low water and warm weather, which have saved so many of us from being skunked under difficult late-season conditions in recent years, as the Jassid, the Letort Beetle, and other *minutae* such as the Black Ant and the Cinnamon Ant, and the many miracle-workers that are to be found in the midge selections now stocked both by Paul Young and by Orvis, and Ed Koch's terrestrial fly selection, which is now carried by Abercrombie & Fitch. These men came to the Midge rod because they had first worked out the tiny flies that gave it its original raison d'être. In contrast to their approach to the problem, that of those of us who went in for light tackle just for added kicks was really mindless.

The other Charlie, *le grand* Charles Ritz, is equally obsessed with experimentation, though from the opposite end, the fisherman's rather than the fish's. He was taking second-hand rods apart, improving their taper, and correcting their balance, as long ago as the teens, when his father first sent him to America to license the use of the Ritz name for a hotel in New York. Now in his seventies, he will go on experimenting, particularly with rods and lines, until the morning of the day he dies.

The most graceful caster of the old school I ever saw, he has now changed his old style, in which with a sort of back jerk of the wrist at the moment of forward thrust he used to drive a line arrow-straight and bullet-fast. Now he's all for the high-speed, high-line technique, and has become the absolute evangel of Jon Tarantino. Tarantino is by all accounts a very nice guy, and one of those rare natural casters of whom there are only a very few in every generation. But he's built rather on the order of Johnny Weissmuller, and Tarzan tactics that are becoming to him just couldn't look right on the slight slender figure of old-world elegance of Charlie Ritz. When Charlie was casting in his own old way, he seemed to achieve and maintain the speed and trajectory of his line as effortlessly as a bird on the wing. Not only did his casting seem as natural and unforced as the flight of a bird, it also seemed as beautiful as its song. He could even impart some of his own easy elegance to those who fished with him, and I never could quite figure out whether he did it by actual instruction or whether some of it just rubbed off on others, by the highly contagious effect of his own example.

One afternoon on the Risle, on the water of Eduard Vernes, he even had my wife emulating his easy natural unforced style. I watched, unable to believe my eyes, as she laid out line like a cable. It seemed to unroll rather than fly through the air, and all I could see to account for it was that tack-hammer, driving-forward thrust of the forearm that appeared to culminate, at the last split second, in a sort of back jerk, or back snap, not really of the wrist but rather of both wrist and forearm as one, acting almost like a recoil, or at any rate a reflex action, and appearing to give a sort of final kick to the impetus of the forward cast. It looked as easy, and as quick and fast, as the batting of an eyelash, but it seemed to send the line a country mile.

From my post on the other side of the river, upstream and across from the spot where they stood in front of the little streamside pergola where we had lunched, I watched this casting and began trying to attempt the trick myself, to see whether I could do it on the basis of monkey-see monkey-do. The result was that on my next cast I scared one of those fat noble Norman trout out of a year's growth, dumping long line on the water as if I had kicked it there with my foot. But Jane, the next day in Connemara and even a week later on the Torridge in Devon, was still batting her line out as if it were jet-propelled, and with energy utterly unreinforced by any other means than the merest momentary back-flick of her anything but mighty forearm.

I stood watching her, bemused and bewildered, as each successive cast of her white line seemed about to bridge the Torridge from the bank where she stood, in a clear space between two fruit trees, to the bank across the river. The exhibition was suddenly interrupted by a strident *yawp*, which could hardly have been warranted by anything less drastic than a snake bite. Easy as the whole thing had looked, she had nevertheless managed to throw something more than the line, and she took to her bed at the George Hotel in Hatherleigh for the next four days, with what the local doctor diagnosed as a tennis elbow. I'm sure it could never have happened if she had had the continuing corrective influence of her preceptor, if Charles Ritz had been fishing beside her then as he had been on the bank of the Risle, but we had bade Charlie goodbye the week before at the Ritz in Paris.

Charlie Ritz and Charlie Fox—what a shame that these two of my four Charlies don't know each other. But I suppose they do in a way: by now they have undoubtedly read each other's books, and in consequence really are better acquainted than if they were to meet at a cocktail party in New York or at lunch within gunshot of Madison Avenue. Meeting on a stream, of course, they wouldn't need an introduction. Real fishermen know each other on sight. It isn't a matter of equipment, or even of technique. But something tells an angler when he's in sight of one of his peers. Maybe the first inkling is in the way each looks at the water. But the sure sign is the care each seems to be taking to avoid interfering with the other's fishing. It's a universal brotherhood and has no need of slogans or passwords or a secret grip.

Charlie Fox and Charlie Ritz both have done high deeds in the handling of truly big fish with consummate skill, but both remain true to trout. Charlie Fox plays big salmon with one hand, photographing them, as they jump, with the other, with a camera attached to his fishing vest. He keeps the pictures and returns the fish, believing, with Lee Wulff, that these noble creatures are too valuable to be caught only once. Charlie Ritz has fished the beats of dukes and kings, taking the enormous fish of the Em, and the Aaro and the Alta, but he comes back ever and again to his true and abiding attachment, the trout of Normandy and the grayling of Austria. He gets extra marks, in my book, for his affection and admiration for grayling, the greatest of insufficiently appreciated fish. And Charlie Fox, who has had as sustained a love affair with trout as any man I know, gets an extra sprig of laurel for having said of a jumping salmon: "Salute him by lowering your rod."

12 · Trout by the Score

If a fisherman is a good sportsman he can play a delightful game of solitaire with himself, of the most interesting kind. I have made a practice of doing this for years on the stream by keeping score of the number of fish seen rising and the percentage of these which are raised to the fly and the number hooked. My temper ebbs and flows with the results. When the great day comes when 90% to 95% of the fish

*I see rising are raised and hooked, I feel like the golfer who
has beaten the best previous score.*
E. R. Hewitt, in *A Trout
and Salmon Fisherman for Seventy-five Years*

I WROTE a couple of pieces for *Field & Stream* comparing
angling to golf, where what matters most is how you do this
time against last time, and how you do against par, which
is supposed to be a gauge of competence for the course. When
I wrote them I had forgotten, though I had read all of Mr.
Hewitt's books, that he had made the analogy cited above. His
form of "solitaire" differed from mine in that it was based on
percentages of fish risen, which I suppose is an even finer
scorecard of skill, whereas mine was a pure and simple game
of numbers. Elsewhere in the book cited he said that he had
long since passed the point where the number or the weight
of fish taken counted much. I am not so jaded, and doubt
that I ever will be. Every least and last trout hooked counts
like crazy with me.

I did not begin to approach my present level of enjoyment
of angling, however, until I began carrying a notebook instead of a creel, and started thinking of angling as an interesting game rather than as an uncertain meat-substitute.

This golfer's attitude toward angling is really a form of
disappointment insurance. Once you've taken it on, you'll
never again know a bad day on any river or stream. I might
equally well call it monotony insurance, because once you've
started keeping score instead of fish, no water except perhaps
that of a swimming pool or a bathtub will ever lose angling
interest for you. You'll find yourself contented, and even
delighted, to fish the same old familiar home waters over and

over again, rather than dashing off in all directions looking for new ones.

Actually, you can't learn any stream by heart in less than three seasons anyway, so you can't begin to savor its enjoyment to the full until the fourth year. I've proved this to my own satisfaction several times, and most conclusively during the first four seasons, from '56 through '59, on the Upper Beaverkill stretch that I fished at Turnwood, when I kept the following careful record of every trout hooked and played.

I never kept such a complete record for other favored stretches, such as the Esopus, from the Five Arch Bridge down to the Chimney Hole, though I'd still recommend that as the most challenging beat I know. Nor the Chichester, above Phoenicia, or the Beaverkill for the mile above Cook's Falls, or the Willowemoc for the mile reserved for fly fishing only, above Livingston Manor—though a record like this could well be kept for any of the four. I've fished them all with approximately equal enjoyment if unequal reward, fishing fine and using what you might consider bookkeeping methods, as opposed to fishkeeping.

Maybe it sounds crazy to suggest that you'll have more fun on stream if you carry a notebook instead of a creel, but just look at my four-year score, tabulated from my angler's log, for the days spent during those four seasons on this one stretch. See if it doesn't suggest, as you look it over, something like the outline of the curriculum for a four-year course in Progressive Angling Enjoyment. I promise you, it's an equally interesting course on any stream you want to take it on.

I began with a fixed idea, in the '56 season, when I saw this water for the first time. Because I'd found a Cahill bivisible spider, size 16, to be a wonderful "locator" on the other Catskill streams mentioned, I started out using it on this new stretch, while trying to get acquainted with its most likely lies for trout. I was going through another purist phase at the time, saying that I preferred to get skunked on a dry fly to catching fish on either nymphs or streamers, so although the scorecard for that first season shows a scattered number of trout caught on other flies, 125 of the 177 fish I took on this water in '56 were taken on the Cahill bivisible spider. I was delighted with the season's scorecard, as it worked out to an average of 13.6 trout per day's fishing. I'd had what I considered a pretty good season's average on the Esopus a couple of years earlier, when I'd been on a Pink Lady kick, using no other fly the whole season through, and had averaged only 6.5 trout per day. So here I was, my first season on some new water, doing twice as well as I had done on water that I thought I knew pretty well.

Toward the end of that first season, I had found the Cahill bivisible spider a bit less surefire than it had seemed at the beginning, and had begun to supplement it with a blue spider. The next year, the effectiveness of the Cahill bivisible spider seemed greatly lessened. It was still good as a locator, but it would provoke bunts more often than solid hits. I tried it first on every pool, but when it produced a bunt I would switch over to the blue spider immediately, floating it over the same spot where a trout had just bunted the bivisible, and found on a satisfying number of occasions that the bunt would thus be converted, on this second try, into a solid smash. So this time, as the tabulation for '57 shows, the blue spider by the season's end had actually outfished the Cahill bivisible, the

FOUR-YEAR SCORECARD FOR ONE CATSKILL MILE

	'56	'57	'58	'59	Four-year totals
	179 ÷ 13 times fished = 13.6 average	237 ÷ 13 times fished = 18.2 average	427 ÷ 18 times fished = 23.7 average	542 ÷ 20 times fished = 27.1 average	1385 ÷ 64 times fished = 21.6 average
TOTAL NUMBER TROUT TAKEN	179	237	427	542	1385
Caddis Grub, size 14			3		3
Jassid, size 20			5		5
Black Nymph, size 20	5	1			6
Mickey Finn, size 12	3	2	6		11
Montana Nymph, size 12		12	4		16
Light Cahill, dry, size 18	2			15	17
Grey Nymph, size 20	7	1		10	18
Supervisor Streamer, size 14			29		29
Ratface McDougall, dry, 14	4	25			29
Quack Coachman, dry, size 14		15	14	4	33
Maribou, white, size 12		18	13	4	35
Parma Belle Streamer, 12	11	17	5	10	43
PHY Nature Nymph, 14			1	46	47
Letort Beetle, size 20			70	10	80
Blue Spider, size 14	19	56	31		106
Hewitt Nymph, size 14			5	108	113
Dry Flies, sizes 20 & 22		37		78	115
Betsy Streamer, size 14	1		95	138	234
Cahill Bivisible Spider, size 16	129	53	146	119	447

favorite of the previous year, by a score of 56 to 53. But in the second season, getting to know the water better, I had begun to fish it with an approach that was a bit more varied. I found that some of the flat quiet stretches, which I had written off the year before as dead water because they weren't so trouty-looking as the more obvious runs, could be made to produce strikes if they were fished in depth, after being floated over to no avail with a spider. Although the two spiders accounted for the largest number of fish that second season, as they had the first year, they now represented only about a third of the total, instead of almost seven eighths. The total take went up, as it should have since I now knew the water better, to 237, for an improved average of 18.2 trout per time fished.

In '58, for no reason that I could think of, the Cahill bivisible spider regained the effectiveness it had begun to lose the year before. It accounted for 146 fish, the biggest total of the four seasons. But two new factors came into play. I discovered a hitherto unsuspected quality in the Betsy Streamer, an old Paul Young fly I'd never thought much of; and a brand new fly, the Letort Beetle, which first became commercially available that year, started off the season with a bang.

The Letort Beetle, a number 20 black nymph first developed by Ernest Schwiebert on the Letort in Pennsylvania, was a dazzling success the first month I used it, giving me seventy nice trout, all well above average size. Then just as suddenly it stopped producing. From one weekend to the next, it turned from a surefire lure into an absolute dud, and I never will know why. It was as if the trout had circulated a petition against it, during the week I was away from them, and had come to a collective bargaining agreement never to touch it again. Still, I don't know—'58 was a crazy season in one other respect. On two different afternoons, over a month apart, the trout went wild over a Supervisor streamer— that gaudy blue, green, and red thing that you would expect to be effective only on the squaretails in fly-in spots in the wilderness—and twenty-nine apparently normal, diffident browns and rainbows impaled themselves on it. In the whole four seasons they never had before and they never have since. It's things like this that will keep fishing from ever being an exact science, no matter how scientifically you approach it.

But the big thing that happened in '58, that third year of fishing this stretch of water, was that the Betsy Streamer, which I'd always bought and classed as a wet fly, suddenly turned into a demon as a dry. Since I always want my line to float and my leader to sink, whether I'm fishing wet or dry, I have a habit of greasing the line a number of times a day as I fish. For this purpose I always let out line with a wet fly on, smearing the line dressing on the line with the thumb and forefinger of my right hand as I retrieve it with my left. I find this way that a silk line will remain just as good a floater as any air-chambered nylon line of the supposedly permanently floating type. One day I must have got some of the line dressing on a Betsy Streamer. As I started the jerky retrieve, occasioned by drawing the line through the line dressing, I noticed that the Betsy, instead of coming back upstream minnow-like beneath the surface, was pulling under, then bobbing back up onto the surface. I was annoyed to notice this, and did not look at the bobbing fly but concentrated on the line to make sure that I was applying the line dressing evenly and equally as I drew the rest of the line between my fingers. At the conclusion of the retrieve I looked at the fly again, just as I was about to lift it from the water to change it, and cursed myself for my clumsiness in having cancelled the effectiveness of that particular retrieve. But as I lifted it from the water, not fifteen feet from where I stood, I saw a tawny shape move away from behind it, and veer away toward the bank. Quickly cancelling the plan to change the "spoiled" fly, I threw it instead with a quick short cast right over to that edge of the bank and retrieved it, diving and bobbing, hurriedly back. The hurrying did it, and bang he was on. I would love to report that he stayed on, and he did for three beautiful jumps. I had plenty of chance to judge his size—a good 20 inches at the very least. Between times, too, on my little Midge rod he felt like a salmon. But after the third jump he felt like nothing at all, because he wasn't there any more. At the hook end of that long leader I had thirty inches of .0039 filament, and though I had lowered my rod tip and prayed each time he jumped, it simply wasn't stout enough—or maybe I was literally too butter-fingered, from the line dressing that was still on my hands. Anyway, he got away. But ninety-five of his brothers and sisters didn't, that third season, helping enormously to kick up my total score to 427, and bettering my average to 23.7 trout per fishing time, as I had learned another way to fish this water.

From then on, I never left any part of that water without trying a heavily dressed Betsy Streamer, both for a full free float downstream and for a jerky retrieve back up. About a third of the time they'd take it as a free-floating dry fly, and the rest of the time they'd nail it on its diving and bobbing

return trip back upstream. By the end of the third season, I
felt I had begun to understand the angling possibilities of this
piece of water pretty well, but I held little hope for the fourth
season, which was '59. That was the year a lot of trout fishermen I know just stopped going fishing after Memorial Day.
The season in New York was two weeks longer by law but
above twelve weeks shorter by weather. By June 1 most New
York streams (except for the Esopus, thanks to the flow of the
Portal) were lower than they usually are by mid-August, and
by mid-August they were virtually vestigial. But by dint of
trying oftener and harder, and because I at last knew the water
well, I had my best season to date, as the '59 entries on my
four-year scorecard show.

As you will see by examining the fly entries for 1959, two
nymphs that had amounted to very little the year before scored
heavily that year. The Hewitt Nymph, size 14, with a dirty
yellow underside and black above, which had scored only five
times in '58, accounted for 108 trout in '59, and the size 14
PHY Nature Nymph, a Paul Young creation that had picked
up only one trout in '58, accounted for forty-six the following
year. Then, too, the trick of fishing the Betsy Streamer as a
dry fly (with a downstream float and a bobbing retrieve back
upstream) worked better than ever, contributing 138 trout
to the score. The old reliable, the Cahill bivisible spider, rang
up a very respectable score of 119. These, together with the
smaller scores representing the use of other flies, such as tiny
dries, size 20 and 22, in ankle-deep water, brought the total
up to the gratifying sum of 542, with an average of 27.1 trout
per time spent fishing this particular stretch of water.

Granted that there are some variables to account for in any

comparison of the different scores for the same water over a span of four seasons, since weather and consequent water-depth make it impossible to consider any stream as the same four years in a row. Still, I think these four scores make a pretty good case for the fact that, regardless of weather, you are very likely to do increasingly better on any water if you keep at it and study it as you fish it.

If I had stuck to flailing that stretch with just one fly, as I pretty much did the first year, the chances are overwhelming that I could not have bettered my score each year thereafter. There are several things in the four-year score that furnish a clue to its progressive improvement. In '56, the first year, I fished the spider only upstream, and did very little downstream fishing. In fact, it was only after the discovery of the two-way effectiveness of the Betsy Streamer, in '58, that I began giving this water as thorough a going over downstream as up. The improvement in the score speaks for itself.

There are those who are still horrified at the thought of fishing a dry fly downstream, but I have found that if you can cast to the far bank, angling your cast about three quarters upstream, you are getting as much fishing downstream as you are up, on each free float. Particularly on a skater like the spider, which you can bring back upstream to your casting position in six-inch jerks, punctuated by slight pauses, you are just as likely to take fish on the surface retrieve as you are on the downstream float. And if all you get out of the spider, either floating it down free or "skating" it back up over the water, is a bunt, then you have an excellent chance to convert it to a hit with a nymph or a streamer retrieved back over that same telltale location. I still feel that if I had to fish any stream on one fly I would choose the spider, size 16, because you can tease trout with it more ways than with any other fly. Next best bet for me would be the two-way stretch I get out of the Betsy Streamer. Third choice would be a Hewitt Nymph, fishing it three-quarters upstream, exactly the same as with the spider, but held just in or below the surface film of the water, by the slow sweep of the floating line, on the downstream float.

In fishing by the score, I have always felt that a trout is a trout, and I've never attempted to indicate size in my notebook. I simply keep count of the number of fish hooked, landed, and released each time, and establish my averages by dividing the total number of fish counted by the number of times I've been fishing. If you are mathematically more gifted than that, it would be very easy to keep a much better point system of scoring. Instead of counting one for every trout regardless of size, you could count one point for every trout under 10 inches, two for those from 10 to 12 inches, three for 13 inches, four for 14, and five for 15, right on up to ten for a 20-incher. For any lunker running from 20 to 25, you could give yourself fifteen points, and twenty-five points for anything over 25 inches.

I sometimes find myself doing better, with this system, on bad days than on good days. I've had days when I might take only eight or nine fish, but all big, and I've had days when I might score three or four times as often, but not have a single trout over 10 inches. With my simple way of keeping score, the latter days look wonderful, but on a qualitative basis they aren't that good. Neither are the other days as bad as my oversimplified scorekeeping makes them look.

I'd a lot rather have a day like one I remember, when I took only six trout but one ran 19½ inches and another 20¼, than any number of days when the little kamikaze brookies come to my spider in droves, hell-bent on hooking themselves. But while those days bulk up my score, the others only lower my average.

All you need is any kind of notebook and the stub of a pencil to keep score right on the stream if you don't want to trust to your memory until you've knocked off for the day. If you can't be bothered taking out your notebook every time you catch a fish, though, you might try one of those counters that women use for toting up their purchases in supermarkets. With such a gadget, all you need do is click it the required number of times to indicate the different sizes of the fish as you catch them, and you keep a qualitative score as easily as I do now the quantitative way. Another qualitative way of scoring, if you fish waters in which there are several species, is to count one point for a brookie, two for a rainbow, and three for a brown. In my experience of the waters I've fished, that's a fairly accurate reflection of their willingness to bite. Of course, if you teach at M.I.T. or are related to Einstein, or if you're an engineer and are used to a slide rule, you could keep a score that would reflect even the size of the hook on which each fish was taken. For instance, five points for 15-inch trout, plus eight points if you hooked him on a size 8 streamer, or sixteen points if you got him on a size 16 spider, or even twenty points if you took him on a number 20 midge. You could score a hundred points with half a dozen fish, while I'm impressing myself with a mere twenty-five or thirty on my simple one-for-one scoring system.

Trout by the Score

Much as I hate angling to be in any way competitive, you could even match scores with somebody else for a given piece of water, the way chess enthusiasts play by correspondence. But be sure to make it clear between you whether you are keeping a quantitative or a more elaborately qualitative score. Any way you keep it, I bet you'll have more fun fishing for trout by the score than you ever had fishing for them by the pound.

13 · Iceland, the Angler's Ultima Thule

*. . . duckes, cootes, herons, and many other fowlys with ther
brodys, whyche me semyt better than all the noyse of
houndes . . .* The Treatysse of Fysshynge
with an Angle, 1496

"THAT'S THE SEVENTH SALMON I've played since noon," I said.
"Don't tell me it's always like this."

"Oh no," said Thor, "you really should have been here a month ago. About mid-July is when it's at its best. This is just average, like any time after that first wild run, when they first come in from the ocean. That's the time to be here."

We were fishing his water on the Haffjardara, and that morning I had taken my first salmon. Not only my first salmon there, but my first salmon ever. Your first salmon must have a name, and mine, a sleek fat hen, had been christened Thora, in honor of my host, Thor Thors. It was mid-August of '55, and I was between wives. It was my first summer as a member of the Big Bend Club on the Neversink, and I hadn't really planned on doing any fishing anywhere else. But Louis Renault, a photographer friend, had an assignment to get some pictures of birds in Iceland. He was taking his wife with him—she was an ardent bird-watcher—and they were going on, after five days in Iceland, to vacation in Europe. He knew how I loved to fish; for the previous two years I had been stocking the one-acre pond he had outside his house in Stamford. It was two-bucket fishing. We'd go to the stocked ponds of his neighbors for several miles around, and as I'd fill one bucket, Louie would run home with it in his station wagon, dump it out in his pond, and then bring it back to exchange it for the other, which would usually be just about filled in time for the swap. That way, we had stocked his pond with several hundred bass and two to three times as many bluegills.

As long as it was only five days and could virtually be squeezed in between weekends on the Neversink—and I'd always wanted to try salmon fishing—it seemed a good idea. So here I was, on Thor's river in the Snaefellsnes, northwest of Reykjavik, with the Renaults gone off to the north for their bird-snapping. And this was my introduction to salmon fishing. That first day I hastily revised my plans and decided to stay on for an additional five days after the Renaults left for Norway, only wishing that there were some way to prolong it even more. Of course it was a first time, and in this as in so many other things there can be only one. In the decade since, I've fished for salmon at every opportunity, but I know there can never be another time like that dream afternoon on that dream river, the Haffjardara.

I was back there again, to the day and the hour, on July fifteenth of the following year, having regarded it throughout the year as the only date I had that really mattered. I was there with bells on, with my new wife Jane and with Al McClane, having filled them both to the bursting point with my tall tales, in the interim, about the dream day I'd had on this dream river, and at a time, mind you, when it wasn't even supposed to be especially good. Now if we could just plan to be there on July 15, when Thor says that first wild run is at its height . . . So we were.

But that year, for no good reason that anybody could determine, we were either two weeks early or the salmon were two weeks late. We went on to other rivers, and came back again, and on the rebound Al did hook two fish, but that was two fish for the three of us, and I could only wonder if I really had been dreaming, the year before, with my seven salmon in an afternoon. Al says no, I wasn't, and that the Haffjardara is a dream river, but he long ago learned, and I've been learning every year since, that there isn't a river in the world where you can be absolutely certain, a year in advance, that you'll raise even one salmon on a given afternoon. And to this day, whenever Al McClane and I meet, we go through a set routine that has become as ritual as the exchange of a password. "Hi, where'd you rather be, or on Thor's river?"

And the only answer is: "Right."

The salmon fishing in Iceland is as nearly foolproof as salmon fishing ever can be, provided you remember that salmon fishing can never be foolproof anywhere. I know this, but the trouble is I never remember it when I should. I've sent people to the Derryclare Butts, in Ireland, their mouths watering after I got carried away in telling them about the salmon fishing there, and those who were still speaking to me after they got back were obviously more than half inclined to sue me. Dare I, then, tell you any more about the salmon fishing in Iceland? Well, in the case of Iceland, the bets are hedged to some degree against utter disappointment, because most of the rivers there also carry both trout and char, either of the migrating or of the nonmigrating variety, and many of them carry both. Even so, we probably ought to put up one of those signs that you often see on certain sections of just-opened highways, where just as the road appears to be at its most promising, you are reminded that from that point on you are traveling at your own risk.

Iceland is the fourth largest island in the North Atlantic, after Greenland, Britain, and Newfoundland. It lies between 63° 24′ and 66° 32′ north latitude, with its north coast just touching the rim of the Arctic Circle. It is a fifth larger than Ireland, a fifth smaller than Pennsylvania. Iceland's sixty salmon rivers have been building their almost legendary fame over the past century, and today there are no waters in the world more jealously held or more zealously preserved. Since 1945, and after passing from Danish rule to independence, Iceland prohibits by law the ownership of a salmon river by anyone but an Icelandic national, so the one way to assure a more or less permanent beat on one of these idyllic streams would be to marry an Icelandic girl. Major General R. N. Stewart, author of *Rivers of Iceland*, an Englishman who has fished there for more than fifty years, beginning as far back as 1912, said in reference to this then-new ruling: "A single angler could go farther and do worse." To anyone who has seen Icelandic girls, the general's remark could seem a mere elucidation of the obvious.

Most people think of Iceland as a remote fastness harboring Eskimo, polar bear, reindeer, seals, and ice floes, and assume that the only proper garb for expeditions there is the type made famous by Admiral Byrd. True, Iceland does lie north of the lower third of Greenland, which is only a couple of hundred miles to the west, and is wholly above the Faeroe Islands, but the proximity of the Gulf Stream gives it a mild oceanic climate, with a spread of only about 20 degrees between average winter and summer temperatures.

There are both reindeer and seals on Iceland, but no Eskimo, and the only polar bear ever encountered is an occasional visiting tourist along the north coast. The average winter temperature is only 30 degrees Fahrenheit, and the summer average is a degree or so above 50. In the three months of the salmon season, from mid-June to mid-September, the noonday temperature is apt to rise close to 70, and there is a midnight sun, at least over the northern half of the island, for almost all of the first month of the season. Even in late August and early September, when the end of the season is approaching, there are only a few hours of real darkness, from around eleven at night until around three in the morning. (Conversely, in the depth of winter in Reykjavik, the country's one real city, there are only about four hours of actual daylight, from late morning to early afternoon.)

Except from the standpoint of his own creature comfort, Icelandic weather need not concern the angler, as the fishing there is as nearly weatherproof as it can ever be anywhere. Since the surroundings of the rivers are volcanic rock, overgrown with tundra, and there are no trees whatsoever, there is also an almost total absence of mud. Hence the clear streams never really muddy up even in the foulest weather. They may "pearl" a bit for a few hours, but they never turn that chocolate color that is so frequently the fly fisherman's despair almost everywhere else. The one fly in the otherwise serene ointment of Icelandic fishing, however, is that high winds are rather more likely than not to be blowing across the treeless landscape. (There are furze-like shrubs here and there, but they stand never higher than about eighteen inches, and the combination of bare rock and tundra is otherwise unrelieved, giving the setting of most rivers the aspect of a scene from the Twilight of the Gods, a bleak and brooding view of surroundings of awesome majesty. Bright intervals between the wind and the rain are frequent, however, and the fish seem to move more briskly at the first emergence of the sun, when the angler's attention is most likely to be distracted by the sight of a rainbow, complete and intact as a croquet hoop, with both of its ends plainly in sight.)

Since there are no trees to worry about, it is relatively easy for the angler to maneuver in such a way as to let the wind carry the fly to the fish, even in a gale. Winds of up to force eight, just short of hurricane velocity, are by no means infrequent, and at such times tossing the fly up in the air, about the height of a tennis ball for an overhead serve, will be enough to launch it sufficiently, letting the line coiled at the fisherman's feet pay out into the wind, as it will. Regardless of the angry weather, or even perhaps especially in such weather, it is almost a certainty that the angler will ultimately be fast to a fish, when the one worry is to keep one's footing. For the light-tackle man, at least, chest-high waders are an absolute necessity.

While Icelandic fish don't run as large as those of arctic Norway—the record salmon for most of Iceland's rivers stands between 30 and 35 pounds—what they lack in size they more than make up in vigor. The average is about 9½ pounds, but since the season is a short one, the likelihood of encountering a salmon recently in from the sea is proportionately higher, and even a 6- or 8-pounder, newly arrived, will lead the angler such a merry chase that he's almost certain to be sloshing around in water above the height of hip boots before finally beaching him, unless his tackle is of such Gargantuan proportions as to permit horsing the fish in. That, of course, is what the Icelanders do. They may by now have heard of the light-tackle trend, but they still use the heaviest rods that Hardy makes, derrick-like devices of 22 to 24 ounces, with leaders of around 20-pound test. Their general practice is to fish from the shore, wearing the trawler boots that are sold down by the docks in Reykjavik, and grab the tail of any salmon that's brought in, heaving him away some thirty feet or more from the edge of the stream, where the odds are overwhelming that he will accommodatingly brain himself on the needle-sharp lava rock. When an American shows up with a fly rod of four ounces or less, announcing his intention of beaching for himself any fish he hooks, they laugh themselves into hysterics. Icelanders are laughers and drinkers on a Homeric scale, and as likable a group of people as are to be encountered anywhere, but it has never yet occurred to them to give a fish anything remotely resembling a sporting chance. Relatively few of them will even fish consistently with a fly, since the matter of terminal tackle is not restricted by law, but will resort to big spoons of pikelike size. Even the visiting English, stout fellows though they are in the matter of suitable tackle—and inclined to sneer at the "toy rods" used by Americans—are horrified by the hardware thrown into their rivers by the Icelanders. Indeed, General Stewart advises giving a good rest to any pool that has been worked over by an Icelander.

The angler going to Iceland will be well advised to take his own rods and leaders, and the rod should not be more than 6 ounces at the very most, since nine out of ten of the salmon hooked will run under 10 pounds. And, since most Icelandic rivers offer a simultaneous chance at two of the five kinds of fish prevalent (that is, salmon and sea trout and seagoing char, as well as the nonmigratory strains of both trout and char), almost any salmon pool is equally likely to yield a trout or a char of from 2 to 4 pounds. The latter, of course, are a picnic on rods of from 2 to 4 ounces, but somewhat anticlimactic if played on heavier tackle. Because of the comparative lack of obstructions on the streams, and the relative ease of finding a bank favorable to beaching the fish, the angler need not feel underequipped with a trout rod and terminal tackle no heavier than 1X.

In Reykjavik there are two excellent tackle shops where rods can be repaired promptly and well and all necessary flies obtained. The rods and reels and leader material of the Icelanders, however, are all likely to be too heavy. As for flies, Silver Doctor, Silver Wilkinson, and Black Doctor are almost a three-way tie for first place as the most dependable all-round fly, with Blue Charm the runner-up. They are all taken with enthusiasm not only by the salmon for which they were patterned but also by sea trout, browns, and both migratory and nonmigratory char. The latter are such voracious takers of virtually any fly, including dries all the way down to number 20 midges, that almost any fly tossed is likely to provoke some sort of action. Large salmon will play with a White Wulff, or other hair-wing dry, clowning with it and passing it back and forth like hockey players with a puck, but will probably not take until given a wet fly. The Thor pattern, among sea-trout flies, seems to be the best single fly, in number 6 and number 4 sizes, after July 10, when the sea trout are in.

The angler who goes to Iceland before July 15 is courting disappointment. The season is open from June 15 to September 15, but the fish are seldom in the rivers in any appreciable numbers much before the first of July. Icelanders generally say that July 15 is the optimum moment, for both salmon and sea trout. But the angler with a choice of dates will do better to take the later one. Unlike the British Isles, Iceland has no early and late rivers, and in a year when the fish are late in coming in, the angler's disappointment is apt to be as great in the rivers of the west coast as in those of the northern section. The big Laxá, near Husavik, has consistently produced some of the biggest salmon ever caught in Iceland, and two other very productive rivers on the north coast are the Hrútafjardará and the Siká. The suffix -*á*, pronounced "ow!," means river, and *lax* means salmon (Icelandic is basically the Old Norse, or the German of the year 1000). Hence almost every section has a Laxá, meaning simply Salmon River. The one in the north is usually known as the Laxamyri, although its full geographical name is the Laxá i pingeyjarsýslu. The Snaefellsnes section, on the west coast, has three outstanding rivers, the Straumfjardará, the Haffjardará, and the Stadará, the latter being exceptionally good as a sea trout stream. Nearer to Reykjavik are the Grimsá, the Sogid, and the Bruará. All of the rivers mentioned have been fished frequently by Americans, but since there are sixty in all, it is obvious that no one American can have fished them all, nor does the mere naming of them mean that any American can fish them.

The best rivers are on the north, the northeast, and the west coasts—rugged streams, flowing fast and deep. There are a few good rivers in the south, shallow and easily waded. The Laxamyri fish average 18 pounds, and expert anglers have taken as many as 20 to 30 such salmon in a single day. Many other rivers provide excellent salmon fishing, and it is a general rule that in large streams the fish range from 12 to 18 pounds; in the smaller ones, from 5 to 7 pounds.

Increasingly, Icelandic rivers are held by syndicates of native owners, and it is by no means axiomatic that permission to fish them can be obtained quickly and easily.

The SUNNA Tourist Bureau, Bankastroeti 7, Reykjavik,

has a two-day angling trip, combining trout fishing in the lakes one day and salmon fishing the next, for $98 for one person, or $35 per person for a party of five. This is mentioned to give an idea of prevailing rates. SUNNA could undoubtedly arrange more extensive trips for anglers interested in doing more than just sampling the Icelandic fishing. (Their trips include provision of tackle as well as thigh boots and warm overclothing.)

Boot-foot waders are preferable to the stocking-foot type, since the abrasive action of the omnipresent volcanic rock dust (even the roads are of volcanic rock) will quickly wear through waders at the ankle, where brogues and wading socks make a too-convenient catch basin for the diamond-hard particles. The lava riverbeds, too, are extremely slippery, so hobnailed wading sandals, or at least a set of chains or a pair of wading grips, are a must.

As for the rest of the outfit, it is important that it be both rain-resistant and windproof. A rain jacket, preferably with a hood, should be in the back pocket of whatever tackle pack, vest, or coat the angler normally wears on the stream. It is almost certain to be needed, for protection from wind if not from rain. The winds serve to keep the water temperatures almost always below 50 degrees Fahrenheit, so it is especially important to be warmly clad from the waist down. Ski underwear and heavy socks are indicated, the latter of the insulated or therm-rubber variety, for those who tend to be at all cold-footed.

Icelandic Airlines (Loftleidir) has at various times offered salmon fishing to Americans on a package-deal basis, providing about ten days of fishing for about a thousand dollars.

The airline has at such times had access to three of Iceland's best salmon rivers, and to several of the trout-teeming lakes. They can still in all probability, given sufficient advance notice —a matter of months, that is, rather than weeks—arrange trips on an individual basis. Unless one has an Icelandic friend who owns a salmon river, it could undoubtedly cost a lot more, both in money and in time and trouble, to try to arrange an expedition on one's own. There are no railways in Iceland, and some of the more remote rivers are accessible only by a combination of plane and pack horse. There are buses to put you within reach of a number of the rivers, but those within easiest reach physically are the least likely to be within reach financially, in terms of fishing rights.

In general, both food and lodging throughout the land are substantial but not deluxe, and the food is more likely to please gourmands than gourmets, since Icelandic portions are Viking size. The lodging is more inclined to comfort than to chic. (Two of the food specialties are smoked mutton, and little birds called rjúpa, delicious but so tiny that they make squab seem the size of turkey.) In Reykjavik, with the exception of the Hotel Borg, which compares to a good small provincial German hotel, there are at present very few adequate tourist lodgings, and outside the city they are of the farmhouse variety, clean and friendly but strictly potluck all around. The independent angler, setting out from Reykjavik, had better have some of the explorer and pioneer in his make-up. And unless his wife is at least as addicted to fishing as he is, she'd better go on to Copenhagen and wait for him there. After two days, Reykjavik would bore her blind.

My own wife made just one stipulation, before setting out

for Iceland with me and Al McClane. She was born cold, and despite the assurances that both Al and I gave her about the mild, Gulf Stream-tempered climate, she insisted on my getting her a set of real cashmere underwear such as she had worn for hunts in the past. I got her the one pair that Abercrombie & Fitch had in stock, at $50 each for the top and bottom garments. I equalized this, however, by getting my own long woolies at an army surplus store, at 25 cents each for the top and bottom, thus on balance making the price right. Her cashmeres saw only one day's service on the trip, so it was fortunate that she also had some ski underwear along, of the fireman's red variety. The first day she wore the cashmeres, she was casting from the bank of the big Laxá, up north near Husavik, and engrossed in Al's advice to turn and watch her back cast, she absentmindedly took a forward step to get a better view of it, and went in over her head. A small crowd of admiring Icelanders, perhaps thinking it was part of the exhibition, had neither time nor apparently inclination to do anything but applaud when she bounced back up out of the water in the gambit of an experienced diver.

But the cashmeres stayed both wet and smelly ("Whew! straight from the camel to you," was how she expressed it), despite being hung up to dry, both outdoors and in, for the next week, and this in July, when the north coast of Iceland is truly and literally a part of the land of the midnight sun. It was a good three months before they could be certified both dry and nonodoriferous.

One other hazard ought to be mentioned, in any briefing of the prospective visiting angler. The Icelanders are the friendliest things on feet, but they just can't drink. And yet they do, ritually and ceremoniously for a start, and then once started, on to oblivion. When you meet them, on or off stream, and no matter how many of them you meet at once, you must "Skoal" each of them, and each must "Skoal" you back. This would be fine in 7-Up or iced tea, though a bit kidney-taxing, but they do it in a lethal-looking black fluid they call Brenntwein, which we came to know colloquially as Black Death. And once any Icelander has whipped one of those black bottles out of his knapsack, he will not replace the cork. The cork is tossed back over the left shoulder, apparently for luck. A bottle that is opened is a bottle that must be emptied.

You love them for their hospitality, but you learn to fear them for it too. "Skoal Jane." "Skoal Al." "Skoal Arnold." "Skoal Christian." "Skoal Hekla." "Skoal Gudmundur." Well, sure, why not, that's only six, all around. But wait. Each must do it to each of the others. And each must do it back, to each of the others. And bottoms up or it's a mortal insult. So that isn't six drinks, it's thirty, by the time each has skoaled and been skoaled by each of the others, because of course you can't sit there like a clod and not participate in each and every toast, whether directed to you or not, without offending the person to whom this particular one has been directed.

Meals are even more hazardous, for while the skoaling continues, other marks of affection and esteem are vouchsafed the visiting firemen. You are a guest and the guest should have the best. In the case of salmon, they seem to feel that this is the eye. If after the thirtieth gulp of Black Death your next gulp can be affirmative, rather than a sudden horrified and involuntary negative one, when you look down at your plate to see a big blue and white poached eye glaring at you balefully, you're a better man than most, and have proved yourself worthy of an Icelandic reception.

The meals are apt to seem bizarre in any event, when you come in off the stream after midnight and sit down in the sunlight, just as you would at noon. The midnight sunshine is only slightly paler—like creamery butter, as compared to the dairy-butter yellow of the noonday sun. You never know whether what you're eating is breakfast or late supper, and the fact that they both appear to share the most familiar aspects of a smorgasbord makes it very hard to tell. The smoked mutton, which you're equally apt to encounter at either end of the endless day, is delicious, even to one who normally avoids smoked things and abominates mutton. As with rattle-snake sandwiches, however, it's probably better if you eat it first and find out what it is afterwards, if at all. Better to think "it's just like chicken," and wonder, than to learn and throw up.

In and near Reykjavik the cuisine is hearty but unexceptional, with no likely surprises beyond the sweet soups, like rhubarb and prune, that all Scandinavian countries favor, and a few debatable staples like dried cod. There is a marvelous dairy dessert called *skyre*, pronounced as if it were spelled "skeer," which is halfway between the consistency of yogurt and cream cheese, which you spoon up after sprinkling it with sugar, like a *petit suisse*. But up north you're more likely to encounter things really worth avoiding, like whale meat or even a reeking dark pink paste called, according to General Stewart, *hákarl*, made of first buried, then disinterred, shark meat.

Icelanders are just as nice when they're drunk as when they're sober, which is fortunate, since they never replace a cork. They don't get sick or nasty or mean, they just pass out quietly. We were embarrassed, the first few times we were entertained, by the intricacies of broken field running required to step around and over our crumpled-up hosts to find our way out when it was obvious that it was well past time to leave. But on subsequent meetings we realized that there was no need for embarrassment, as it was evident that the parties had ended as planned, not with any sort of rude bang but with a gentle guttering out, as of candles.

There are no tourist attractions, unless you count Thingvellir, the site of the Althing, where the world's oldest parliament met a thousand years ago, and the Geysir, the source of piped hot water for many miles in every direction, and a flight over Hekla, the volcano that erupted as recently as 1947. But, in general, Iceland's attractions must be counted as the fish, the people, and the birds, and all these are wonderful.

Although there are no railways, there are many bridges and excellent roads, and when you stop at a bridge to look down into the water, you are almost always rewarded by the sight of salmon. The water is so clear—and the absence of trees makes for a corresponding lack of obstructions below the surface—that if fish are there you'll see them. In my mind's eye I'll see two forever which were resting side by side beneath one of the bridges between the Straumfjardará and the Haffjardará, big and smoky blue-gray, holding in the current with the merest occasional flick of a fin, and looking, in the magnifying glass of the clear water, the size of zeppelins.

Almost every river has a succession of *fosses*, most of them from five to fifteen feet high, though many lead past these negotiable *fosses* only to the point where they come to a real big *foss*, from fifty to a hundred feet, up beyond which there can be no salmon. One is over three hundred feet, the Gullfoss, which would probably make it a tourist attraction, too, to people who have never seen Niagara Falls.

"Mama, what's a *foss*?" I thought I heard a small voice say, one day when I was fishing in the big Laxá. Jane and Al were a quarter of a mile or so downstream, where I had watched them pulling in sea trout, from 4 to 6 pounds, until I couldn't stand it and had come upstream to hunt for salmon.

"Why, this is a *foss* that we're coming to now," I seemed to hear a maternal voice answer, much nicer than, but still reminiscent of, Donald Duck's. And there, not thirty feet beyond my rod tip, was a parade of ducks, and Mama had indeed just said something, though whether my translation was correct I couldn't yet tell, to one of the five ducklings swimming along in Indian file behind her.

As they neared the *foss* I could no longer hear her, in its noise, but I could see from the way she kept talking over her shoulder that she was giving them a most detailed briefing, much like the constant chatter of the barker on a rubberneck bus. I wanted to yell: "Hey, look out, Mama, pay attention to the falls there," but she couldn't have heard me in the roar —the *foss* was about six feet high—and besides, she seemed to know much more about it than I did. As she went over the brink of the falls, still saying something over her shoulder, I almost wanted to hide my eyes at the horror of it all, as I saw those five poor little ducklings going right on over behind her. Isn't nature cruel, I was thinking, and wasn't Mama stupid but weren't those little ducks brave? Or were they stupid, too, and I thought of those German soldiers, saluting one by one as they stepped into the open trap door of the zeppelin over London, to lighten it enough so it could get away, in that long-ago picture *Hell's Angels,* and wondering which I thought they were, stupid or brave, or both, and if you're stupid, can you be brave? The monologue was interrupted by the sight of Mama first, and then one after another, one, two, three, four, five, yes her entire train of ducklings, bobbing up out of the water beyond the edge of the foam, a good fifteen to twenty feet below the foss, in alignment so perfect that it was like looking at a film of a shooting gallery run backwards, with the ducks popping up in the order in which they went down. And Mama was talking, again or still, over her shoulder, and though by now I could no longer even pretend to hear, she was saying, I'm sure: "Now that, children, is a *foss.*"

14 · Salmon in Connemara and in Devon

Fishing, if I a fisher may protest,
Of pleasures is the sweetest, of sports the best,
Of exercises the most excellent,
Of recreations the most innocent,
But now the sport is marred, and wott ye why?
Fishes decrease, and fishers multiply.

Thomas Bastard, in
Chrestoleros, 1598

MOST TROUT FISHERMEN I KNOW, in these latter days of greatly heightened fishing pressure on streams, where the anglers appear to outnumber the fish, approach their sport with the attitude of the gambler who, on being told that the roulette wheel was crooked, said: "I know, but what can I do? It's the only wheel in town."

The alternative, to the monotony and frustration of seasonal servitude spent whipping the riffs and eddies of overfished or fished-out streams, is to take off for as long as you can get away, for one of the places where the fishing is, well, never guaranteed—as we all learn sometime, and some sooner than others—but so carefully tended and preserved and reserved that, by contrast at least, it's likely to seem so wonderful that you remain in a state of euphoria verging on beatitude for a year after you get back, and figure you're still way ahead on points even if you go fishless for the rest of the season.

Ireland is one recommendation. A great advantage it has is that your wife will probably like it, and if the only way you can get in any far-away fishing is by combining it with a vacation trip, then Ireland is a good bet. So many people just assume that fishing takes you to such interesting places, but in general the places with the most interesting fishing are the least likely to be interesting for any other reason. Ireland is a blessed exception.

Now that the jets overfly it, Shannon Airport is more of a treat than it was when all the flights by the northern route had to stop there. And it still is, as it was then, the world's greatest bargain basement, and particularly succulent to the tastes and wants of women shoppers. The restaurant there, too, is one of the best anywhere, and if you were to come away from the bargain counters of the duty-free shopping center for no longer than it takes to sample their bread and their tea, you still might go away saying it was one of the taste sensations of your life. Irish bread and Irish butter are both so superb that, whenever you get back to them, you wonder how in the meantime you could have made do with less. Their tea, too, is highly habit-forming, made, as our ghillie Lawrence O'Malley said, "strong enough to trot a horse upon." And as for Irish coffee—not that you have to go to Shannon Airport any more to get it—it will still remind you of Shannon wherever you get it afterward, if you first sampled it there. With its witty recipe and its inimitable flavor, it's as close to nectar as the gods will ever let us get:

> *Cream rich as a brogue,*
> *Coffee strong as a friendly hand,*
> *Sugar sweet as the tongue of a rogue,*
> *Whisky smooth as the wit of the land.*

Before you ever get to where you're going to fish, you're very likely to be so well disposed, and so is your wife, that the fishing may seem better than it is. For one thing, since salmon fishing has been so long known as the sport of kings, you'll feel that in one respect at least you're living up to its name, if you do it from a hotel that is a castle, like Ballynahinch, at Ballinafad, County Galway, or Ashford Castle, at Cong, County Mayo. Paradoxically, the best fishing at Ashford Castle is, or at least was, away over in the very shadow of Ballynahinch in Connemara, some thirty miles west of Cong, where Noel Huggard, the proprietor of Ashford Castle, has, or at any rate had, a magnificent beat, or stand, at the "butt" of Lough Derryclare, at the point where it forms a bubble in the flow of the Ballynahinch River to the sea. This, and the other beats on the Ballynahinch River that belong to Ballynahinch Castle, are superb spots for the postgraduate trout fisherman who wants to take salmon on his trout tackle. The fish are unlikely to run much over ten pounds, but will give you a very lively show on any rod under five ounces, and a real picnic on rods under three.

Ashford Castle itself is on Lough Corrib, at Cong, which is in County Mayo, just over the line to the east of Connemara, and most of its guests fish from boats, on the lake. So before you go there, unless you're ready to settle for boat fishing, you'd better check to see whether Noel Huggard still has any river beats for salmon, such as he had in the past, or can arrange some for you. If he can, then Ashford Castle is the place to stay. You come to the castle through the twisting streets of Cong, the picturesque little village where the movie *The Quiet Man* was made. As you go past the pub of the film, which turns out to be a general store in actuality, you see the spot in the river where the film showed the priest engaged in a Homeric battle with a salmon. We both suspected that salmon of being no fish when we saw the film, and sure enough we met him personally when we got to Ashford Castle: a six-footer named Laurence O'Malley, one of Ashford's ghillies. He it was who was tugging like a Trojan, out of sight of the camera, at the other end of the priest's line, in a scene that was funny but wouldn't have fooled one fisherman in ten thousand. You turn in to the gatehouse at the entrance to the grounds of Ashford Castle, passing the majestic ruins of the Royal Abbey of Cong, which dates from the twelfth century, when it was erected on the site of a twice-burned monastery founded in A.D. 623. The oldest part of the castle dates back to the year 1228, and this and successive additions to it had fallen into ruin by 1852, the year of the great famine, when Guinness, the famous brewer of Guinness Stout, bought it from the Ashford Estate and set about restoring it. His son, Lord Ardilaun, spent well over a million prewar pounds on the castle alone, before his death in 1915, to say nothing of what he spent on the grounds, which by his time had grown to 35,000 acres.

As a hotel, Ashford Castle dates back only to the early summer of 1939, when it was acquired, with three hundred acres of the surrounding grounds, from the trust representing the Guinness interests, by Noel Huggard, whose family owns other distinctive hotels in Waterville and Killarney. He and his wife Angela are the perfect prototypes of a county hunting couple, and staying as a hotel guest in their company gives you the illusion of living in a sporting and holiday residence of more than baronial affluence. For this "small hotel" is small only in the sense that the space set aside for the accommodation of the paying guests is proportionate, in relation to the sprawling splendor of the whole, to the exposed portion of an iceberg. For Ashford Castle has its own farm, dairy, slaughterhouse, and butchery, as well as a fishery and salmon smoking plant. Its grounds include a maze, a beach, a cinema, a tackle shop, flower gardens, and vegetable gardens, as well as an ornamental Japanese garden, a deer park, an eel weir, tennis courts and garages, and a slipway for seaplanes. Edward VII spent a month there, as a Guinness guest. Today's guest is likely to feel that the treatment now can hardly be less royal than it was then. Paul Gallico, for instance, went there once for a week and stayed three months.

Noel Huggard has fished for salmon all his life, and if he sizes you up as a truly addicted angler, which he can do after one swift glance at your fly boxes, he will send you to his choicest beat, the stand at the Derryclare Butts. If he sizes you up as a Sunday fisherman, he'll stick you in a boat and figure you'll be happier there, and of course quite possibly you will, because it's no trick at all to pull in hefty brown trout, mighty salmon, or fearsome pike, trolling in Lough Corrib, practically within the shadow of his castle walls. But once you've left the lush greenery of County Mayo and begin the climb into the highlands of Connemara, where there's almost always a rainbow somewhere over the winding roads, over the heather and the gorse, and once you've crossed the bog from the high road down to the butt of Derryclare, you'll have the time of your fishing life—that is, you will if you go any time from mid-April to the end of May, when the salmon are almost sure to be in.

If your tackle is as light as it should be for maximum enjoyment—a bamboo trout rod with a tippet of no more than 2X —you'll lose a lot of salmon, because you can't follow them off the jetties where you hook them, but you'll be storing up memories, in the process, that will last you for decades. And losing them in decent proportion to the number you land is the only way to be sporting about this fishing, because the fish belong to the hotel, and the ghillie works for the hotel all the time and for you only while you're there. The ghillie gaffs the fish, and a fish gaffed is a fish done for. Jane had an 11-pounder, which took her twenty-three minutes to play, on her two-piece

8-foot 4¼-ounce Orvis, with a 16-foot leader tapered to 2X, hooked on a size 4 Mar Lodge. The fish had given her a great show, running out the backing beyond the first hundred yards. The backing was black for the first hundred yards; beneath it I had wound another hundred yards of white backing around the core of her Landex reel, and she and Laurence O'Malley both shouted across the jetty, to where I was fishing from the other side, that the fish was running all the backing out. I shouted back that it couldn't, but they insisted that it was, as they saw what they thought was the bare reel spool appearing beneath the last black strands of the first hundred yards. Within seconds the argument was settled, as the fish tore on out, and the white backing unreeled to follow him. That will give you an idea of the head of steam that a spring-run Irish salmon, fresh in and with the sea lice still on him, can build up when you're playing him on tackle light enough that you don't dare do anything but let him run.

When the fish was reeled in to where the leader was starting to come through the guides, Jane said: "Laurence, that's a noble fish—I want to release him."

Laurence, poised with the gaff, gave her such a black Irish look as to make it questionable whether he intended to use the gaff on the fish or on her, and muttering something about the one way to put an end to any such talk as that, strode in over his boot tops to gaff the fish with merciless finality.

Our salmon at Derryclare ran 10, 11, and 14 pounds, and that's about the range you can expect most of them to be, although they have been taken there as small as 6 and as large as 20. One wonderful afternoon in mid-June of 1936, three rods took ten salmon there, from 6½ to 20, and in 1921 one rod killed thirty-six salmon there between mid-April and the end of May. The record of the Ballynahinch Castle fishing is even more impressive, one rod having taken fourteen salmon there in a day. Their stretch consists of the Ballynahinch River, below Derryclare, flowing for about three miles from Lake Ballynahinch into Cashel Bay; the beats consist of a series of pools and flats, practically every yard of which is fishable except in spate, down to the Tombeeola Bridge.

Between Ashford Castle and Ballynahinch Castle you pass through the Joyce's country, which at first hearing you of course associate with *Ulysses*, until you find out that it is so named because it is full of Joyces, not one of whom ever heard of James. North of Ashford Castle, and a bit east, is Lough Carra, between Ballinrobe and Castlebar, all full of associations if you're old enough to be a George Moore fan; but he wasn't a fisherman, and there's no special attraction there for the angler. Lough Carra does have some very big brown trout, averaging twice the size of those of Conn and Corrib, but as far as I'm concerned all three are just so much more boat fishing. But where you go in Ireland depends largely on when you can get away, and for how long. If you have a month, you can get around to several districts.

The big fish are in the Blackwater, of course, and especially in the famous beat at Careysville, owned by the Lismore Estates Company, Lismore, County Waterford. Four salmon of over 50 pounds were taken in the Blackwater between 1903 and 1930. There were even more of that size, six to be exact, taken in that same period from the Shannon, but the hydroelectric scheme ruined the fishing there for a matter of decades after that, and the Shannon has only recently shown signs of coming back. So if it's size that matters to you most, then your first choice practically has to be the Blackwater, between Fermoy and Lismore. Your next choice would probably, on this basis, be the Suir from Carrick to Clonmel, where the largest Irish salmon ever caught on rod and reel, a 57-pounder, was taken back in 1874.

But while there's a status-factor, in that there's a certain amount of dining-out to be done on the mere fact that you've fished the Blackwater, I'd opt for Connemara if I had time for only one district. Connemara is Iceland, but with trees, for the wild and rugged aspect of its landscape, and for the quick comings and goings of its showers and its sunshines. There's something awesomely Wagnerian about the lowering clouds that wreath the hills among which you wind and turn, in Connemara as in Iceland. And there's the same effect on the fish, it seems: I often noticed, in both places, how the emergence of the sun for a brief bright interval between the overcast and the showers would seem to wake them up like an alarm clock, and as the sun broke through you'd tend to grip your rod a little tighter, bracing for the sudden savage pull that so often came at just that moment. The two places are alike, too, in the infrequency with which you encounter traffic other than horse-drawn, as you motor to and from your fishing spots. In Ireland, however, the carts turn out to be pulled, more often than not, by donkeys. But when it comes to the frequency with which you pass pubs, then all resemblance ceases. In Ireland the pubs are delightful, and seemingly omnipresent, and on the days when you've taken salmon, you are a clod if you don't stop in at some of them, to buy your ghillie a Guinness. In Iceland, on the other hand, since there are no pubs to be passed, you have your own Black Death right on the stream, in any Icelander's haversack, so there's no occasion for this ritual that adds such a warm touch to the Irish fishing.

Much depends on time and money, but if neither is too limited, an ideal month in Ireland, from mid-April to mid-May, could be divided, more or less equally according to how the luck sped you on or held you back, among these four spots, any of which can be reached within three hours' driving time from Shannon. First, a week fishing out of either Ashford Castle or Ballynahinch Castle—and I say first because there's always the chance that things might be popping enough at either that you'd say the hell with the rest of the schedule and just stay on. Second, a week on the Blackwater, anywhere you can get on it, from Mallow to Lismore. Third, a week at the Butler Arms, Waterville, County Kerry, fishing the Currane. It would be good to have this particular week abut the week at Ashford Castle, since the same family owns both places and if you wanted to arrive early or late at either, depending on the way your luck was going, you could let them straighten out your schedule between them. Fourth, a week on the Ilen, at Skibbereen, if only for the piquancy it would lend your future small talk, to be able to refer to "one time at Skibbereen." If any of the last three didn't work out, when it came time to nail down definite dates and reservations, you could always take a week on the Maigue, fishing out of the hotel at Adare, County Limerick. It's a lovely little village and the hotel is quaint. It's very close to Shannon, and you could make it either your first week after arrival, while the dates for some of the other places might be firming up, or your last before leaving.

Whatever you do, and before you do anything, get a copy of *The Angler's Guide to Ireland*, published by the Bord Failte Eirann (the Irish Tourist Board), which is frequently revised, comprehensive and knowledgeable, utterly without puffery, and tells you all you need to know, in angling terms, about all the places you might want to fish. As anglers' reading it is delightful: it tells all about the right flies and the right sizes for the different times and places, and is as witty as it is wise.

As refreshing as Connemara, in its remoteness, its utter "awayness" from any angling scenes or surroundings you're likely to have known at home, is Devon, to which I was sent by a book about fishing, so if you should ever happen to go there after, if not directly because of, reading this, then it would be a double dose of poetic justice. In Devon you feel that you're five hundred miles and five hundred years away from everything you've ever seen or known. Every inn seems to date from 1450, and every church seems to date from 1140. You drive on the left because it's in England, but the distinction is academic, since there's really neither right nor left to roads that have only a middle. You poke about the lovely Devon countryside, going to and from your fishing, in narrow country lanes that seem like so many green tunnels, with their borders of hedges that are anywhere from shoulder to head high. You meet other cars, of course, but when you do you'll get out and he'll get out, and you have a nice friendly and ever so sporting discussion concerning the relative distances which one of you will have to drive backwards to get to the nearest of those occasional spots wide enough to permit you to pass each other in your opposed directions. These chance encounters turn out to be a large part of the fun, and in between times you're enjoying the narrow winding roads in a way that you'd long since forgotten roads could be enjoyed. You find yourself trying to remember whether it was Chesterton or Belloc who memorialized "the rolling English drunkard who laid out the rolling English roads."

Getting there was half the fun, just as the Cunard people say about crossing the Atlantic, though in my case it turned out to apply to crossing England, by a slow train out of Waterloo Station. I had read about Hatherleigh, in Devon, in Bernard Venables's then newest book, *The Angler's Companion,* published in London in 1958 by George Allen & Unwin, Ltd., and distributed in this country by Macmillan. The British Railways people in New York seemed to know no more about Hatherleigh than I did; in fact, much less, since I had just been reading Venables, and apparently they hadn't, so they said the best they could do would be to sell me a ticket to Torrington, thirteen miles away, and I would have to shift for myself from there, by cart or by cab or however. Bless them forever for their ignorance, because the slow train to Devonshire wound up toward the Bristol Channel and back down again, making a sort of shepherd's crook beyond Exeter, until it came back down again to Torrington. That part of the ride must have consumed more than an hour of the five hours and some minutes that the train took, in all, to come from London.

It was the best part of the trip. Up to Exeter the stops had been for towns, whereas beyond, the train seemed to be stopping for every cow-crossing. Literally, those last fifteen or twenty stops seemed almost all to have to do with picking up milk pails. But the train ride was, in and of itself, so wonderful —with the hominess of its old-fashioned plush-lined compartment, the unhurried pleasure of frequent ambles back and forth to the restaurant car, which seemed to be run, like a Central European café, on the principle that you were welcome at all hours, however little or much you cared to eat or drink on any one visit to it—so that, between the two places, we were both sorry when the journey ended, like coming to the last page of a book you have loved.

It was only after we'd been in Hatherleigh a while, and were thinking about the arrangements for our return trip to London, that we discovered that Exeter, which we had passed through before undertaking that last shepherd's-crook ride up along the Bristol Channel for the lovely last hour of the trip, is only nine miles from Hatherleigh. Since the hour we would have saved, if we had got off originally at Exeter, would have lost us a dozen memorable sights, and would itself have no doubt been forgotten within a day, we both felt grateful for the ignorance of the British Railways clerk in New York who had booked us to Torrington—"as near as you can get" to Hatherleigh from London. Since the only possible point of traveling for pleasure is the way it papers the walls of memory, that slow train to Devonshire had given us the extra dividend of an hour's added pleasure.

That was 1959, and the trains may no longer be so bucolic. I remember, a year or so ago, being told that the only good train left in this country is *The Lark*, from Los Angeles to San Francisco, and that in this day of being uncomfortably buffeted about, faster than you care to go, from pure jet to turbo-prop and back again, it would be worth taking, just as a pleasure trip. *The Lark* didn't leave until nine at night, but it would be wonderful, I was told, to get on it any time after six o'clock in the evening, dine leisurely and well, enjoy the sights of the beautiful coast from the big dining-car windows, and then get off in the morning in San Francisco. Since I had successive dates in the two cities, I decided to try it. It wasn't easy. I had to book my ticket from Los Angeles to San Francisco and pay for it in advance from New York, and then go pick it up at the station in Los Angeles. This had to be done before a given hour or the reservation might lapse, despite the fact that the ticket had been paid for. When I got to the station to pick up the ticket, I asked the man at the ticket window about dining on *The Lark* "any time after six o'clock."

"Well, hell, the train don't go till nine," he answered.

"I know," I said, "but I was told that one of the big attractions is the nice dinner you serve from six o'clock on."

"They *is* a snack car," he admitted, "where they might could give you a san'wich 'n' a coke 'er somethin' by say maybe quarter *of* nine."

So much for the wonderful tips you get from your friends about travel. The next time I saw my friend who had touted me onto *The Lark*, I asked him if he had been larking me, or had it been that long since he had taken *The Lark* himself.

"Oh well," he confessed upon reflection, "it must be five or six years since I've taken it, come to think of it."

So, come to think of it, in this epoch of change that wonderful slow train to Devonshire, out of Waterloo Station, perhaps should not be urged upon you too insistently as being the better half of the fun of getting to Hatherleigh. Maybe, although at the time nothing could have seemed less likely, even Hatherleigh itself has changed. And we all know—don't we?—how fishing can change, not only from season to season but even from one day to the next.

Our Christmas card lists reveal the fact that, even in the course of these relatively few years of its long history, the George Hotel at Hatherleigh (established 1450) has changed, at least to the extent that its very gentle proprietor, Mr. Herbert Simmons, is no longer there. So, before you go to Hatherleigh, you'd better check the guide called *Fishing in Britain and Northern Ireland*, put out by the British Travel Association, to see whether the George Hotel is still listed. If it isn't, or if they can't or won't have you, or if the place has been torn down, you're still all right. Try the Half Moon Inn, the hotel in Sheepwash—I swear I'm not making this up—which is as close to this particular spot on the Torridge as the George Hotel in Hatherleigh is. The Half Moon, Sheepwash, Devon.

But before I assume that you're going, just listen to what got me to go there, and see if you can resist it any more than I could. Hear now Bernard Venables, in *The Angler's Companion*, a book you ought to read anyway, if you ever go to England:

> Close to Devon's north coast on the Cornish border the River Torridge starts. At its mouth it empties into Bideford Bay, sharing an estuary with the Taw. Between it runs a circuitous course, making a great horseshoe into the warm and rolling Devon hinterland. It is not a great river as Wye and Tay are great; there is no sense of majesty, wild or stately, which is often the association of salmon fishing. It is a small river by such standards; it runs intimately with its landscape rather than with splendour. Its prospects usually are short ones, steep and enclosed.

But it has a beauty, of its special Devon kind, to enchant and still a troubled mind. In its deep valley, under the tree hung crests, there is a seclusion as gently rurally perfect as is to be found in England. The river runs quietly, except in spates, swirling a little, in places breaking over the stones, but only seldom being riotous, making a lulling dappling sound. The sheep in the fields that hang on the falling faces of the hills bleat gruffly, pigeons coo; the lark rises in a placid ecstasy. The buzzard flies in leisurely sweeps, quartering the valley and calling continuously in its mournful mewing voice. At Hatherleigh, in April, where the river is on the bend of its horseshoe shape, the feeling of the valley's removal from the harsher farther world saps all sense of urgency.

There, there is a beat that the author knows. The road runs to it from Hatherleigh, running narrowly and inconsequentially, into the valleys and over the hills, up into the looming sight of Dartmoor, down into the high-hedged hollows, past a village, past a pretty pub. Then falling twisting under a shade of trees and past stone cottages to a bridge where the water starts, an ancient narrow massive bridge, patched with golden lichen on the stone, grown with ferns, little and leathery, in the crevices.

The beat runs upstream from there, with the bank on the narrow flatness of the close-turfed meadow under the forest of the sudden hillside. The road is little frequented; off the road and up the bank, even that small traffic is forgotten, and there will be no more intrusion than, once in a while, the bailiff treading his mildly admonitory rounds, insuring that the fisherman does not lawlessly fish without a license.

The river's run of spring fish is at its best in April, and that is as happy a circumstance as there could be. Under the edge of the hand of the hill, against the hedges, down to the water, there are the primroses; the milkmaids grow with them, and out across the meadow. There are the early purple orchids, and on the warmer days there are the first bees humming and the brimstone butterfly on the wing. Then, to confirm the rising glow of hope, a salmon jumps in the pool above the bridge.

Where the fishing usually starts, in the pool by the hut, by a bend in the river, the water has so promising a look on a fine April day, and when the level is right, that it can hardly be envisaged that a salmon will not be caught—and indeed, on that pool, one often is caught. It is so encouraging a pool to fish, unlike the vast expanses on some greater rivers; its nature can be encompassed by the studying eye. Where the fish are known to lie, the reason for their lying is plainly to be seen—so often not the case in salmon fishing. Each cast is made in warm expectancy. The fly is coaxed and worked along the submerged sheltering shelf of rock, with expectation tingling in the senses from moment to moment. But, when the joyful emergency does come, the rod does throb and bend, and then presently the fish— always so unimaginably big—does show, there is always the same amazed delight that so big and far-travelled a fish could come out of this small river. But indeed, this sense of scarcely believable revelation is an inseparable part of all salmon fishing so far as the author is concerned. Every salmon caught is as hard to believe as the first one was.

There is, broadly, and for no reason that has so far emerged precisely, a connection between the size of a river and the size of its salmon. The Torridge is not a big fish river. In the spring some will weigh no more than eight pounds; most will be about ten or twelve pounds. One of fifteen pounds is a big fish.

Oh 'tis true, 'tis true. Oh excellent author, oh venerable and venerated Venables, every blessed least word turned out to be true, down to the last one, for no fish exceeded fourteen pounds. And the beat described was instantly recognizable, from "the looming sight of Dartmoor" on, around the bends and past the hedges, and the pretty village and the pub, until the ancient narrow lichened stone bridge hove into view. Going over the hills from Hatherleigh, we soon learned enough Devonian weather lore to know that if you can see Dartmoor plain, then tomorrow there'll be rain. Dartmoor, where there's a big prison, is probably a grim sight close up, but it's beautiful from far off, though its beauty may be lost on you if you have something on for the morrow that can be spoiled by rain. In the blessed Devon sunshine, when we ran the little Wolseley up to the crest of that one hill, we always hoped to see it wreathed in mist. In Devon, though, much as I hate to indulge in the pathetic fallacy, even the rain somehow seems friendlier than it ever felt anywhere else. For one thing, after you've been there for more than a day or so, you find yourself dressing for it, and for another, as in the classic case of hitting yourself on the head with a hammer, it's so wonderful when it stops.

It was on that beat, in lambent sunshine between the flowering trees, that Jane cast not wisely but so well, across the river and into the *crise* of a tennis elbow, and it was on that beat, so well portrayed in words by Venables, that the last word of his prophecy was fulfilled, for the bailiff, the man from the river board, duly found us there on his "mildly admonitory round," and though he was polite and friendly, almost genial, in exchanging gossip about what fish had been taken when in the previous few days, he still didn't fail to bring the conversation at last around to the point where, after a deprecatory little cough, he said: "Of course you both have your licenses." And upon being assured that we did, he still wondered if we "didn't mind" showing them to him. So every word that Bernard Venables wrote about Hatherleigh and the Torridge was true.

How many angling books, do you suppose, would pass such a test?

But there were other beats in the vicinity, no less wonderful, that he had not mentioned, and one of them was at another bend in the river, at Iddesleigh, bordering the plowed fields of Mr. James Banbury, a gentleman farmer with racing cars in one of his barns. Mr. Jim, wearing riding breeches and a venerable tweed jacket, and using a small tractor as his cock-horse, would come riding over his hills to point out the best lies on his water, and there the stream was even smaller, making the fish seem even more "unimaginably big." The one trouble with Mr. Jim's water, almost every time we fished it, was that it was full of jumping salmon, but jumping in that high pole-vaulter's leap that always means they are jumping for joy, or to get rid of sea lice, or for no good reason at all, except that the one thing they won't do then is take a fly. When they leap in the low arc of a man diving off a bank, instead of a high board, then they mean business and you'll take them, but you won't as long as they're jumping.

At one of the favorite salmon lies on his water, which Mr. Jim was kind enough to point out to me, I saw a salmon that looked "unimaginably big," as advertised by Bernard Venables, meaning that it probably ran about 14 pounds, and this one, for once, was holding still and not jumping out of the stream like the popping kernels in a pan of popcorn, as so many of the others had been. I cast to him, very carefully, using Mr. Jim's favorite fly, a number 5 low water Black Doctor. The fly lit well above him, and I was grateful to see that it was swinging on a straight line, with no slack, just below the surface, where in a few seconds it would pass right over his head

—upon which a 14-inch brown trout swirled up from nowhere and made off with it.

Oh irony—back home on the Beaverkill or the Esopus, I'd have wanted to give that 14-inch brownie at least a fourteen-gun salute, but here on the Torridge, where he came between me and a fish that might well have gone as many pounds as he represented in inches, I cursed him roundly, and couldn't wait to get him in and brush him off the hook. I tossed him back so cavalierly, giving him the bum's rush without a thought as to how and where he landed in the water, in contrast to the loving stroking I would normally give such a fish when heading him gently back upstream to give him the benefit of the revivifying effect of the current, that after a few minutes I began cursing myself. That was only after the salmon, utterly unperturbed, had twice snooted the same fly when it swung over his nose on subsequent casts that achieved his lie without in any way being impeded or intercepted. I cursed myself for having given in, if only in a momentary fit of temper, to the salmon fisher's snobbish attitude toward trout.

This is a one-way snobbism, for though I've often heard salmon fishermen speak contemptuously of trout, and had in this instance just done so myself, though fortunately in nobody's hearing—unless you want to count the trout himself— still I have never heard a trout angler speak of salmon in any tone other than one of worshipful awe. Maybe I might have, if I had been privileged to spend a lot of time hanging around the Houghton Club quarters at Stockbridge on the Test, but at least I never heard an American trouter low-rate the salmon. Perhaps this is because trout never seem as easy to catch as when they're encountered in a salmon river, and most trout fishermen only rarely get a chance to go after salmon. Nobody has ever bragged about catching a sucker since the time of Texas Guinan, nor has anybody, I imagine, ever had one mounted. But there are times and places—and this day on Mr. Jim's water on the Torridge was one—where trout are to salmon as suckers are to trout. It's just that there are no times and places where anything else in the same water makes a sucker out of a salmon. There are those, and Lord Grey of Fallodon was one of them, who contend that a sea trout is pound for pound an even better adversary than a salmon. But the comparison is never made in any invidious way, and it's always carefully stated to the effect that they love not salmon the less, but only sea trout more.

The same snob value that accrues to salmon, in waters that they share with trout, also accrues to trout, and I've always thought most unfairly, in waters that they share with grayling. Mention a grayling to an American trout fisherman and his eyes will light up. But on the classic English chalk streams, like the Test and the Itchen, they'll look at you askance if you're so naïve and provincial as to get enthusiastic about a grayling. Yet there's hardly a sight to be seen anywhere more beautiful than, say in Austria, a grayling between you and the sun, shaking a shower of diamonds from that lavender dorsal fin. But a grayling admittedly is a relative cinch to tempt into striking, compared to the almost legendary difficulty of fooling a chalk-stream trout.

I had long since learned, in Iceland, that in ratio of performance to size—the index of performance, as they say in automobile racing—there's nothing finer with fins than a sea trout. But if one comes between you and a bigger sea-run member of the same *salmo* family, then you're ready to cuss him out for a cussed nuisance. Twice this happened in Connemara, when a perky "white trout" of about 14 inches— could it have been the same one?—came between me and a salmon that appeared to be about to take my fly. It may have been the same sea trout, though it was a salmon in a different lie, and interested, both times, in a different fly, a Black Dose once and a Thunder & Lightning the other time. God, was I mad! Long afterward, though, when you're away from fish and fishing entirely, and find yourself looking back in your mind's eye at different waters you've fished, you may recall him or them, as I do now those two or that same "white trout," with a pleasant fondness verging on downright affection. At the moment of fishing, however, all that seems to count is the scarcity value of the particular fish you're after. Though if we still had salmon by the thousands coming up and down our Eastern coastal rivers as far south as Delaware, as they once did, instead of being coaxed back by the dozen into a few Maine rivers, as they have been in recent years, we wouldn't stand in such awe of them. But today, as Al McClane says, you practically feel as if you ought to tip your hat at the sight of them.

And as for grayling, it is only since Alaska's statehood that we can now say again that we have them in more than one state. At the turn of the century we had them in Michigan, where there's a town named after them, where my father as a young man fished for them. It was along about that time that Michigan gave quantities of grayling for stocking purposes to Montana, where they were threatened with extinction. Then, not too many years back, after grayling had long been extinct in Michigan, Montana tried to reciprocate. But it was too late. The lumber barons had in the interim done too much dirty work. The Montana grayling wouldn't "take" again, in those same Michigan waters that their forebears had come from in the first place. So now, if you want to fish for grayling, you must go either out to Montana or up to Alaska. Actually, if you live in the East, it's almost simpler, in this phase of the jet age, to go after them in England, or even in Bavaria or Austria.

The English, in an extension of that same sporting snobbery already noted, persist in classing the lordly grayling as a "coarse fish," which, to any American who has ever so much as seen a grayling, seems to be the ultimate in insults. On the other hand, Englishmen will happily fish for, and in some instances even blithely eat, certain species, such as chub, dace, roach, and rudd, that we would consider not only "coarse," but positively vulgar. The grayling is neither. I caught, and immediately afterward cooked, a beautiful big fat one once on the Itchen just above Winchester, and it was heaven out of water.

There are no grayling on the Torridge, but it is a great sea trout river, though very few had been seen in April when we were there. Mr. Jim was all for having us back in June, for the run of the "peal," as they are called in Devon. In Ireland, when you say "peal" you mean grilse, which they refer to as "salmon peal," whereas they call the peal of the Devonshire man by their own Irish term, white trout. To add to the confusion, just a few miles away from North Devon, in Wales, they call the sea trout "sewin." And, of course, wherever you see "salmon trout" on the menu, you know it means sea trout, even if you don't know that they are also known by such varying regional or developmental names as herling, whitling, sprat, scad, mort, pug, herring-sprod, and finnock. It's a progressive puzzlement.

The invaluable Bernard Venables, whom I shall forever include in my prayers for having led me to the Torridge, says in *The Angler's Companion*—and what a companion it became —that the Torridge is a good sea trout river:

> From time to time a peal will be taken in April, invariably a big one; but the real run starts in June, and then the fish swarm up the river if there is water for them. Thereafter they will continue to come until the end of the season. Many fishermen, once the sea-trout run has started, will bother no more about the salmon. The sea-trout, taken by fly on the shallows after dark, offer such wonderful sport. They may be taken at other times and by other means, spinning; but it is by fly fishing that the cream of the sport is had.

The Torridge can be so beautiful in April, it's hard to imagine what it would be by June. If Byron could have known this lovely river, where the salmon are to be taken from between banks so benignly close together, in surroundings of such pastoral beauty, it is hard to believe that he could ever have called angling "the cursedest, coldest and the stupidest of sports."

15·Salmon in New Brunswick and Quebec

'Tis blithe the mimic fly to lead,
When to the hook the salmon springs
And the line whistles through the rings.

Sir Walter Scott, in
Life in the Forest, 1822

"THE WEALTHY MAN who may take a beat on one of the best rivers for the season . . . will have a wire from his keeper when

all is right; he will come to the river . . . and almost certainly
he will catch salmon—but he will have known very little of
the ardent pleasures that poorer men find in the sport. Poorer
men may go salmon fishing as precious leisure falls; as they
find their river so must they fish it. Their days will be more
often fruitless than favored; there will be whole holidays that
will show nothing. To such men a week in which two salmon
are caught is not one to be forgotten."

So wrote Bernard Venables, in *Fishing,* in the series British
Sports: Past & Present (published in London in 1953 by B. T.
Botsford, Ltd. and in the United States by The British Book
Centre, New York). While he was undoubtedly talking, in
that instance, only about fishing in the British Isles, it would
not be doing too much disservice to the contrast he noted if
one read the passage through again, and this time substituted
"Quebec" where he says "wealthy" and "New Brunswick"
where he says "poorer." Quebec and New Brunswick both
afford excellent Atlantic salmon fishing for the American
angler, whereas the revival of Maine's once splendid salmon
fisheries has not yet progressed to the point where it provides
much more than enough sport to go round for the local fishermen. Salmon are to be taken by the score in Quebec, and by
the hundreds in New Brunswick, for every dozen to be taken
at this stage of the game in Maine.

In general, the waters are deeper and the average salmon is
larger in Quebec than in New Brunswick. Although both
places offer fishing from canoes and wading, the former pre-
dominates in Quebec and the latter in New Brunswick. And—
again to generalize—the average cost per day's fishing in Quebec is apt to be just about as much higher as the fish are

larger, in comparison to New Brunswick. Similarly, the tackle required is proportionately heavier in Quebec. Guides are required by law, for nonresident anglers, in both provinces. But in Quebec they tend to behave like servants, and do things *for* the visiting angler, whereas in New Brunswick they tend rather to do things *with* their "sport" than for him, and to show him the ropes rather by example—sometimes to the extent of showing him up—than by respectful suggestions, as would be the case in Quebec. There are exceptions, of course, in both provinces, but the generalization is as accurate as any generalization can be. The fishing in Quebec tends to be more leisurely, more luxurious, more sedate, and less demanding than in New Brunswick, where roughing it is more likely to be the rule than the exception, whereas in Quebec the reverse is the case. And whereas public fishing, such as on the Matane River, is very unusual in Quebec, where most waters are privately held by individuals or clubs, the opposite is the case in New Brunswick, where only a small portion of the water is leased or otherwise restricted. For the trout fisherman who simply wants to do some postgraduate work with larger members of the *salmo* family, the change from his native streams and the alteration of his present tackle and fishing habits would be much less abrupt if he were to go after salmon in New Brunswick rather than in Quebec.

In general, and again with exceptions in both places, the best fishing is early in Quebec and late in New Brunswick. There are successive runs in both, but the Quebec rivers in general start earlier—June 5, say, for Quebec, as opposed to June 25 for New Brunswick—and while the bigger fish come early in Quebec, the opposite is the case in New Brunswick. (Although the bright salmon run later in New Brunswick, it is the only one of the Maritime Provinces that allows fishing for black salmon, the spent kelts, from ice out to May 23.) A 25-pounder is average in June in Quebec, for instance, whereas a fish of that size would be exceptional in New Brunswick before September, and unusual even then. Rivers such as the Matapedia and the Restigouche average about 20 pounds over the entire season, whereas the average for the entire season on the Miramichi is just under 10 pounds. Another contrast—again subject to exceptions in both places—is in the best taking time. In the Quebec rivers it is late morning—say, 10:30 a.m. to noon—whereas it's early evening—say, 6 to 8 p.m.—in New Brunswick.

Both provinces limit legal fishing for salmon and grilse to artificial and unweighted flies only and from two hours before dawn to two hours after sunset. And—always allowing for exceptions, as indeed one must in everything that pertains to angling—these rules are much more scrupulously observed in Quebec than in New Brunswick, where outright poaching and "bending" of the game laws seems to cause much less horror to the citizenry in general, exclusive of the wardens, than in Quebec. In New Brunswick the neighbor's boys who "sweep the pool" by night, netting out every last fish, are almost openly admired and regarded, if not as Robin Hoods, then at least as pretty dashing fellows.

The angler in Quebec will need at least an 8-foot rod, with a 3½-inch reel, to take a GBF or GAF line, and 200 yards of backing as an absolute minimum. He will be unhappy with lighter tackle than this, first because he's apt to find it difficult to get adequate casts from a canoe with a shorter rod or a lighter line, and second because in the heavy water he is very likely to need 1/o size flies, or even larger, to get down to where the fish may be under given water conditions. Favored flies are Silver Rat, Green Highlander, and Jock Scott. Sizes should run 1/o, 1, 2, and 4, with little likelihood that he will need more than an occasional and exceptional fly either larger or smaller than that range.

The guide anchors the canoe, in successive "drops," from the head of the pool to its tail, and the angler casts alternately across to the right and left, letting the line swing the fly, from both directions, to a point directly below the canoe. The great majority of the takes are directly downstream from the angler, in line with the bow of the anchored canoe, and most often within twenty to thirty feet below the canoe. Once fast to a fish, the angler contents himself with keeping the rod tip up, and confines his playing of the fish to the irreducible minimum until the guide has had a chance to raise the anchor and start getting the canoe toward shore, where the angler will then make an earnest effort to regain his backing and his line and to bring the fish within range of the enormous net that the guide has by now taken out of the canoe.

In contrast, the angler in New Brunswick will wade out within casting range, raise his rod tip when the fish takes, stumble and scramble back toward shore as best he can, meanwhile letting the fish run until the fisherman can get out of the water and chase after him along the river bank, trying to get below the fish and head him back upstream, where the current will help to play him out, then finally beaching him. The chances are better than equal that the guide will not even be in sight at this point. He will be either somewhere else along the same beach, chasing after another fish (because when salmon take they're very apt to take in sudden flurries), or he will be off at some other pool on the presumed pretext of casing another "hot spot" for the sport's benefit. There is a third possibility: he might have found a patch of blueberries, and be intent on indulging the native's apparently insatiable passion for them. Whenever your particular fish interferes with his own fishing or his exploration, don't count on him to be around when you beach it.

The angler accustomed to the use of a short light rod will find it no more of a handicap fishing for salmon in New Brunswick than it has ever been on his own trouting haunts. Nor will he need a heavier line. What he will need is at least 200 yards of backing. Even a 4-pound grilse will be as likely as not to run into the second hundred yards of backing before the angler gets to a position where he can start regaining it.

Black Dose and Jock Scott are the two most effective flies, among the standard patterns. The former will bring strikes from both grilse and salmon, whereas the latter seems to exercise a slight degree of selectivity, being a bit more likely to be taken by salmon than by grilse. The latter, however, seem especially devoted to the Conrad, a black-bodied, silver-ribbed, black hair-wing fly with a bright green butt. The butt is of almost Day-Glo or gantron vividness, and appears to be visible to an extraordinary degree. This fly can be murderous when the grilse are in a taking mood. In general, hair wing flies have been increasingly favored in New Brunswick in recent years, although such staple standard patterns as Silver

Doctor, Silver Grey, Silver Wilkinson, Silver Blue, and Blue Charm still take fish when the fish are taking. So, for that matter, do trout flies, including streamers and bucktails. In New Brunswick it is very rare to need any fly larger than size 6, and after the first week in July, size 8 and smaller can be used effectively. In the September fishing, when the dry fly comes into its own, spiders down to size 16 have been used successfully.

In both provinces, guides are prone to try to get the sport to use heavier terminal tackle than he needs. They will try to get you to use tippets of 20 pound test in Quebec, and 10 pound test in New Brunswick. Ten is heavy enough for the former and 6 pound test for the later. You will lose a measurable percentage of fish hooked in both places, and rather more in New Brunswick than in Quebec, but the fly will come back to you almost every time.

The angler should not go to either New Brunswick or Quebec without a reminder that money spent in pursuit of Atlantic salmon ranks midway between money invested in backing a Broadway show and money invested in an Irish sweepstakes ticket. The rewards are glorious in all three cases, but no crying towels are provided in the event of failure to cash in. Charles Ritz, who has fished for salmon for fifty years, has an inviolable rule not to accept any salmon fishing that may be offered him (not even if the King of Sweden were to offer his own beat) unless he can go and stay for four weeks, as his experience has been that there will never be more than one good week out of every four spent fishing for salmon, and there is no way that anybody can know in advance which one of the four it will be. Unless you have four weeks to devote to it, the odds are three to one against you, that the good fishing will be either the week before you get there or the week after you leave.

Par for the course, the world over, is a fish a day, but very rare is the salmon angler who consistently breaks par.

Not for nothing has it become known as the sport of kings. In Quebec it can cost you, for the rod fee alone, from a low of $5 a day (now raised to $10) on the Matane to a high of $50 a day on the Matapedia. To the rod fee must be added meals, accommodations, transportation, guide fee, license, and tips. The going rate for guides in Quebec is $12 a day. In New Brunswick, perhaps because they are there more with you than for you, it never exceeds $10, and can even nowadays sometimes be shaded below that. All guides expect tips, but Quebec guides look for money (an extra day's pay for a week's service), whereas a New Brunswick guide would much rather have the equivalent in fishing tackle, although he probably needs the money more, since New Brunswick is the poorest of provinces. No Quebec guide would presume to ask you for a fish, assuming until told otherwise that you have your own plans to dispose of them. All New Brunswick guides have twelve to fourteen children, and act as if any fish you might want to eat or send to someone were being snatched out of their mouths. No Quebec guide will ever let you carry anything, unless possibly you insist on carrying your rod yourself. Any New Brunswick guide will let you carry everything, including *his* rod, except your own fish, which he insists on carrying in the evident hope that you won't try to take it away from him by main force. No Quebec guide would make so bold as to "try a few casts" without your express permission, at the very least, or your urging at the most. (They sometimes get elderly sports who *make* them do all the fishing, and just sit back in the canoe until the guide has the fish well hooked, whereupon they take the rod to play it.) Conversely, your New Brunswick guide not only carries his own rod, expecting to fish with you, but is very apt to regard any demands you may make of him on stream as an unwarranted incursion on his fishing time.

Quebec is where you can take your wife, knowing that even if she doesn't fish, she'll enjoy the surroundings. New Brunswick is where you leave your wife at home, unless she's a better scout, and less of a tenderfoot, than you are. In either place, if you're there the wrong week, you'll feel that it's the world's most outrageous gyp. But if you're there the right one, you'll think it's the greatest bargain on earth. You'll feel the same way about the cost of the license, which in both places is $15.50 for the season or $5.50 for three days.

16 · Lee Wulff and Light Tackle for Salmon

Fly casters have long been judged by smoothness of line
flow and easy grace of movement, even when changes of
direction are involved. But all that goes by the board when
you're using a featherweight rod. . . . An angler's form in
casting may be important to himself and other anglers. To
the fish, who will be the final judge of his prowess, form
matters not at all!

Lee Wulff, in *The Atlantic Salmon*, 1958

As IF IN ANSWER to the plea of Bobby Burns for "some power the giftie gie us, to see oursels as others see us," comes the following quote, from *Lake and Loch Fishing for Salmon and Sea Trout*, by the veteran British angler W. A. Adamson (published in London in 1961 by A. & C. Black, Ltd.):

In the past two years there has originated in America a vogue for the ultra-short and ultra-light rod. It is made of split cane, is six or seven feet long, and weighs as little as one-and-a-half-ounces. Note that these rods are being used for salmon . . .

The action of casting is quite foreign to British practice (outside tournaments) and it may even involve the arm fully extended, the line in the left hand frantically sawing away to shoot line *in the back cast* as well as forward. The whole process is fairly strenuous and more akin to a tennis service than casting, as we know it, with ease and grace . . .

Mr. Arnold Gingrich is the publisher of the American magazine *Esquire*. From time to time, in that periodical, he gives his comments on "the light tackle trend in angling." After a successful trip to Iceland when he caught many fish of three to seven pounds on an ultra-light rod, he had some rather scathing things to say about the "hop-poles" used by British salmon fishers. Since then he has gone overboard for Mr. Lee Wulff's vigorous casting methods with ultra-light rods.

Let nobody be misled by Mr. Gingrich. He fished for small fish from the treeless banks of Iceland's small rivers. I like to imagine Mr. Gingrich attached to a forty pound fresh-run salmon on the Spey. I like to think of him with his six foot, one-and-a-half ounce rod, leaping over bushes, dodging round trees, swinging from bough to bough like Tarzan, glissading down screes, and abseiling down sheer rock faces, in a mad rush of half a mile or so to get on terms with his fish!

Second the motion, and may nobody now or ever be misled by anything I have to say about the pleasures and advantages of light tackle in pursuit of both salmon and trout.

Whoever gave Mr. Adamson his figures on the size of those fish in Iceland was pretty snide, though. If you count only the salmon, they were 6 to 14 pounds, but if you count the sea trout, and on the Midge rod I count everything, then they ran from 3 pounds to a little over 5. There were char, too, of 2 to 4 pounds.

I thought for a moment that the difference in Icelandic pounds from ours might have created the confusion, but the difference is only ten percent. The Icelandic pound is half a kilogram, or one and a tenth pounds, so if an Icelander weighs your fish for you on his scales and tells you it's 10 pounds, well, so it is by his measure, but by ours 10 times 10$\frac{1}{10}$ makes 11. But that wouldn't account for the strange shrinkage down from 14 to 7, the sea change undergone in transshipment to Mr. Adamson's pages. On the other hand, Mr. Adamson would be just as nearly right, in his terms, in contrasting a 7-pounder as in contrasting a 14-pounder to a 40-pounder. In either case, there certainly is no comparison.

For that matter, and to make Mr. Adamson feel even more secure in his statement, he should have seen me floundering in and out of the Miramichi, just last summer, three times to clear my line from rocks around which it had been wrapped by a 4-pound grilse. That fish led me, certainly not a half mile but very nearly a quarter mile, and took out well over a hundred and fifty yards of backing in the process. The third rock around which he had caught the line turned out to be just beyond reach, though I waded out to the suspender buttons on my chest waders. While I was thinking, "What would Lee Wulff do now? Or Al McClane?" the wait for further action grew longer than that grilse could stand. He just had to swim back from the other side of that rock, to see what happened to me in our little game of follow the leader, and why, having only followed him around two rocks, I was now dogging it on the third. In doing so, of course, he freed the line from the third rock, the one that was out beyond my depth, and when he saw me, and saw what he had done, he was off again for another hundred yards. But this time he found no more rocks to wrap the line around, so we called the game for reasons of mutual exhaustion. It took the better part of a half hour's treatment, in a little keeper pool that somebody had made with rocks, as if playing with blocks, at the stream's edge, before he was in any shape to go back into the river again.

As against that, I've had 14-pounders come in to the beach in as little as eleven minutes, which is well under the traditional minute per pound, and shows that you can't blame your tackle entirely for the differing times you take in playing different fish. The time spent playing that one possessed 4-pounder had to include about twelve minutes of "time out" while I splashed, from shore and back again, out to those three rocks.

But to get back to Mr. Adamson, which I did by the speediest possible return of print, I told him that I shared his curiosity to see what would happen to me and my 6-foot, 1½-ounce rod, if we were both attached to a fresh-run 40-pounder on the Spey, and urged him to try to arrange it. Alas,

I never heard from him again, and I have yet to fish the Spey.

But not long after that, in a communication to the *Atlantic Salmon Journal*, there was a similar pejorative comment on ultra-light rods. It was made by Donald Rudd, the real name of the veteran angler who writes under the pseudonym of "Jock Scott," and it said something to the effect that Lee Wulff, for all his success on our easy streams over here, couldn't "skin a pudding" with a rod like that, were he to attempt to use it on a Scottish river. Lee Wulff, who has forgotten more about fishing than I can ever hope to learn, was not one, either, to let a challenge get fluffed off so lightly. On the Dee, in the summer of '62, the great Lee Wulff–Jock Scott match was duly held, and it proved very little beyond what everybody already knew, which is that salmon can never be counted on to appear anywhere, even on the Dee, according to anybody's best-laid plans, even if the planners are such redoubtable salmon fishers as Jock Scott and Lee Wulff. After all, these two between them wrote what a lot of salmon anglers now regard as virtually the old and the new testaments of the cult: Jock Scott's *Greased Line Fishing for Salmon* and Lee Wulff's *The Atlantic Salmon*.

The one fish caught was taken by Lee Wulff, but in a sense it was comparable, as far as their match was concerned, to a punch landed between rounds. It was a 10-pounder, taken "accidentally" while, during an off-moment, Lee Wulff was demonstrating the action of his light rod to Captain Tommy Edwards, the great professor of English casting. During the whole week that Lee Wulff and Jock Scott were actually fishing against each other as a test of their opposed concepts of proper tackle, neither hooked a fish. It was all very genteel, and aside from its constituting another proof that all men are equal in the eyes of fish, each contestant finished the match saying nice things about the other, and hoping they could fish together again.

But while Lee Wulff won the match only on a technicality, it did give him a chance to prove that his methods, of wading in up to his vest and reaching out to the fish by shooting a long line from a short rod, could cover the water just as effectively as the single throw of a measured line from a long rod cast by an angler standing at the edge of the river. He has since shown this technique, even more effectively, on some widely seen television programs, and has done more than any other man to familiarize the public with the idea that a big fish can be mastered with a small rod.

Actually Mr. Hewitt first demonstrated, as far back as forty years ago or more, the scientific basis for the method that Lee Wulff has since dramatized: to let a fish wear himself out, with minimum strain on the *rod and the leader,* by holding the rod up high, at the absolute vertical, as we all tend to do when playing a fish at a distance with a short rod. In *Secrets of the Salmon,* first published in 1922, Mr. Hewitt showed in diagrams, with different rods of all weights, from 1½ ounces on up, how much less strain the rod exerted on the line and leader when held at the vertical than at each of the successively lowered angles pictured. It was a startling demonstration, but nobody, seemingly including even Mr. Hewitt himself, was temperamentally disposed to do much of anything about it. Then, after some thirty-five years, Lee Wulff began to exploit the technique, and to explain it, as he did in his 1958 book, *The Atlantic Salmon.*

The proof of the principle was there all the time, as pro-
pounded first by Mr. Hewitt, and in effect it was giving the
lie to all the huffing-puffing heroics of the "give 'em the butt"
technique of anglers of the "heave-ho, my hearties" school.
If anybody had bothered to study the significance of Mr.
Hewitt's diagrams, it would have been immediately apparent
that to rear back and "give 'em the butt"—meaning to thrust
the lower end of the rod forward and thus force its arc into
the truest vertical that the pull of the running fish will permit
it—was the only thing to do to *ease* the strain on both rod
and leader, instead of increasing it, as those hell-for-leather
fishers thought they were doing.

The peculiar thing is that dozens of English books on
salmon fishing, over the past eighty years or so, have dwelt at
some length on how often the trout fisherman finds himself
confronted with the necessity of playing a salmon on trout
tackle. Of course, maybe it isn't so peculiar, when you reflect
that to this day most English trout fishermen use rods that
we would now consider heavy for salmon. But in 1922, in
Secrets of the Salmon, Mr. Hewitt mentioned taking salmon
on a 1½- ounce rod, by way of explaining why he had included
a rod of that weight in the comparative diagrams. Both he
and all the English authors always spoke of this as if it were
some dire catastrophe and said the angler had been lucky not
to lose both fish and rod when put to such an extreme test.
Nobody else, before Lee Wulff, to my knowledge ever pointed
out in print that it is actually an advantage to play a strong
fish on the small rod, rather than on a bigger one. This is the
revelation of his book, *The Atlantic Salmon*, in which he
shows, with word and picture, that the less the fish has to pull

against, the fewer are his chances to break off, during the jumps and rushes that wear him out faster than you could ever wear him out by main force. I've seen the Icelandic artist Gudmundur Einarsson, a veritable giant of a man, stand on a high rock in the middle of the big Laxa, and haul in a 25-pounder, using his Gargantuan rod as if it were a derrick. But I've seen Lee Wulff master a fish of the same size, or even a little larger, and do it in not much more than half the time, on tackle one tenth as heavy, by letting the fish run and wear himself out, rather than attempt any of the pull-devil pull-baker tactics that, in any event, his tackle couldn't permit. And it was a lot prettier sight to watch.

Gudmundur was one of the two Icelanders to whom we gave our giant Paul Young salmon rods, which we found so stiff as to be unusable. And while he wouldn't have dreamed of using his on the Laxamyri, where he wanted a really stout rod so he could cast "mit schpoon in statt of fly" and stand his high ground against any fish, he was delighted to use it on the smaller rivers, where he doubtless felt that he was at last getting in line with "the light-tackle trend." The rod was the 6-ounce 9-foot stick that Paul Young had originally devised for Bobby Doerr, for steelheads on some of the big West Coast rivers, and it had Jane's name on it. On it I had put an Arnold reel with a GAF white line, and Gudmundur for years thereafter sent us countless pictures of slews of salmon, "taken on the Jane rod and the Arnold reel."

Gudmundur could throw a line half way to Reykjavik, from anywhere in Snaefellsnes, but he wouldn't have had any possible use for my Midge rod, except perhaps to use it as a toothpick. Gudmundur's stance and actions, as he swung his huge rod, always reminded me of the statue of the discus thrower; my own, with the light rod, have always seemed to me to be most nearly comparable to those of a tennis player with a big serve. Lee Wulff, however, thinks of his own action with the light rod as being more nearly like that of throwing a baseball than anything else. He thinks of it as being a cross between, or a combination of, the old style of casting and the trick of casting with the line alone, without using any rod.

I know, for myself, the exact moment when I found the knack of getting around the apparent disadvantage of the little Midge rod. I was fishing for some of the larger bass that had taken to holing up in one corner of Louis Renault's pond in Stamford, and particularly for one that had weighed 2½ pounds when I took him out of Gene Tunney's pond to put him in Louis's, and had weighed in at 2¾, 3, and 3½, on subsequent occasions when I had taken him out for periodic check-ups. He had formerly been very fond of a blue spider, but lately had evinced no interest in anything but a *Vivif*, a lure the size and shape of a small sucker, which Louie had tossed him, via a spinning rod, and which he had bunted a couple of times without taking.

I knew I couldn't cast anything as monstrous as that on any rod I had, but I thought I would like to try him on a few big streamers and rubber bass bugs. But how to do it, without snapping the fragile tip of my slender Midge, which I was using at the time, and especially how to get such a heavy lure both back and ahead about forty feet, to reach the spot where I had last seen him? I thought I'd try doing it without the rod, so I propped the rod against a bush, drew the line out through the guides, and tried casting it as a free line. Both Al McClane and Ellis Newman had tried to teach me that trick, which they did easily, on the lawn between the lodge and the dining pavilion up at Turnwood. But though I'd managed, up there, to master a few tentative and wobbly pitches on a line and leader bare of any fly, I now found it hopeless, when the leader carried the extra burden of a bass bug. After one attempt, I spent the next ten minutes unsnarling the resultant tangle. So with great fear, and the vivid recollection of Paul Young's warning not to use *any* of his bamboo rods on "so-called fly-rod plugs and lures," I decided to try it with the rod, but to "throw the rod away" only in a figurative sense, having just proved to my own extreme dissatisfaction that I couldn't do it by actually throwing the rod away literally. But I could try *pretending* that the rod wasn't there, using its guides only to help me keep the line in the air and not at my feet in an unholy mess. This time it seemed more promising. Within a few minutes I found that, casting *through* the rod, as it were, and using the rod really only as a direction-change stick, between back casts and forward casts, keeping my rod hand almost out of it and letting my left hand do all the work, in the *whee-whee-ew* rhythm of the quick successive tugs of the double-line haul, the line began to sing out fore and aft, and I could feel no real sense of strain on the rod itself at all.

By the time I got the trick working I had forgotten all about the big old bass in the corner of the pond, until he suddenly took off for the pond's farther shore with my bass bug in his mouth, reminding me of his presence by a sort of reverse application of the adage about the watched pot that never boils. Boiling was what he was now certainly doing, and my Midge rod, which I had been shooting around with such elaborate care in my casting, was now thrust into the starring role of this most impromptu production. I was delighted to see, after a few minutes, that he now weighed 3¾, but even more pleased to see that the Midge had suffered not at all from being a party to the 80-foot travels of that big bass bug back and forth through the air over Louie's pond. From that moment on, I never had another qualm about using the Midge on streamers and salmon flies, up to size 4. Beyond that size I still drew the line, preferring on sizes 2 and 1 to use the stouter tips of my Hardy *C. C. de France* or the Pezon & Michel that Charlie Ritz had made for me as his answer to my Midge. These rods, though both 6½-footers, have more wood in them at the tip, and though I "throw the rod away" in using them on larger flies, particularly on false casts whenever more than thirty-five feet of line is extended in the air, I have the added sense of security of knowing that they could take it better, if I should inadvertently let too much of the strain of that much line weight fall on them.

Lee Wulff did a lot of experimenting with the possibilities of featherweight rods, between 1940, when he wrote *Leaping Silver*, and 1958, when he published his findings on the capabilities of the light rod, in *The Atlantic Salmon*. Of course, his tactics were much more scientific than my crude do-it-yourself fumblings. He demonstrated, first of all, that a salmon could be played with no rod at all, by way of establishing a *ne plus ultra* in the arguments for ultra-light tackle. Then, as a pilot, he applied the principles that he had found most successful, as a seat-of-the-pants bush flier, in outwitting the wind. He showed that if you can just make a fast enough cast, you can often take advantage of the vagaries of even strong winds, by getting a quick cast in between puffs. With a stopwatch he timed his own efforts with two of his own rods, both Orvis rods. He gave both his best performance and showed that there was a distinct advantage in speed in his little 6½-foot, 2-ounce rod over his 9-foot 5-ouncer. The time he needed, on the former, to straighten out his back casts and forward casts averaged only 18.4 seconds, whereas on the latter, the larger rod, the operation took 23.1 seconds. More astonishing still, the rate of travel of his line on the little rod worked out to 96 mph, exactly twenty miles per hour faster than the 76 mph rate of travel of his line on the larger rod.

Don't be misled by this into thinking that speed is in itself any great desideratum in fly casting, whether with light rod or heavy. For as Al McClane never stopped dinning into my own thick head, through all the time he spent remodeling my casting, the best and longest casts are slow and smooth. I cite this difference in speed here only to point out that, when you *have* to get off a quick cast, between puffs of wind, it's comforting and perhaps surprising to realize that you can get it off faster with the small light rod than you can with a long heavy one, even though the two rods are in every other respect as nearly equal as the same maker can make them.

Look at the pictures of Lee Wulff playing large fish on his light rod, and you'll see things that are wrong, by the old-timers' dogma, in almost every picture. He casts, at ninety-six miles per hour, with his forefinger fully extended on the top of the grip of his rod. Heresy, says Charlie Ritz, on the ground that while the forefinger grip may be an advantage for accuracy of placement of the fly, it impedes speed and power, in the "high-speed high-line" theory of casting. Lee holds his rod as high as his long reach can lift it, and well back too, bringing the rod to the full vertical, against a running fish—a sight that would make Paul Young turn in his grave, remembering how he always used to warn us not to raise our little rods higher than 45 to 60 degrees to the angle of pull. On his back cast, his arm is fully extended, a good eighteen to twenty inches behind his head—to the horror of every old-time casting instructor who ever stressed the necessity of confining the rod's motion to a gentle arc from ten o'clock to one o'clock on an imaginary clock face. And on the forward cast, his whole body goes forward in a follow-through reminiscent of old pictures of pitchers like Christy Mathewson or Walter Johnson, with no remote resemblance to the casting form of their contemporaries, with its easy and graceful rocking-chair motion of the forearm alone.

The only one of the old-timers who wouldn't have had to feel that Lee Wulff's exemplification of the modern style of casting made him eat his own words would have been Mr. Hewitt, because in a sense all that Lee Wulff is doing today is merely a colonization and consolidation of ground that Mr. Hewitt staked out over four decades ago. But Mr. Hewitt was such a weirdly opinion-bound old codger, at least in those last years, that he wouldn't believe anything, even if he knew it was so, unless he'd said it first. (I wonder if Mottram influenced Hewitt's diagrams?) Now that you look back over his old writings, though, you wonder why he didn't do, or at any rate advocate, the very things that Lee Wulff is doing today.

Over forty years ago Mr. Hewitt took a 25-pound salmon, on the Upsalquitch, in the presence of George La Branche

and Ambrose Monell, on a size 14 of his own Neversink skater
—and this is the mark a lot of us are shooting for today, although I believe Charlie Fox has equaled it more than once,
on skaters Mr. Hewitt gave him. Hewitt took a 12-pounder
on a 1½ ounce rod, before 1922, but Mills still lists today
10-foot rods as made to his specifications and still sells his
gut leaders too, stained with silver nitrate, for those Bourbons
in their clientele who to this day consider Nylon, Perlon,
Platyl, and Tortue as, collectively, only "imitation gut." So
the circle of contempt is as vicious as ever, and Mr. Adamson
will have to line up for his turn in taking potshots at those of
us who are trying to set up some kind of par for the course,
in terms of worthwhile goals of "do-it-the-hard-way" angling.

Meanwhile let Mr. Adamson, too, be not misled. We do
our fishing in what to him may appear to be the hard way,
even perversely so, and often we do it, perforce, without the
least semblance of ease or grace. We do plenty of running, to
get and keep on terms with large fish, when we use light
tackle. But this is not, as Mr. Hewitt first proved and Lee
Wulff has since demonstrated, because of the lightness of our
rods, but rather because of the delicacy of our terminal tackle.
There is our Achilles heel, during the first five minutes of
playing a large fish. And that's why we need at least 150 yards
of backing, and sometimes twice that, to let the fish enjoy
his first run, while we in turn run like hell to try and get below
him.

Lee Wulff has solved this problem of backing, in terms of
light tackle, in a wonderfully common-sense way. Take your
rod and line out on a lawn and cast as close to a country mile
as you can, double-line haul and all. Then cut the line off, at

the reel, and fill up the rest of the space you've saved on the spool with extra yards of backing. This is how I can squeeze 300 yards of 9-pound backing, far exceeding the strength of my 6-pound tippet, on even an L. R. H. Hardy Lightweight 3¾₆ inch reel, to equip my Midge for salmon fishing.

It is at precisely this juncture, when the fish that is playing you has managed to run out enough line to wrap you around one or more rocks, that you will display no semblance of "ease and grace" and you may well amuse the chortling likes of Mr. Adamson by incurring one or more pratfalls. But you will also experience, by way of compensation for that ever present hazard, the satisfaction of realizing that you are giving that noble fish the nearest thing to an even break that he ever gets during his whole hazardous life cycle.

It's strange that this seems to have no appeal to the English anglers. They, who have for so long been the custodians of our angling heritage, who have such a punctilious regard for other points of protocol and such an almost superstitious reverence for doing things the most sporting way, they seem to consider us eccentric in our devotion to light tackle. This is indeed a sign of America's coming of age, when we can appear eccentric in the eyes of the English.

Meanwhile, let us all unite in praise of Lee Wulff, who must stand, until somebody else comes along, as the only appropriate bearer-aloft of that banner with its strange device, *Excelsior,* and as the best of arbiters among us. For, while most fishermen here and abroad agree that any fishing is better than no fishing, there's precious little else on which they do agree. Each of fishing's many forms has its devotees, so passionately addicted to their particular form of the pastime as to be anywhere from surlily noncommittal to downright contemptuous of all its other forms. It often seems that the contempt of the trout purist for the spin or bait fisherman is only exceeded by the dedicated salmon angler's contempt for the trouter, which in turn is only exceeded by the tarpon man's contempt for both of them. (Overlooked in this vicious circle is the contention of the great but now almost forgotten Dr. Henshall that the black bass is inch for inch and pound for pound the greatest fish that swims.) Lee Wulff has attempted to turn this circle of contempt into a charmed circle of content, by positing the following angling equation: It is equally hard, and equally a matter of pride, he says, to take on a fly rod, and with a fly, a tarpon of over a hundred pounds, on a leader of 12-pound test, or a salmon of over 16 pounds on a size 16 fly, or a trout over 20 inches on a number 20 fly.

Lee Wulff, on his Orvis Superfine (which as a one-piece stick is slightly stouter and 3 inches shorter than the two-piece Paul Young Midge at approximately the same 1¾ ounce weight) has taken many salmon in the neighborhood of 30 pounds, but it is the way he does it that separates this man from us boys. Most of us, when we're lucky enough to land salmon of any size on our light short rods, are so impressed with the delicacy of our tackle that we're practically afraid to breathe every minute the fish is on, and figure we have to play him (or, to be more truthful, let him play us) anywhere from two to three times as long as we would with the normal 5- to 6-ounce salmon rod. But Lee Wulff will subdue a salmon of anywhere from 15 to 30 pounds on his little rod with his right hand, meanwhile photographing his jumps with his left hand, and will have concluded the entire performance, including the release of the "tailed" fish by the tailer of his own invention, with the pictures as a better souvenir than any stuffed carcass mounted on a wall, well within the minute-per-pound that salmon fishermen have traditionally considered par for the course. That he does it on a small dry fly and on the short light rod is not exactly news, since Mr. Hewitt anticipated him there by four decades, but what will be news, whenever it's done, is the capture of a salmon of any size on a size 20 fly. Those sizes go down awfully fast, below 16, and to the best of our knowledge this hasn't yet been done.

On his record to date, though, it wouldn't be a bit surprising if Lee Wulff should be the first to do it. And when it's done, then 20/20 anglers will have to look for new points of pride.

Meanwhile, Lee Wulff comes closer to it every time he hits a salmon river. Although he set up the goal, of a 16-pound salmon on a size 16 fly, only in the spring of '64, twice within the summer he exceeded it on the Moise, where he devised a new skating fly, on a size 16 hook, that looks like a cross between his own stone fly and the one known as Whiskers. It has a surface-riding action, like a small hydroplane, as opposed to the semi-submerged swath of the Whiskers fly. The forepart is of white bucktail with white hackle aft, and with a ring of badger hackle slightly abaft of midship. He has called it the Prefontaine, in honor of his host on the Moise, where he took two salmon on it, the first 23¾, and the second an even 24 pounds. He hooked but lost five others on it, all of which pulled out the small hook to a gap wide enough to be liberating. The hook he used was a Mustad, but maybe the next move is up to the House of Hardy. Nobody else has made a small hook as strong as their size 12 for their smallest stand-ard-pattern salmon flies. All they have to do now is to preserve its strength while getting its size down to 16. If they can do that, then some of the rest of us will have a chance. In the meantime Lee Wulff will go on doing fine on his Mustads, just as he surmounts with apparently effortless ease the handi-cap of a dragless Beaudex reel, out of which I, for one, could hope for nothing but a scorched forefinger the minute I tried to temporize with either a salmon or a grilse, to say nothing of—what could lose me, on that reel, the whole finger—a tarpon.

17·The Angling Heritage

*To write on Walton is, indeed, to hold a candle to the sun.
Had Montaigne been a fisher, he might have written somewhat like Izaak, but without the piety, the perfume, and
the charm.*   Andrew Lang, in
                    preface to *The Compleat Angler*, 1896

G. E. M. SKUES wrote to Patrick Chalmers that Izaak Walton was "a miserable old plagiarist who owed what he knew
about fishing to a lady, to Dame Juliana, in fact, of the first

part, and, of the second, to 'that good young gentleman' Charles Cotton." But the author of *The Compleat Angler* has been generally regarded as "the gentlest teacher and the powerfullest preacher" of the art of angling and the science of conservation. Walton lived from 1593 to 1683, and *The Compleat Angler*, first published in 1653, was issued in five editions within his lifetime. This "darling book," as it was called by its first American editor in 1847, had appeared in 284 different editions in English by the end of 1935 and has appeared at the rate of between two and three editions a year since then, making its author one of the best known and most loved figures of all English literature, and his name as much a synonym for an angler as Nimrod is for a hunter.

The book's original appearance in the author's sixtieth year brought him the friendship of Charles Cotton, who, though thirty-seven years younger, was to outlive Walton by only four years. For the fifth edition, in 1676, Cotton wrote Part Two at Walton's invitation. This second section, devoted to fishing "fine and far off" for trout and grayling in a clear stream, has become an integral part of *The Compleat Angler*, and has been included in all but a small portion of the subsequent editions, most of which give equal billing to the two authors. As a handbook of practical utility to modern anglers, Cotton's part is vastly more pertinent today than Walton's, since the younger man was an accomplished fly fisherman, whereas his master, Walton, was primarily a bait fisher and had been obliged to rely heavily upon second-hand sources at best, with open acknowledgment, and third-hand material at worst, and without acknowledgment, for the fly-fishing portions of his work. Thus, while Walton has remained for three centuries the patron saint of fishing in general, it is his disciple Cotton who has actually held that relationship to dedicated fly fishermen. But in the world of letters quite the reverse is the case: Cotton has been rescued from an otherwise obscure position as a minor Restoration poet only because of his association with Izaak Walton, the renowned literary figure.

Walton was that great rarity of the days before the Industrial Revolution, a self-made man, whereas Cotton was a gentleman to the manor born, though plagued continually by pecuniary troubles. Yet it was "meek Walton," rather than the high-born Cotton, whose literary style made of *The Compleat Angler* one of the most joyous pastorals ever composed in any language and a work that has been revered, over the centuries, less because of its subject than in spite of it. And although Charles Cotton, the squire of Beresford, knew his subject better at first hand than the Stafford yeoman Walton, he was content to ape Walton's style, to the best of his ability, in the second part of the "booke." More, he saw fit to include, wherever possible, adulatory references to "his father" Walton.

Most of the early editors and biographers of Izaak Walton were clergymen, beginning with Moses Browne in 1750, who at the suggestion of the great lexicographer Dr. Samuel Johnson reclaimed *The Compleat Angler* from the literary oblivion in which it had lain for seventy-four years, and gave it a new edition that was issued at intervals until 1851. Both Reverend Browne and Reverend Thomas Zouch, another early biographer, stressed how good the book was in spite of the fact that it was about fishing. Throughout the eighteenth century this attitude prevailed pretty generally, and it was not until the latter part of the nineteenth century that Walton's editors were inclined to dismiss, as "irrelevant and garrulous," many of those highly moral and spiritual discursive passages which were regarded as the book's chief ornament by its earliest admirers. And although the book has been praised by many literary figures—such as Wordsworth, who wrote of "meek Walton's heavenly memory"; Alexander Pope; Richard Brinsley Sheridan; Charles Lamb, who said: "It would sweeten a man's temper at any time to read it"; Washington Irving, James Russell Lowell, Richard Le Gallienne; and Andrew Lang—it is only Lang who, apart from being a man of letters, enjoys any stature in his own right in angling annals.

It is true that after the comparatively simple first edition of 1653 Walton becomes progressively long-winded and preachy, and this element of his style reaches an apex in the fifth edition of 1676 (when he was eighty-three). Still, nothing could destroy the spirit of innocent mirth with which he continued to invoke the rustic pleasures and honest enjoyments of the angler's life in an idyllic setting that has become analogous, in our time, with Merrie England. That the England of Walton's time was not so merry makes his work only the more remarkable, for in the pages of *The Compleat Angler* that England now seems to us a land of sweet leisure all compact. But for Izaak Walton, an ardent Royalist, the time of Cromwell was a time of trouble, and Walton more than once risked his purse and his head by remaining true to his convictions.

Though born in Staffordshire in the Elizabethan era, Walton early made his fortune in London, where he became a member of the Ironmonger's Company. His first biographers were under the impression that he was a wholesale linen draper, but later researchers tended to render that assumption questionable, although they were not able to substitute, with any exactness, any other specific role to his business activities. In any case, by the time he was fifty he had amassed enough worldly goods to permit his retirement to the country, and for the last forty years of his life he was able to devote himself entirely to writing and fishing. There was the added advantage, for a Royalist, of being able to keep out of harm's way better in the country than in London, during the era of conflict between Cavaliers and Roundheads, and particularly during the long years of Cromwell's reign.

According to Anthony Wood, a contemporary, he left London "in 1643 (at which time he found it dangerous for honest men to be there) and lived sometimes at Stafford and elsewhere, but mostly in the families of the eminent clergymen of England, of whom he was much beloved." This retirement, like many other purported facts of his life, was disputed and debated by later biographers, notably Sir Harris Nicholas in his monumental edition of *The Compleat Angler* in 1836, but it is beyond question that after 1640, when his life of Dr. John Donne was first published, Walton was a man of letters first and a man of leisure second, and no longer a man of business. Apart from *The Compleat Angler*, his literary output consisted almost entirely of biographies of such worthies as Sir Henry Wotton, Chancellor of Eton, the poet Herbert, and the Bishops Hooker and Sanderson. Without *The Compleat Angler*, Walton would have been known to our time, if at all, only as a tediously pious Plutarch, and Cotton as a reprobate poet and parodist, and both would have been largely forgotten and almost entirely unread.

The remarkable durability of this sporting classic is best attested by the avidity with which its various editions are continually sought, not only by bibliophiles, but by anglers otherwise utterly uninterested in book collecting. Of the various editions, after the original five which appeared in Walton's lifetime between 1653–76, the following are the most noteworthy. The Moses Browne, which first appeared in 1750, and in four subsequent editions until 1851; the Hawkins, which appeared in fourteen editions between 1760 and 1826; the Major, which enjoyed fifty-six printings between 1823 and 1934; the Rennie, with twenty printings between 1833 and 1851; the Nicolas, with five editions between 1836 and 1931; the Bethune, the first American edition, which was printed five times between 1847 and 1891; the Ephemera (Fitzgibbon), which had nine editions between 1853 and 1893; the Jesse, which also had nine, from 1856 to 1903; the Davies, which had eleven between 1878 and 1930; the Marston, which made the hundredth of the various editions and appeared in four printings from 1888 to 1912; the Lang, which had twelve editions between 1896 and 1932; and the Le Gallienne, which appeared six times between 1897 and 1931. All of these are sought by collectors.

There have also been numerous translations, and one interesting novelty, a Japanese edition in English, with introduction and notes both in English and in Japanese, in the Kenkyusha English Classics series, published in Tokyo in 1926. There have been many limited editions, such as that of the Peter Pauper Press, and these have been illustrated by such artists and designers as Arthur Rackham and W. A. Dwiggins. Among the modern editions, what was probably about the three hundredth appeared in 1953, on the tercentenary of Walton's first edition. It was sponsored by the Izaak Walton League and published by Stackpole and was revised and edited by Eugene Burns.

The exact number of editions, as of 1965, is difficult to determine, although it is certainly in the neighborhood of 350, with five in the seventeenth century, ten in the eighteenth, 164 in the nineteenth, and all the rest since 1900. Those interested in the comparative details of all the editions published in English up to 1935 may find them described in *A New Chronicle of the Compleat Angler* by Peter Oliver, published in 1936 by The Paisley Press, Inc., New York, and Williams and Norgate, Ltd., London. Virtually all of the editions may be seen in the New York Public Library.

The famous Fifth Edition of 1676, which was the first to include Cotton's Part Two, was actually the sixth printing of the book by Marriott, the original publisher. It had been preceded by printings in 1653, 1655, 1661, 1664, and 1668. It also included, as Part Three, *The Experienced Angler*, by Colonel Robert Venables, another Marriott author and a veteran of Cromwell's armies but sufficiently rehabilitated in Restoration times to earn a flattering and friendly dedicatory letter from Izaak Walton. For that one edition, the book was entitled *The Universal Angler*. However, except for a later facsimile reprint of this edition, the Venables work was not carried in subsequent editions of *The Compleat Angler*.

Just as Lindbergh was not the first to fly the Atlantic, although his subsequent fame led many to believe that he was, so Izaak Walton was by no means the first to write a book on fishing in English. That distinction is generally accorded to Dame Juliana Berners, the abbess who contributed *The Treatyse of Fysshynge with an Angle* to the second edition of *The Book of St. Albans* in 1496. Other works to appear ahead of Walton's were *The Arte of Angling* (1577), *A Booke of Fishing with Hook and Line* by Leonard Mascall (1590), *Hawking, Hunting, Fouling and Fishing,* by W(illiam) G(ryndall) (1596), *The Secrets of Angling* by John Dennys (1613), *A Discourse of the General Art of Fishing with an Angle* by Gervase Markham (1614), and *The Art of Angling* by Thomas Barker (1651).

Walton openly acknowledged his own indebtedness to Barker's work, though saying that he was repeating Barker "with a little variation," but all of the authors named had leaned heavily upon Dame Juliana's original list of twelve artifical flies, and some, such as Markham, had simply cannibalized all preceding works on the subject. Walton followed Markham in some of his errors, as well as some of his borrowings. Walton was generally supposed, by most of his early editors, to have patterned his dialogue form on some of the many books which had been written in this form in the preceding century, *Herebaschius' Husbandry* (1577) and *A Treatise on the Nature of God* (1599) being the two books cited as most closely resembling his. And, of course, the casting of discourses in dialogue form was as old as antiquity— dating back to the Socratic dialogues of Plato's time. Thus although the question of plagiarism was often raised in the earlier notices of Walton's work, chiefly because of the vicious attack on him for "plagiary" by Richard Franck in his *Northern Memoirs* (written in 1658 but not published until 1674), honest Izaak was not impugned with borrowings beyond those sanctioned by the very liberal literary practices of his day. The question has been raised again in recent years, however, since Carl Otto von Kienbusch's discovery, in London in 1954, of the one known copy of the 1577 volume, *The Arte of Angling*. This little book, which had somehow escaped being recorded anywhere at all, is in general structure the exact prototype of the first edition of *The Compleat Angler*. It is a series of episodes in dialogue form, with two characters, Piscator and Viator, the former undertaking the instruction of the latter. After the first edition, Walton changed *his* Viator to Venator and added a third character, Coridon. Cotton, on the other hand, when he wrote Part Two for the fifth edition of *The Compleat Angler*, stayed with the original two characters of the first edition, Piscator and Viator.

Much has been made of the number of exactly parallel passages in *The Arte of Angling* and *The Compleat Angler*, and it would be fair to say that *The Arte of Angling* does, in its general structure and outline, bear very nearly as much resemblance to the first edition of Walton's work as that simple first edition itself bears to the greatly expanded fifth edition. To say that *The Arte of Angling* bears the same relation to *The Compleat Angler* as a preliminary sketch might bear to a finished painting is another matter, for that would be to assume that it served Walton, wholly and simply, as a source book. Otto von Kienbusch, in his introduction to the facsimile reproduction of *The Arte of Angling* which he generously had issued by The Princeton Library in 1956, does so characterize the earlier book's relation to Walton's, and this opinion is shared by its editor, Gerald Eades Bentley, in his preface.

That Walton was widely read is evident on almost every page of *The Compleat Angler*, and that he was willing to give credit where he knew it to be due is almost equally evident. He gives the name Jo Davors as that of the poet who wrote *The Secrets of Angling*, though Dennys later came to be known as the angler's "glorious John," but the orthography of the time made many names hard to untangle. In any case, Walton did not try to palm off the quoted verses as his own. He even acknowledged foreign sources, such as Rondelet and Gesner, who wrote in France and in Germany a century before him. He need not have worried about them, as he might have about a contemporary such as Thomas Barker; they would not be around to plague him if he quoted them without credit.

Even if it were conceded that Walton had *The Arte of Angling* propped up before him as a source book when he sat down to write *The Compleat Angler*, this still could not account for more than some of the more rudimentary elements of his work. The unknown author of *The Arte* is crude and blunt where Walton is subtle and sensitive, and though they both be "merry men," the earlier unknown's humor comes in quick, short jibes, whereas Walton's flows on as gently and continuously as, in his own words, "these silent silver streams which we now see glide so quietly by us."

For his is, as John Buchan said of it, "about the best cheerful prose in our literature, prose which is all air and dew and light." If *The Arte of Angling* does, admittedly, whistle the selfsame tune that Walton picked up in *The Compleat Angler*, still it is his own orchestration of it, his weaving of it into a garland of imperishable beauties, that has given it its immortality. He gave angling not a how-to book of enduring utility, though even that could be said of Cotton's part, but the greatest literary idyll that any language has ever bestowed on any sport. In this respect it may still be said of him, as Andrew Lang said in the nineties: "He is not so much unrivalled as absolutely alone. Heaven meant him for the place he filled, as it meant the cowslip and the mayfly." And, in spite of latter-day revelations, Lang's can still stand as the last word, since it is only reasonable to concede, with him, that *"The Compleat Angler,* the father of so many books, is the child of a few." As to Walton's borrowings, it is perhaps not overcharitable to regard them as we do Shakespeare's. In that sense, we could say again, as Lang said, that Walton "is indebted to none but his maker and his genius." Patrick Chalmers made another point about old Izaak with which it is hard to disagree: "His influence has made almost every poet a bit of a fisherman. And, beyond a doubt, it has made of every fisherman a bit of a poet."

It is not so easy, however, these three score and ten years after Lang wrote the preface to his edition of *The Compleat Angler,* to let his dictum stand unchallenged that, of all angling literature, it could still be said that "Walton alone gave it style." It is perhaps enough to say that, of all authors, Walton gave it its greatest single impetus. For, exceeded as it is in its antiquity only by the literature of hunting, the literature of angling is now even greater in its extent and diversity, and is today generally acknowledged to be the largest body of literature devoted to any single branch of sport. Could we but find all its lost books, as Otto von Kienbusch found *The Arte of Angling,* an argument could perhaps be made that it was still older than the literature of hunting. For even Dame Juliana, in the 1400's, referred to "books of credence" on the subject of angling. Presumably one of these was a manuscript treatise, mentioned by Robert Blakey in *Angling Literature of All Nations* (London, 1856) as having been found among the remains of the valuable library belonging to the Abbey of St. Bertins, at St. Omer, which was supposed to have been written about the year 1000. And W. J. Turrell, in *Ancient Angling Authors* (London, 1910), said that Aelfric's *Colloquy*, written by Aelfric the Abbott about the end of the tenth century to teach his pupils Latin, with the Latin translation beneath each Anglo-Saxon line, was the oldest English treatise on fishing.

Though you could count on your fingers the number of known books between Dame Juliana in 1496 and Walton and Cotton in 1676, after the latter still-verdant classic came the deluge. While a definitive bibliography of angling literature has not been attempted in recent decades, it is obvious that any such masterwork, if attempted today, would have to embrace in excess of five thousand titles in English alone. Even so, it would still be only fractional in relation to the full bibliography on ichthyology, which would exceed fifty thousand entries.

The most-written-about single fish, considered as a quarry for sportsmen rather than as the subject of commercial or scientific study, is by all odds the trout. And of all the many branches of sport fishing, fly fishing, with its attendant studies of entomology, has received by far the greatest amount of literary attention. Since the kindergarten of angling is still fishing with a pole and a worm, and serious anglers generally agree that the progressive education of an angler culminates in stream fishing with a fly, it is only natural that the highest reaches of the literature should be concerned chiefly with this form of fishing.

The two chief milestones in almost five centuries of angling literature are, and will undoubtedly remain, the *Treatise* of Dame Juliana Berners, first printed in 1496, although presumably written some fifty years earlier, and *The Compleat Angler*, with its all-important second part by Charles Cotton, of 1676. As classics, the Berners and Walton books are in a class by themselves, but there are eight others which, together with these first two, have earned, through their longevity and the frequency with which they have been reissued, the distinction of constituting The Big Ten of angling classics. They are, arranged alphabetically between Berners and Walton, the works of Thomas Best (1787), "John Bickerdyke" (1889), Richard and Charles Bowlker (1758), Gervase Markham (1631), Alfred Ronalds (1836), Thomas Salter (1814), J(ohn) S(mith) (1696), W. C. Stewart (1857). The well-read angler ought also to include, on a par with The Big Ten, but never heretofore counted among them because it was for centuries a lost classic and was only recently rediscovered, *The Arte of Angling* (1577), as reproduced in facsimile at Princeton in 1956.

At the risk of seeming to oversimplify the subject, one can blaze a trail through the thousands of titles that all told form the almost impenetrable thickets of angling literature, by adding, to the ten all-time classic best sellers already mentioned, merely another ten authors of vintage works (1828–1935) and still another ten authors of modern works (1950–

63). Thus, by reading thirty books, any angler can qualify as being truly well read, without attempting the almost insuperable task of reading everything that has been written about fishing in the last five centuries. And while it is unlikely that any of the scholars in the field would agree exactly on the ten moderns, it is equally unlikely that they would disagree seriously on the ten classic or the ten vintage selections.

After running this short course, those whose reading appetites have been whetted to read on would still do well to seek further guidance, in the form of one of the several good "books about books about fishing," before striking out for themselves. Otherwise the unguided angler will have to plough through many for every one that he finds in any substantial way rewarding. Inevitably there has been endless duplication in the literature of angling, which has been as repetitive as it has been discursive, ever since Old Izaak stamped its style. It would not be too severe to say that not more than one in every hundred of its thousands of books has represented a truly original contribution, either from the standpoint of adding to the attraction, through literary distinction, or enhancing the instruction, in the sense of adding to angling knowledge.

One shortcut across these trackless wastes is, of course, An Angler's Anthology, and there are at least two good ones, an English one by A. B. Austin, first issued by Country Life Ltd., in London in 1930, and in this country by Scribner's, and the other, American, by Eugene Burns, published by Stackpole in 1952. Both browse delightfully among the books on angling, back to the Treatise, culling choice blooms from the vast gardens, but their gatherings, like cut flowers, leave the

interested angler with nothing that he can plant and culti-
vate and make his own. Like all samplers, the more he enjoys
them, the more they make him want to look for more, and
yet by their very nature they can't give him any idea of where
to find more of the rare and fragrant blossoms without getting
bogged down among the weeds and brambles.

Three books which can give such guidance to angling
literature, and which are at the same time worth reading in
themselves, are *Notable Angling Literature* by James Robb,
published by Herbert Jenkins Ltd. (London) in 1945; *A History of Fly Fishing for Trout* by John Waller Hills, published
by Frederick A. Stokes Company in 1921; and *Walton and
Some Earlier Writers on Fish and Fishing* by R. B. Marston,
published by Elliott Stock (London) in 1903, although first
published in 1894. On the last page of the second of these
books Hills spoke just as truly for the other two as he did for
his own when he said: "There are some who read everything
which is written about fishing, for I am of that number . . .
there must be others also like myself, whom the history of the
sport attracts, who are fascinated by the devices of other
days, and who are never weary of going back to the old
writers, of reading them again, of getting at their real meaning, and of seeing where they have anticipated us and where
we have improved on them." All three of these writers—Robb,
Hills, and Marston—get at the real meaning of the old
writers, quote them and characterize them, point out the
significance of their contributions, and show both where they
are still valid and where later developments have improved
upon them. Robb, since he is the most recent, is the most
valuable as a guide to further reading.

The thirty books that together bridge the five centuries from the *Treatise* to our own times are generally available in metropolitan and university libraries, and the identification of them here given should be sufficient to permit access to them. For anglers who wish to have copies of their own, the services of a sporting bookseller will undoubtedly be required. Two who between them can be counted upon to furnish copies of virtually all these books are Sporting Book Service, Box 181, Rancocas, New Jersey, and E. Chalmers Hallam, Earlswood, Egmont Drive, Ringwood, Hampshire, England.

The Thirty Books

* indicates attraction (literary value)
+ indicates instruction (technical value)

CLASSIC

****+ Dame Juliana Berners: *A Treatyse of Fysshynge Wyth an Angle*, 1496 (see McDonald: *Origins of Angling,* below, which contains two versions of *The Treatise*)
** Thomas Best: *A Concise Treatise on the Art of Angling,* 1787
** "John Bickerdyke": (Charles Henry Cook): *The Book of the All-Around Angler,* 1889
** Richard and Charles Bowlker: *The Art of Angling Improved in all its Parts, especially Fly-fishing,* 1758
*** Gervase Markham: *Country Contentments,* 1631
***+ Alfred Ronalds: *The Fly-fisher's Entomology,* 1836
** Thomas Salter: *The Angler's Guide,* 1814

** J(ohn) S(mith): *The True Art of Angling,* 1696
**+ W. C. Stewart: *The Practical Angler,* 1857
***** Izaak Walton and **+++ Charles Cotton: *The Compleat Angler,* 1676

VINTAGE

**+ Sir Humphrey Davy: *Salmonia, or Days of Fly-fishing,* 1828
***+ Francis Francis: *A Book on Angling,* 1867
***+ Sir Edward Grey (Lord Grey of Fallodon): *Fly-fishing,* 1899
**+ Frederic M. Halford: *Dry-fly Fishing in Theory and Practice,* 1889
*++ Edward Ringwood Hewitt: *A Trout and Salmon Fisherman for Seventy-five Years.* Charles Scribner's Sons, 1950
**+ George M. L. La Branche: *The Dry Fly and Fast Water* and *The Salmon and the Dry Fly* (together in one volume). Charles Scribner's Sons, 1951
*+++ "Jock Scott" (D. G. H. Rudd): *Greased Line Fishing for Salmon* (compiled from the papers of A. H. E. Wood). J. B. Lippincott Co., 1935
***+ William Scrope: *Days and Nights of Salmon-fishing in the Tweed,* 1843
**+ G. E. M. Skues: *The Way of a Trout with a Fly,* 1921, and/or *Minor Tactics of the Chalk-stream,* 1910
**++ Eric Taverner: *Trout Fishing from all Angles,* 1929

MODERN

**++ Ray Bergman: *Trout,* revised ed. Alfred A. Knopf, 1952

*+++ Charles K. Fox: *This Wonderful World of Trout.* Foxcrest 1, Carlisle, Pa. 1963

**++ Alvin R. Grove, Jr.: *The Lure and Lore of Trout Fishing.* Stackpole Co., 1951

**+++ A. J. McClane: *The Practical Fly Fisherman.* Prentice-Hall, 1953

****+ John McDonald: *The Origins of Angling* (and a new printing of *The Treatise of Fishing with an Angle.* Doubleday & Co., 1963

*+++ Vincent C. Marinaro: *A Modern Dry-fly Code.* G. P. Putnam's Sons, 1950

**++ Charles Ritz: *A Fly Fisher's Life.* Henry Holt & Co., 1959

*+++ Ernest G. Schwiebert, Jr.: *Matching the Hatch.* The Macmillan Co., 1955

++++ Helen Shaw: *Fly-tying.* Ronald Press, 1963

**+++ Lee Wulff: *The Atlantic Salmon.* A. S. Barnes, 1958

The first dividend to be derived from reading the old angling authors is the realization that there is nothing new under the sun, and that every angler practices his pastime under the conviction, voiced by all his elders, that fishing isn't what it used to be.

In 1890, in *Angling Sketches*, Andrew Lang (**) summed this up: "It was worth while to be a boy in the South of Scotland, and to fish the waters haunted by old legends, musical with old songs, and renowned in the sporting essays of Christopher North and Stoddert. Even then, thirty years ago (1860), the old stagers used to tell us that 'the watter was ower sair fished,' and they grumbled. . . . ' 'Tis gone, 'tis

gone: not in our time will any man . . . need a cart to carry
the trout he has slain.' They are all gone now, the old allies
and tutors in the angling art. The companions of those times
are scattered, and live under strange stars and in converse
seasons by troutless waters. But, except for the scarcity of
fish, the scene is very little altered, and one is a boy again, in
heart, beneath the elms. . . . However bad the sport, it keeps
you young, or makes you young again, and you need not
follow Ponce de Leon to the Western wilderness, when, in
any river you knew of yore, you can find the Fountain of
Youth."

That passage has as much truth as poetry, for from the
time of Walton himself, who lived to be ninety, the great
fishers have generally kept young enough to fish to a ripe old
age, as witness Scrope, who was eighty, Francis, Halford,
Grey, and Hills, who all made it past seventy, and those two
fabulous old friends of our own time, Hewitt and La Branche,
who both died in their nineties within the past few years.
Further back than Andrew Lang, the angling reader will
pick up the same old refrain from the querulous voice of the
American Charles Hallock, who complains, in *The Fishing
Tourist* of 1873, that it now ran the angler virtually a dollar
a pound to find trout and, almost in the same breath, that
the ease of modern travel was making them too easy to
find.

There is repetition, surely, throughout the literature that
is available in such abundance for the angler who would learn
as he reads, but in a twofold sense even the repetitiveness
of it constitutes another dividend, for one of the best ways
to acquire a solid education as an angler is by having the

fundamental lessons drilled in, by hearing them taken up again and again by the many voices of the old masters, beginning with Cotton's insistence, away back in 1676, upon the most essential point of all, that of fishing "fine and far off" in a clear stream for trout. Starting with the *Treatise* itself, the reading angler acquires successive layers of learning, like the successive coats of lacquer on a job of custom coach-work, feeling a growing sense of the traditional as fundamentals are reiterated across the centuries, and enjoying successive thrills of enlightenment with the continuous revelations of the various great break-throughs of angling knowledge and mastery that have been made by the half dozen or so "great originals" across the years down to our own time. All this is certainly included in the thirty volumes that constitute the "short course" already recommended. And while not all of the authors mentioned are of anything like the same stature, and not more than half of them are today of full and unimpaired instructional value, virtually all of this better half have made truly original contributions. And it is worthwhile to read the other half too, either for pure enjoyment or as a basis on which to measure the stature of such mighty figures as the most important of them are.

With the thought of furnishing a further guide to anyone who would become an angling scholar, the thirty authors have been given stars and/or plus signs, as a purely arbitrary way of indicating their relative importance. The stars indicate the comparative and approximate degree of the value of the books as purveyors of the attractions of angling, and the plus marks indicate their value as instructors to the angler who wants to read more to be taught than to be entertained. Walton, for example, wears five stars simply because he is and will remain peerless as long as the well of pure English stays even reasonably undefiled by the gathering vulgarities of our assorted gobbledygooks of technical newspeak, but he carries no plus marks at all because he ceased, over a hundred years ago, to have any actual instructional value for a sophisticated angler. Cotton, on the other hand, is accorded only two stars, to show how far he fell below his "father" Walton in communicating the pastoral delights of the angling scene in the days of merry England, but in compensation ekes out his five-star rank with three plus marks, to indicate the simple truth that after almost three hundred years his is still the best school the aspiring clear-water fly fisher can hope to attend. James Chetham, however, who wrote in Walton's lifetime, is accorded but the single star, indicating that he is of interest only to the reader who is more "book-worm than angle-worm," delighted as the latter may be to come across, in Chetham's (*) *The Angler's Vade Mecum* (1681), such a wonderful complaint as the forthright pronouncement that "this night fishing" was "unwholesome, unpleasant and very ungenteel" and that he would have none of it, since it was "to be used by none but idle pouching fellows."

Since comparisons are at least as odious in this field as in any other, and perhaps even more so in the light of the reflection that fishing is, at best, one of the world's few truly non-competitive sports, it may be a matter of passing regret that the stars and plus signs here used may seem to assign purely arbitrary rankings to writers the way a Michelin guide would assign them to restaurants. The device is used to aid the beginning angling scholar to know what books to look for first, depending on whether he is more interested in entertainment or in instruction, and the stars and plus signs merely aim to indicate which books are of greater interest in each of these two respects, with the possible added service that the angling reader aiming to acquire his own library may want to set about it after the manner of first things first.

Even the briefest outline of history could not possibly attempt to confine the account to events of absolutely equal interest and importance, and however egalitarian and democratic might be the aim to make all good books on fishing equal, there must always be some authors in any field, such as Marlowe and Shakespeare in dramatic literature, and Berners and Walton in angling literature, who will be "more equal than any others." In his excellent *History of Fly-fishing*, Major J. W. Hills made the fair statement that "there are four names which stand above others in the history of the fly: the author of *The Treatise*, who started it; Cotton, who established it; Stewart who converted the world to upstream fishing; and Halford, who systematized the dry fly." The good major is, since 1938, beyond reach for consultation, but even he—on record though he is as being of that number who would read everything ever written about fishing—would not argue that all four of those names, though he picked them out from hundreds of others, were therefore and by that act made equal to each other. Their only equality, by even the major's omnivorous interest in the subject, would be in the sense that any book about fishing is better than any book that isn't about fishing. By the same token, one of the most endearing statements ever made by an angling writer was the one attributed by Hills to Francis Francis: "Some fishing is better than others; but there is no such thing as bad fishing."

Thomas Best, whose *Concise Treatise on the Art of Angling* ran through thirteen editions after its initial appearance in 1787, can be of interest to an American angler of the 1960's chiefly for the purely antiquarian fact that his was the first book to mention the multiplying reel, though in its relation to other books that came before and after it, his book was, in Robb's estimation, both practical and sensible. There is not much more to be said for Thomas Salter, by today's standards, though his book too, from its first appearance the year before the battle of Waterloo—as a best seller of wide influence—was a worthy stone in the arch of angling knowledge. One piece of advice he gives is as fresh as ever: "Notice that by rubbing gut . . . which has laid in coils, with India rubber, it instantly becomes straight, especially the pieces to which hooks are tied, as these pieces usually are kept coiled up."

"John Bickerdyke" (Charles Henry Cook), though Robb terms him "one of the elect," particularly in the field of coarse fishing and for his pioneering in sea fishing, is a giant of diminished stature today, and though his time (1887) is much closer to our own, *The Book of the All-round Angler* is still chiefly of interest as background and for the continuity it provides with others of more lasting originality both before and since. For that matter, Gervase Markham, though regarded by his peers in 1631 as something of a rascal and an opportunistic jack-of-all-trades, has more to say to those of us who are today still intent upon "matching the hatch," for it was he who first gave us the idea, as follows: "Now for the shapes and proportions of these flyes, it is impossible to describe them without paynting, therefore you shall take of these severall flyes alive, and laying them before you, trie how near your Art can come unto nature by an equall shapes and mixture of colours; and when you have made them, you may keep them in close boxes uncrushed, and they will serve you many yeares."

As for Richard and Charles Bowlker, Hills dated the start of modern fly-dressing from the first appearance of their book in 1747 (begun by the father Richard and continued in subsequent enlarged editions by the son Charles). There were so many, in fact, as to earn their *Art of Angling* the appellation of "the most successful purely fishing book ever written," and certainly this one of its dicta still stands: "When you see a fish rise at a natural fly, the best way is to throw a yard above him, rather than directly over his head, and let your fly move gently towards him, by which means you will show it to him more naturally." A half century earlier, J(ohn) S(mith), in *The True Art of Angling* (1696), had written another enormously influential book that went through twelve editions and remained a standard work for seventy-five years. It advised fishing upstream in clear water, though with a natural fly, but downstream in thick water or with an artificial fly. It remained for W. C. Stewart (**+) to combine those pieces of advice, in *The Practical Angler* (1857), the first advocate of upstream dry-fly fishing: "The nearer the motions of the artificial flies resemble those of the natural ones under similar circumstances, the greater will be the prospects of success." As Hills pointed out, this sums up the creed of the dry fly: "He was not the discoverer of upstream fishing any more than Darwin was the discoverer of natural selection, but he was the first for nearly two hundred years to take the trouble to make the case, and the first of any age to do it completely."

Even so, the contribution of Alfred Ronalds (***+) was the more lasting, for where Stewart began something that was later pushed to the point of senseless mania, Ronald's *The Fly-fisher's Entomology* (1836) started not only a whole school of writers but a whole school of thought, and gave fishing a new dimension as a science. From 1836 to 1921 it was the only book of its class, and is for all time, in Hills' phrase, "the creator of the race of angler-naturalists."

Although Francis Francis, like most of the writers before him, treated of all forms of fresh-water fishing, in *A Book on Angling* (1867), he showed his estimation of their relative importance by devoting two thirds of his more than five hundred pages to trout and salmon. And though Francis, standing on Ronald's shoulders, raised "the right fly" to gospel, and Halford right after Francis pushed the mystique of the dry fly to a point of snobbish mania, both are richly rewarding reading even today, and both, in view of the near-fanaticism of their insistence on glorifying the proper fly even at the expense of angling results, are still surprisingly human. Here is Francis: "And so you walk on, sometimes musing, sometimes marvelling, as each new voice salutes you, 'the voices of the evening,' that you never noticed before, though you may have heard them a hundred times; but it is your mood to hear, and note them, too, tonight, and you do so wonderingly, as though they were all new things and this some other hemisphere, and so you tramp on homewards under the moonlight. Is your creel light, friend: What then 'Your heart is light too, and there are other things to admire in the world besides fishes,' so take that by way of consolation."

Halford, too, despite his insistence on the dry fly as the be-all and end-all of fishing, could still be cherished for this one passage alone from *Modern Development of the Dry-fly:* "I have as many disappointing days as any of my readers, perhaps more. I fail continually. I leave flies in the fish's mouth; I am weeded and broken. Some evenings I get home dead beat, tired out, depressed, and ready to declare that I will give up dry-fly fishing altogether. I hope however that I have learned to look at sport from the optimistic point of view, and so the next morning I wake up keener than ever, and once more sally forth to the river resolved to do or die." That Halford was a man of high resolve, and no egomaniac, is shown in the fact that he quit all business at the age of forty-five, to devote the next twenty-five years of his life to fishing and writing about the dry fly, not only formulating his own theories but also playing Boswell to Captain Marryat, a great nonwriting fisherman. He also served as the historian and systematizer of the dry fly and, as well, as its transatlantic spark-gap. It was he whose patterns, sent to the sainted Theodore Gordon, started the development of the dry fly in America.

It was the one-two force of Stewart and Halford that raised the dry fly to the almost tyrannical rule that it exerted over fishermen in England in the last third of the nineteenth century, but by the century's last year its exaggerated importance began to be undermined. In 1899 Sir Edward Grey

(***+) emerged, in *Fly-fishing*, as "the first writer of importance on the dry fly who really knew what the wet fly meant . . . and he started that restatement of values that Skues carried so far." Skues brought the English angling world back to its senses with the revelation that there was no real need to exalt either the dry fly or the wet fly at the expense of the other: "There are days and hours when the wet-fly has not a chance against the dry-fly, and there are days and hours when the dry-fly has not a chance against the wet-fly."

On the salmon side, Scrope in *Days and Nights of Salmon Fishing in the Tweed* (1843) took up where Sir Humphrey Davy had left off in 1828, and although he too wrote only one fishing book, it was—and is—one of the brightest volumes in the whole literature of angling. Scrope is a character, one of the most colorful personalities ever to put pen to paper about angling, and everything he wrote is as individual as a fingerprint. But if the literature of salmon fishing had to wait several centuries to get started, and poor Sir Humphrey, dictating his *Salmonia* from his bed of pain, had to play the role of its Berners, then Scrope was well worth waiting for, and he can serve as its Walton and Cotton combined. Probably every man who ever fished has sometime had the thought, when taken to task about fishing, that only Scrope ever put into so many words. Has man the moral right to deprive these, his fellow creatures, of their God-given lives?

Yes, bellows Scrope, and on these grounds: "Let us see how the case stands. I take a little wool and feather and tying it in a particular manner upon a hook make an imitation of a fly! then I throw it across the river and let it sweep around the stream with a lively motion. This I have an undoubted right to do, for the river belongs to me or my friend, but mark what follows. Up starts a monster fish with his murderous jaws. It makes a dash at my little Andromeda. Thus he is the aggressor, not I; his intention is evidently to commit murder."

Scrope's beguiling logic also conferred dubious immortality upon that warden of Selkirk, who "as a water bailiff was sworn to tell of all he saw; and indeed, as he said, it could not be expected that he should tell of what he did not see. When his dinner was served up during close time his wife usually brought to the table a platter of potatoes and a napkin; she then bound the latter over his eyes that nothing might offend his sight. This being done, the illegal salmon was brought in smoking hot, and he fell to, blindfolded as he was, like a conscientious water bailiff—if you know what that is; nor was the napkin taken from his eyes till the fins and bones were removed from the room, and every visible evidence of a salmon having been there had completely vanished . . ." But Scrope is unquotable if not quoted in full. He must be read, as Walton must (though not without Cotton), by every man who would aspire to any status beyond that of the most casual tourist in the rarefied realm of the kingly sport of salmon angling.

Though hundreds fish for trout for every dozen who can afford to fish for salmon, the literature of salmon angling is, in view of that restricting circumstance, surprisingly large. But as far as mastery of the sport's technique is concerned, and forgetting all the purely literary attractions (like Chaytor's *Letters to a Salmon Fisher's Sons*) that beckon down innumerable bypaths, the whole art can be learned from just three books that came after Scrope's. They are *Greased Line Fishing for Salmon*, in which the pseudonymous "Jock Scott" (Donald Rudd) played Boswell to the great A. H. E. Wood; La Branche's *Salmon and the Dry Fly*; and Lee Wulff's *Atlantic Salmon*. These are three of the "great originals," each representing an all-time break-through in angling technique. When A. H. E. Wood, of Cairnton on the Aberdeenshire Dee, discovered by accident the greased-line method, he made it possible for the first time to take salmon with any consistency in low water and in warm weather. In this method a sparsely dressed fly (he used only three, Blue Charm, Silver Blue, and March Brown) is cast across the stream and the line consistently mended whenever drag threatens, with the result that the fly barely sinks beneath the surface, the taking fish is seen, and, when it takes, there is no striking, since it hooks itself in the corner of the jaw where a good hold is generally secured. Similarly, when George M. L. La Branche, teamed with Hewitt, established the possibility of taking salmon on the dry fly, he went on, again almost by accident, to a further discovery that has since been put to use by many more anglers than the comparative handful who fish for salmon. His great contribution was the invention of a deadly method for taking almost any fish that refuses to be taken by conventional offerings, the creation of "the artificial hatch" whereby repeated casts are floated over the same spot often enough to convince even the most skeptical fish that a hatch is on and that he'd better take before it's over. On a par with these two earlier break-throughs is the establishment, by Lee Wulff in *Atlantic*

Salmon, that the light-tackle angler, though seeming to do things the hard way, actually enjoys an advantage, in playing large or difficult fish, over the more conventionally equipped angler. With this, and the techniques of the skittered or riffled "hitched fly" and the semi-submerged fly, the salmon angler is brought up to the minute in the applied knowledge of his sport.

This mention of Hewitt should probably not be left with the mere indication of his godfatherly role in relation to dry-fly fishing for salmon with La Branche, for in the course of his long life he also undoubtedly played the greatest single role in the establishment of nymph fishing in America, and he must also be credited with the invention of one of the most versatile of all lures, the spider as he first fished it in the guise of the Neversink skater. He was taking salmon on a size 14 spider as long ago as the early twenties—a feat that not even now can be regarded as exactly routine.

To get back to the English, Taverner in *Trout Fishing from All Angles* compiled a book that gives the impression of being comprehensive to the point of being exhaustive, as an exposition of all their methodology and knowledge. Fortunately the last word is never written, or angling would be a science rather than a sport—this book almost makes the reader forget that it isn't.

Bergman, in *Trout,* became for Americans what Taverner is to the English, for his is still their best all-around and, to many people their only, book on trout. But Bergman's book, though revised in 1952, was originally written in 1939, and in this sense A. J. McClane's *Practical Fly Fisherman,* first published in 1953, virtually stands on Bergman's shoulders.

Until somebody now in knee pants comes along to do it the same disservice, it must stand as the most comprehensive and useful single volume on all forms of fresh-water fly fishing available to Americans.

Other essential books of the last decade, to enable the angler to feel that he is at least as well educated as books alone can ever make him, are more specialized, but, taken with McClane as a prerequisite, like the required reading demanded of freshmen before they are allowed to progress to more diversified studies, will bring the angling scholar up to date. He who would implement, by today's standards, the most refined application of Cotton's immortal exhortation to fish fine and far off must now sit at the feet of the three Pennsylvania masters of the *minutae*, Fox, Grove, and Marinaro, who will certainly some day seem as legendary to us all as Hewitt and La Branche are already beginning to seem within a decade of their death. And he who would follow, to today's most demanding exigency, the perfectionism upon which Francis and Halford insisted in the natural imitation of artificials, cannot do without Schwiebert. And he who would try today to lead a fly-fisher's life will surely miss a few tricks if he doesn't, somewhere along the way, take time out to study the one now near sundown, led by Charles Ritz, one of the most gracious as well as one of the most graceful of its modern practitioners.

No man can call himself a fisher, within the meaning of the masters, unless he ties, or at least tries to tie, his own flies. Some earnest souls, born with ten thumbs, who have often tried but failed, may be heartened by the knowledge that at last (1963) they have a woman's help, so that, even for them, this art while still possibly difficult is at least no longer impossible. For with the aid of her photographer husband, Helen Shaw in *Fly-Tying* looks over your shoulder and guides your hands as she performs with her own, to let you see just how you do it, step by step. Although this is the most elementary last word on the how-to-do-it side, in a brief survey of angling literature to date, scholarly mastery is not yet lost. The same year, 1963, saw, in John McDonald's *The Origins of Angling (and a new printing of "The Treatise of Fishing with an Angle")*, one of the most intensive and perceptive feats of angling scholarship ever performed over the centuries in which fishing has been written about. McDonald, who, although of a later generation, had served the memory and preserved the contribution of Theodore Gordon (in *The Complete Fly-fisherman*, Scribner's, 1947, in which he collected and annotated Gordon's notes and letters), just as Halford had done for Marryat and "Jock Scott" had done for Wood, has now done the same service for Dame Juliana herself. Thus, in one volume, McDonald serves today's reader as a guide back to the very beginning of the most voluminous literature ever devoted to any one sport and, in that service, attains the stature of one of its stars—those bright lamps that, in Milton's phrase, nature hung in heaven, to guide the wayworn traveler: in this instance, any man who would know the story of his pastime, his hobby, his addiction, or, in more advanced cases, his mania.

18 · The Boys Upstairs at Manny Wolf's

". . . you cannot please him better at meat than to talk of angling . . ."

"But what do I among hunters?"

The Arte of Angling, 1577

SINCE MOST PEOPLE who fish are forced by climate or by circumstances to spend more months in the year thinking about it than they can possibly hope to spend doing it, any book about fishing enjoys an enormous built-in advantage. For to the passionate fisherman the next best thing to doing it is to read about it. Like General Grant, who knew only two tunes—one was *Yankee Doodle* and the other wasn't—the fisherman is prone to divide all literature into two categories, books that are about fishing and those that aren't. By this rough and ready standard, any book that is becomes vastly preferable to any book that isn't.

I've seen die-hard dry-fly purists, who wouldn't be caught dead in the same county with anybody carrying a spinning rod, wade through volumes about ocean fishing, and commercial fishing at that—trawlers, netting, and things of that sort—just because they were "the only thing I could find about fishing" in the otherwise well-stocked shelves of inns and lodges in trout and salmon country. I feel the same way about talk. I divide all talk into two categories, not large and small, as most people do, but simply talk that is and talk that isn't about fishing. And this is why every Wednesday finds me in a grubby little room, reached by traversing the kitchen, upstairs over Manny Wolf's Restaurant, at Third Avenue and Forty-ninth Street, in New York. The little room is adorned by one small picture of a horse and one large picture, a dubious nude, the kind of painting that would have been too daring for a candy-box cover but would have seemed appropriate over a bar back in the days when women were not otherwise to be seen in barrooms. There is a steel desk, some wooden filing cabinets, a beat-up sofa, and a lunch table set for ten. There may, sometime, have been a Wednesday when the number of places set at the table meshed with the number of lunchers who showed up, but usually the number of places prepared in advance turns out to be wildly inappropriate, attendance usually ranging from a not too infrequent low of three to a seldom-achieved high of nineteen. There are thirty members of record, all supposed to be more than casually connected with hunting and fishing, and in consequence rather more likely than not to be out of Manhattan on almost any given Wednesday.

The only truly regular attendant, for fifty Wednesdays out of the year's fifty-two, is Little Joe, the waiter, a character, and a sort of perpetual understudy to Vince Barnett, of the famous insulting-waiter routine. Little Joe treats everybody alike, except guests, to whom he is polite. Lunch is supposed to be at twelve-thirty, but hardly anybody is ever there by then, not excepting Little Joe.

The little room is the unprepossessing home of an organization so loosely organized as to stretch even a term as elastic as club. It is known, if only to itself, as MTYPA, for Midtown Turf, Yachting & Polo Association. In its own billing this social entity professes to be incorporated, but none of the members has as yet been interested enough to look at the proof that it actually is. The group is far better known, to the readers of Ed Zern's column in *Field & Stream*, where it is so characterized, as The Midtown Rod, Gun, Bloody Mary and Labrador Retriever Society, than it is under its own name or even to most of its members. The readers of *Field & Stream* have long since concluded that the organization is fictional, like the membership of The Lower Forty in Corey

Ford's column in the same magazine, and in many respects they are more than half right.

The members, at last count, numbered thirty, and in journalese, which some of them speak fluently, that is supposed to mean the end. But people are always moving away, to the West Coast, say, or forgetting that they belong, so the little room, which is comfortable for six, adequate for eight, tolerable for ten, and murder for more than twelve at a time, will probably remain as it has been for some time, just about right as a container for the weekly meetings. The days when there are more than a dozen lunchers, the steel desk is turned into a second table, uneasily accommodating four or five, and is sometimes supplemented with cocktail tables, big enough to accommodate two drinks and a small plate of peanuts, but stacked instead with a precarious piling up of the components of two man-sized lunches.

The weekly meetings are not meant to be mere talkfests about rods and guns and dogs, but rather are supposed to be devoted either to the planning and arrangement, or to the subsequent postmortem discussion of, various field meetings, such as hunts and shoots and trials and assorted fishings. It is in the course of such activities that the organization is credited, by dim legend, with having started in the first place. To most of the present members, legend is an even bigger liar than it is normally expected to be, because the only such activities scheduled within memories of reasonable length have drawn an attendance confined entirely to the presence at the ordained scene of the particular member who had been prevailed upon to play host to the group. So the weekly meetings are talkfests, and the subjects are, though not necessarily in that order, rods and guns and dogs. The sublime chance of the seating arrangements, combined with the house-arranged acoustics which muffle everybody's voice but that of Little Joe, which they amplify, results in a complete breakdown of communications among those who want to talk about rods, who are seated between those who want to talk about guns, who are both outflanked and outshouted by those who want to talk about field trials.

There are nineteen steps back down to the kitchen, and another nineteen steps back up, and this is the only precise information ever both clearly imparted and fully understood every Wednesday by every member and guest, because it is announced by Little Joe, every time anybody wants anything that isn't in sight. Everything else that is said is subject to subsequent speculation, as to what it was or even who said it, and it is only lucky that neither is very likely to matter very much. Yet the thing that brings back such members as do come back, every Wednesday, is the realization that some of the best talk to be heard on your choice of the three subjects, is heard every Wednesday among the boys upstairs at Manny Wolf's, and it is worth going back again and again in the hope that sometime you will hear that part of it in which you might conceivably be interested. I always hear every last whisper about either guns or dogs, neither of which interests me, and usually don't catch what I'm sure must be being said about rods at the end of the table where I can't hear anybody but Little Joe on the subject of the nineteen steps.

Just from what I've already told you about him, even if you didn't already know it yourself, you'll have to agree that it would be worth going across town to hear Lee Wulff say anything he might say about rods, won't you? And it is, and he is very faithful in his attendance, on the Wednesdays when he is in New York, and not in Canada, or Florida, or Africa, or Montana, or Alaska, or Scotland, or Maine, or New Hampshire. And because he also shoots, and is very likely to be seated between two shooters, he is more apt to be engaged in answering their questions about such arcane matters as loads and spreads and so on than he is in telling you what you'd like to hear about the Moise or the Miramichi.

But as compared to going, say, to The Council on Foreign Relations, where you know you won't hear a damn word about the Moise or the Miramichi, or even the Mississippi, most likely, isn't it worth broaching the waiting lines downstairs at Manny Wolf's, and dodging waiters with loaded trays as you cross the kitchen, to get upstairs to that unlovely little room, where nobody ever eats or drinks quite what, or as much as, they want, because of those nineteen steps, on the off-chance that, if not Lee Wulff, then anyway somebody may be just back from somewhere, Ernie Schwiebert from Sweden or South America, say, and you might hear something you wouldn't otherwise know, about the fishing somewhere?

It might be Ed Zern, back from fishing with Dave Bascom at West Yellowstone, or Gene Anderegg, just back from Germany, or Art Smith of the *Herald Tribune*, or Oscar Godbout of *The New York Times*, home again from wherever, although you could read either of them for a dime.

More probably, of course, it's Dick Wolters of *Business Week*, our peerless leader and president *per petuum*. (I remember one of my kids once asking me: "Was President Roosevelt always the president of the United States of Amer-

« 258 »

ica?" and when I said no, remarking: "Oh yes, I remember now, when you were a little boy I suppose President *Lincoln* was President of the United States of America.") Dick Wolters hasn't been president since Lincoln, but it seems longer than Roosevelt. Anyway, what he's back from is one of those countless field trials, they must be held daily, about which I've already heard so much more than I ever did care to know. Or maybe it's Jim Rikhoff, of Winchester, or Jim Dee, of Winchester, or John Falk, of Winchester, all dedicated gunners, and I think of Scott Fitzgerald writing to Scottie about paying her bills at Peck & Peck & Peck & Peck. Or maybe it's Rolf Coykendall, of *Guns & Ammo*, or Peter Barrett of *True*, that gunnish magazine, or Jack Simpson of Union Carbide—and don't they have something to do with guns, or anyway ammo?

But I'm unfair. These gun types all seem most ready to talk about fishing, too, whereas it's only nuts like me and maybe John Groth who seem to have a low tolerance for listening too long at any one time to talk about guns and shooting instead of rods and fishing.

John Groth might be there, if he can squeeze it in between a date with his doctor and a date with his health club. Why are all these frantic exercisers such chronic hypochondriacs? But if he's there to talk about any fishing, it's more than likely fishing that I've done with him, and in any case we don't have to cram into that crummy little room at Manny Wolf's to see each other.

There are others of the *Field & Stream* family, such as Clare Conley, the managing editor, and Herman Kessler, the art director, husband of Helen Shaw, that wonder woman already mentioned in connection with her, or their, book on fly-tying, who tied me the only size 28 midges I've ever seen. Clare Conley is queer for literature. Up to his eyebrows all day in the outdoor stuff at *Field & Stream*, when he gets out of the office he'd rather talk about William Burroughs or Norman Mailer or Mary McCarthy, when all I want to talk about is Rat Face McDougall or Hairy Mary or Jock Scott. Oh well, greener pastures.

Herman Kessler professes not to fish. Married to a great fly-tier, and he doesn't fish! He doesn't say he dislikes it, just that he hardly ever does it, which is admittedly a difference, although it could be construed as only one of degree. Dangerous talk, I think, for a *Field & Stream* type, and I wonder if he means it, because it's next thing to playing in the Philharmonic and saying you don't like music.

Some Wednesdays it's one of the three Genes, Gene Brown, Gene Hill, and Gene Smith, though rarely all three at one sitting. Gene Hill is the only one who ever gets what he wants for lunch. The rest of us all have fruit salad, with a wide range of choice from "with cottage cheese" all the way to "with sherbert." But he gets veal parmigiana with spaghetti, maybe because he once told Little Joe that he liked it. Sometimes it's Lawton Carver, though not often, because Pappy has been ailing on and off, though he had us all over to a very V.I.P. lunch at the Coliseum in connection with the sports show, and getting reaccustomed to our little room upstairs after that gave us all the emotional bends, having had no intervening decompression chamber to cushion our return to our familiar austerity. Some Wednesdays it's Sid Latham, or Don Layden—or Buzz Fawcett back from shooting jaguars with a bow and arrow, and wanting to know if somebody won't provide a good home for a nice snake, though seldom now, since he's moved to the West Coast. And it's never Larry Koller, down from Monroe, though he's a member of record, and I wish he would show up now and then, because he wrote one good and useful book, *Taking Larger Trout*, and he's since done a lavish and spectacular *Treasury of Angling*.

Often it's Bob O'Byrne, giving out maps or brochures issued by his *Sportsmen's Vacation Guide*, the project on which he was widowed, as it were, by the death of his partner Ray Camp. Pretty often it's Berni Schoenfield, when he isn't on location photographing something for somebody. Less often it's Dick Wolff, especially since the Garcia Corporation moved its offices across to Jersey. And it's almost never Bob Rose any more, first because he was sick a long time, and then because he moved to Vermont. More frequently seen on these Wednesdays than many of the members are some of the guests, such as Hugh Grey, the editor of *Field & Stream*, and even Al McClane, up from Florida and pausing in town only while poised for flight to somewhere like Austria or Australia.

It used to be Ted Rogowski, nearly every Wednesday, stirring everybody up to do something about what the extension of the Quickway beyond Liberty and Livingston Manor was threatening to do to the Beaverkill, but rarely now since he's set up something of a competing attraction with Tuesday lunches of The Theodore Gordon Flyfishers at the Williams Club. But happily of late it's John McDonald, almost every week, and this gives some much needed tone to the joint, because it's nice to know that however motley the membership may ever be or become, thank God and St. Peter there's at least one real angling scholar in the group.

And it's me, oh Lord, every blessed Wednesday, standing

in the need of prayer, up to my ears in hunters, surrounded by dog breeders and field trialers, outranked by wine experts like Zern and O'Byrne, buying belts that I don't need from Gene Hill, borrowing station wagons that I do from Gene Anderegg, listening to everybody arguing about what should be the next outing, because after all that's how this organization got started, and remembering that nobody showed up for the last one, and wondering, when I think of the infinite riches in a little room that this crazy club does occasionally represent on some odd Wednesdays, in terms of the aggregate of angling knowledge gathered around the table, wondering what? Well, just wondering. In other words, it wonders me.

But, it shouldn't. It's a lot like angling itself, really. So frequent the casts. So seldom a strike.

19 · The Earmarks of Aptitude

This is not a moody work; it keeps a man alive and stirring. Patience, indeed! Wm. Scrope, in Days and Nights of Salmon Fishing in the Tweed, 1843

I never use a leader any finer than necessary, but always try very fine tackle if fish will not rise to my regular leaders. Of course, I lose a lot of fish, but don't I have a good time doing it. E. R. Hewitt, in A Trout and Salmon Fisherman for Seventy-five Years, 1951

IF YOU'VE NEVER FISHED AT ALL . . . oh but that's ridiculous, because in that case you would never have reached this page in this sort of book. So we can't start out that far back. But if you've fished only casually, the kind of fishing that's done only "because it's there," among other things to do in the course of a vacation trip, or if you've never really taken it up, so to speak, but have had "a fishing rod" around the house, just the way you have a lawn mower, or a typewriter, or a spade, or a pair of garden shears—just as one of a number of purely utilitarian objects to which you've never given any special thought and on which you have certainly lavished no special amount of attention or affection, then maybe this chapter marks the spot where you might want to take a sort of mental litmus test, to see whether or not there's anything in all this for you.

If anything said up to this point, by me or by anybody I've quoted, has in any way stirred your interest to the extent of making your hand itch to wrap itself around one of those dinky little fly rods, then here's where we ought to try to check you out, to determine whether you do or don't have the makings of an addict.

Always mindful of Mr. Adamson, who warned you not to be misled by anything I might say about light tackle, it's only fair at this point to give you a chance to get off at the next corner, because if you stay on for the ride through the next chapter, that's where this is very apt to cost you money.

The money part doesn't matter so much. It's the wear and tear on your nerves that I'm thinking of, and also what it might mean to your marriage, eventually if not now. The latter consideration is none of my buttinsky business, I realize, but it's pretty silly, just the same, for me to be so elaborately concerned with the physical well-being of the prospective quarry, the fish—which is a feeling I have several times expressed—without giving at least equal time and thought to the emotional well-being of the putative fisherman.

Patience is one thing you don't need, for instance, though it's the one objection nonfishermen always voice. "Oh, I just wouldn't have the patience." Those are the people who have watched the fishermen from the bridges of Paris, or studied, over a highball and through the picture window of a seaside cottage, the picture of persistence afforded by a lone surf caster. I never have seen one of them catch a fish either, and I don't have the patience to watch until one of them might. As for those types on the Seine, Hemingway said some of them sometimes did, and I've asked some of the second category, and they've assured me that every so often they do.

"Patience, indeed!," as the inimitable Mr. Scrope snorts, you don't need patience to keep at something that is in itself interesting enough to keep you "alive and stirring." Patience is for the still fishers, who sit watching a bobber, while a live bait swims or drifts around beneath it. It is only very occasionally that patience pays off in fly fishing, as in cases where you "create a hatch" by repeated casts over a spot where you just plain know there are one or more fish, and you deliberately enter a contest to see whether they, or you, will first be driven to distraction by your endless casts over that same spot with that same fly. It doesn't always work, by any means, but surprisingly often it does. It had better be a spot where you've taken fish before, and with a fly that has worked there under conditions reasonably comparable to those prevailing at the moment you try the trick, or you'll find that you are wasting their time and your own, and they will outwait you, having more time than you have.

Actually, in my own experience, I find myself consistently outfished by the types who are more restless than I am, who can't stand sticking around in one spot for any appreciable length of time, and can't wait to try the next one. They're right, as a general rule, as it's the first cast that counts most, assuming that it is not a disastrously bad one, in any place where trout are.

Remembering what old Thomas Masaryk said, "Wherever trout are, it's beautiful," I'm all too prone to stick around too long, drinking in the sights and sounds, hearkening to "the voices of the evening," and changing, changing, changing flies. Nineteen times out of twenty, this persistent changing of flies fails to pay off. It's how you present it to them, rather than what you present, that counts most. Changing sizes makes sense, particularly if they've shown some interest in a fly, but not enough to seize it. Dropping to the next size of that same fly is practically mandatory under that circumstance, but otherwise it's almost always better to change locations, rather than to stay rooted as long as I do in the same spot, changing flies.

So patience doesn't count, and too much is a liability. How about rhythm? Do you dance well, and can you remember tunes and identify them readily—that is, so you can tell whether it's a tango or a waltz? Great, because this will help you enormously in your casting, and especially in mastering the double-line haul. I dance like a bear and I'm tone deaf, so I had to learn those things the hard way, lacking any intuitive or instinctive knack for them. A good sense of rhythm, then, while it helps, is certainly by no means essential.

Are you tall and long-legged, the natural tennis-player type, like Lee Wulff? So much the better; his long legs and his reach are both helpful: they enable him to wade out farther and hold his little rod higher. But Mr. Hewitt was small and looked fragile, and Al McClane is built like a toy bulldog and Charlie Ritz always appears unlikely to weather the next stiff breeze that blows in off the Place Vendôme. So, obviously, size is in itself no criterion. John Wise, Jr., a marvelous old fisher, well up in his eighties, looks like one of Washington Irving's dwarfed Catskill bowlers, somehow strayed to the Poconos. But, and maybe this is more to the point, do you tire easily? I must be the reincarnation of a delivery horse, because I seem to be able to walk and stand or wade and balance against a current, hours on end, and still feel ready for more. On the Miramichi I'm up at twenty of five, starting the walk through the woods that will put me on the stream with the first light, and except for hastily grabbed meals (that my mother always said I ate like a dog afraid the dish will be snatched away), I'm out there maneuvering around those rocks and bucking that current until the last light at around twenty of ten. Until my mid-fifties, I never felt a semblance of fatigue from fishing, though I could never stand in an office more than ten minutes without looking for a chair. But then I began to get a localized pain, like a hot knife across the small of my back. A polo belt fixed it fine, and when I don't forget to wear it, I feel no pain. Al McClane tires much more readily than I do. I often noticed it, in Iceland and up at Turnwood. He would never fish more than a third to a half the time that I would. But he's got talent, which is more than an equalizer for my stamina. On weekends when I might take a hundred trout in two days, and people who are always quantity-minded anyway would comment on it, Al might have taken eighty. But he'd have done it in a tenth of the time, just because he wouldn't fish very long at any one session, and second because when he did he always had to spend so much of his fishing time helping other people correct their faults—at their request, of course—or explaining how he did certain things. So I could always point out the necessity to put in a corrective factor, as they do after yacht races, based on Al's known and often proved ability to outfish me at an absolutely predictable ratio of six to one.

But that brings up another factor. Are you competitive? Do you like to gamble? Then stay the hell away from this kind of fishing, there's not a thing in it for you. Go out on the party boats, where they have a pool at a dollar a head for the first fish caught, biggest fish caught, most fish caught, and so on. Because if you really give a good goddamn about who catches what, and especially if you particularly care whether or not that "who" is you, then this is the wrong kind of fishing for you entirely. To enjoy this, you've got to be temperamentally inclined to say, and to feel, and to honestly mean, that some of the best times you've had fishing are times when you didn't touch a fish. You've got to be able to say, with Hermann Deutsch: "I do this for the fishing, not for the fish." What is this, you ask, some sort of Zen? Well, yes, in a queer 'tis and 'tain't sort of way it is, because the idea of the thing becomes, after a while, a lot more important than the thing in itself. If you're interested enough in what you're doing, you really don't need applause, and you know that in most instances the applause is at the wrong time and for the wrong things. And fish, despite what monkeys they can often make of us, are not really very intelligent. They're dumb creatures, even dumber than people, and it's easy to find out how people are.

PEOPLE: Well, where are the fish?
YOU: Never keep 'em.
PEOPLE: Hah! Hey, wait—look—he ain't even got a creel!
YOU: No, I put 'em back.
PEOPLE: Put 'em back! Whatja do that for? What was the matter with 'em?
YOU: I hope to go back and catch them again.
PEOPLE: Yeah? What are ya, some kinda nut?

So while the applause of fish is much more meaningful than that of people, it isn't all-important, either.

Sometimes some of the fishing you will be doing will be just too good for the fish. I know that sounds fatuous, even as I say it. But it isn't as crazy as it may seem, because the thing you have to remember about this fishing, first and foremost, is that in it the fish is not so much your quarry as your partner.

He can't know that, of course, but in that you have every intention of catching him, but none of keeping him, the play between you really is a sort of partnership. And there are times, whether in bridge or business or in this fishing, when your partner can't for the life of him figure out what you're up to. Let's take a more or less random instance. Suppose you have diagnosed the situation as that classic one that was expressed this way by the Earl of Buxton: "There is the 'smutting' fish,

greedily taking down the tiniest of insects, and utterly oblivi-
ous of your finest cast and smallest fly . . ." So you try your
finest cast—meaning leader tippet, of course, and it's probably
.0040 if it's the German Platyl or .0039 if it's the French
Tortue, and thirty to forty inches of that as the terminal point
of your leader is really pretty fine stuff. And you try tiny
midges, size 20 and maybe 22, and try to keep them neither
on nor really in the water, but half way between, in the surface
film, because that seems to be where those smutting fish are
doing their steady taking.

Nothing happens, so you try little nymphs, also 20 and 22,
gray ones and black ones and maybe cream and maybe yellow, and these swing just below the surface film, and then
you retrieve them, very carefully, hand weaving line. The fish
go right on feeding, paying no attention to your nymphs, any
more than they did to your midges. So now you get out some
tiny dries, some of them just little puffs of hackle, variants
with no wings, and some with minuscule wings, delicate, di-
aphanous, and translucent, also in 20's and 22's, and so exquisitely made that you're half ready to bite at them yourself.
You spray them with fly dope, in the case of the winged ones,
or just touch them with the least dot of silicote line dressing,
in the case of the variants, so they ride right up on top of the
water, like microscopic sailboats. You let the winged ones
float, free of drag, on a slack line, which you mend carefully
each time you sense that it's about to drag. On the variants
you give an occasional six-inch twitch, treating them like
miniature versions of the Neversink skater.

So what happens? Maybe, this time, not a damn thing.
Those stupid fish go right on feeding on whatever it is they're

feeding on, and paying you and your offerings not the least mind. Or, maybe once or twice in a season, what happens is that a twenty-incher grabs your size 20 variant, and despite the slenderness of your leader, which you think your very breathing is going to break, you manage to hang onto him to the point where, holding him very carefully, you succeed in removing your little fly from his jaw and putting him back, no worse, if somewhat wiser for the workout. More often, maybe four or five times as often, what happens is that a fish like that takes, breaks, and is gone. But still, he's paid your casting performance a lovely tribute, before he up and left.

But this time nothing happens. Not a thing. They just go right on feeding. Are you downhearted, disheartened, or discouraged? Not in the slightest, because you know that the very fact that they are still feeding, and that in running through your entire repertoire of selections of *minutae*, casting tiny flies on a slender tippet, you have not once goofed: you have not "lined" them, you have not "birdnested" your leader; in other words, you have done nothing to put them down or scare them away and make them stop feeding.

You don't need their applause. The hell with them. You know you've just put on a very fine show, and you don't need them, or anybody, to tell you so. You know that, other times and other places, this has worked, and will again. This just happens to be one time and one place where it didn't.

And if, before you've left the vicinity, some oaf with a worm or a minnow or a cluster of salmon eggs comes along and without style or finesse plops his live bait in and pulls out one or more of those same stupid fish, you're perfectly ready and willing to applaud his performance, because he doesn't know any better, and if you didn't you'd appear to be jealous or envious and a poor sport. He takes away whatever fish he catches, and it's just as well, because his way of hooking them, on his live bait, would have harmed them irreparably, if it even had occurred to him to put them back, whereas your way they would have been so slightly lipped, or caught in the corner of the jaw, as to be unharmed. So your fishing *was* too good for them, and it's a pity they couldn't have realized it, and played with you, instead of succumbing to somebody who plays for keeps.

But you have every reason to be proud of it, and if it's any satisfaction to you to do a thing that's hard to do, and do it well, then you've just had a very satisfactory session with your light tackle, and the fact that you didn't once goof, as shown by the fact that you didn't put them down, should really rank this particular session higher in your memory book, though it probably won't, than if you had taken one or two fish and then made some such horrendous blunder as to scare away all the rest.

Is it still too Zennish? Of course the object of the game is to catch, or to try to catch, some fish. But that isn't the only object, nor is it even the most important object, of the game. The key word is "try." If you made the kind of try that is, in itself, something of a triumph to bring off successfully, which, of course, you just did, then it outranks by a wide margin some other fishing session, your own or anybody else's, in which success was achieved without really trying, or at any rate without anything like such a hard try. If you've come along through all this apparent quibble over the *idea* of the thing being more important than the thing in *itself*, then we ought to be about ready to tell each other that what seems to distinguish this kind most from all others is that this is the thinking men's kind of fishing, and I guess we would if it didn't sound so damned pompous.

So let's back away from the philosophy and the ratiocination and all that, lest this subject get too sicklied-over with the pale cast of thought. Let's try a different tack entirely, and let's forget whether you're big or little, young or old, sturdy or frail, since none of those considerations seems to be a truly valid determinant in any case. Just think of Hewitt and La Branche and Skues and old Izaak himself, all fishing until they were ninety. Do you go in for hobbies? Or have you ever collected anything? This may get us to the point faster than any other line of inquiry. If your hobbies have had anything to do with nature, that's probably a plus. Still, if you're a frantic butterfly chaser, you probably don't need another mania, so let's leave you with your nets and bottles and whatever you use, and feel that we're leaving well enough alone. But if you've ever made things, like model airplanes, or ship models, or models of cars, any of those things where pesky niggling bits and pieces of minute detail have had an important role, then you're probably a prime prospect for a full-fledged case of this particular addiction, and you may wind up not merely making your own leaders, but your own flies, with a light over a magnifying glass in some cluttered corner you can call your own, and you may eventually make them all the way down past size 28 and even, *mirabile dictu*, unto size 30. And I will tip my hat and call you mister.

And on the collecting side? If you've gone in for collections of milk glass or matchbook covers, or campaign buttons, or school and college pennants, I just somehow have the feeling that you wouldn't be happy with all this. But if you've collected stamps—and had to monkey with tweezers and little glassine hinges and things of that sort—or books, and you got to the point where you had to have copies of the edition that did have the single misprint on page 97, as well as those that didn't, and complete runs of prior printings ahead of the first edition in book form, or limited editions so limited that they were confined to a few copies only for interstate trade or copyright purposes, well, hell, you're in, and you will probably be or become our peerless leader.

It helps if you like gadgets and gadgetry, but this is not an unmixed attribute. You may be too crazy for the latest thing, and the marvels, in that respect, are all on the other side, and it's the wrong side, you understand, among the paraphernalia of spinning. That's how spinning, for a while, lured away some otherwise worthy and honorable fly fishermen, from about 1947 through 1949, although the worthiest of them have since come back, sheepish and chastened, never to stray again.

Probably a better sign is a tendency toward go-without-ism. If you haven't worn rubbers or overshoes since you were ten, and can't remember when you last wore the tops to any underwear, and can't be bothered with gloves, you're probably a prospect. In this kind of fishing, it goes without saying, you don't carry a creel, because you have no use for it, and you don't carry a landing net, because that makes it too easy. Conversely, you do tend to carry more flies than you need, and extra spools with alternate lines and leaders for whichever reel you happen to be using, and you may even, after either enough years or enough operations, be ready to accept the burden of a wading stick, because you don't mind doing the wading an easier way, and particularly if it aids you to do the fishing itself the hard way.

If you like doing things the hard way, you'll like this. One excellent sign is preferring, as a means of diversion, sailboats over powerboats. Liking handmade music, as opposed to mechanical, is a good sign. Liking originals rather than imitations or copies or facsimiles is another. So is liking to drive, and especially liking to shift gears. And if you thrill to the sound of an Alfa Romeo, it's almost certain that you will respond to the whirr-into-whine of a Hardy reel, one of the nicest noises ever made by mechanical means, and you will avoid like the plague the models with the silent check that have "improved" all that beauty out of them.

What you're headed for, it seems, if you go in for this kind of fishing, is something that may have its origin in sport, but is immediately transmogrified into being equally a hobby, a collection, and a creed. So the mere fact that you're "interested in sports" may be no asset at all, particularly if you mean spectator sports, as opposed to participant sports. If it's the former, the chances are overwhelming that this would bore you blind. So maybe you ought to think it over, at this point, and maybe you ought to cut out here, and not go on to the next chapter. On the other hand, if you have to think it over, then that's as good a way as any of knowing that this is not for you.

20 · Counting Tackle Instead of Sheep

VIATOR: *I have been an angling all night in my dreams . . .*
PISCATOR: *Ney, then you will prove to be an angler indeed.*
The Arte of Angling, 1577

SUNT ORNAMENTA MEA, these are my jewels, said Cornelia in the picture in our beginning Latin book, forever ago, pointing to her two sons, manly little fellows too, for all that their small togas looked like nightgowns. It was the third page in the primer, each page of which had a line of Latin beneath a picture. It came right after the picture of a sailor squaring off with his hands raised in a manner suggesting that he was a sucker for a left hook, captioned merely *Nauta pugnat*, and was followed by a scene showing a farmer's daughter throwing grain from a tray to a flock of chickens, underlined by the legend: *Puella dat cenam gallinis*. Now maybe that's what you'll say when you—huh? oh the first picture wasn't very interesting. Just a bearded bumpkin pushing a plow, which read *Galba est agricola*. But to get back to Cornelia. Maybe that's what you'll say, some fine day about your reels: these are my jewels.

That's what they really are, too, the fine reels for trout and salmon, and if you start this as a sport and then get addicted to the degree that it has aspects of a hobby and a collection, you'll find yourself acquiring reels first because you need them, second because you enjoy them enough, as objects interesting in themselves, to start fooling and fussing with them, oiling them and greasing them, and wiping them with gun cloths, and indulging in a certain amount of fondling them, and almost without realizing it you wake up to the fact that you're collecting them, and that you have, indeed, quite a collection. Reels come to mind first because in the old days fly fishermen tended to low-rate them, lavishing all their attention on their rods and lines and flies, and dis-missing the reel's function, in fly fishing, as "merely a con-venient place to store your line," on the assumption that in the actual playing of the fish you could be bringing the line in by hand, as the logical follow-through of the same finger-weaving, or stripping-in of the line done on the retrieve, rather than reeling him in. Hence the traditional Cinderella status of the reel among the implements of fly fishing.

But on short light rods, even for larger trout and of course for grilse and salmon, since you're almost always going to let the fish run, the natural thing is to get all the line up onto the reel, from the loose coils in which it has been lying on the water or on the ground, as of the moment the fish was hooked, before you start playing him, and then you play him on the reel, and reel him in with your left hand, with the reel above the rod rather than below it. It's like the English and Continental way of eating, with your knife and fork kept in the same hands as you eat, rather than our way of laying the knife down and transferring the fork from left hand to right, between the cutting and the eating of each mouthful. Trout and even salmon fishermen over here used to fish the way we still eat, with that inefficient transfer of the rod from right hand for casting to left hand for reeling, just like our silly exchanging of hands with our forks. That's out, with the small light rod. You've got enough to do, with big fish on a midge rod, to make it wise to forego any waste motions, and any fish above eleven inches is a big fish on a midge.

You put the backing and line on *clockwise* over the spool (regarding the reel's face, where the handle is, as the face of the clock), so when the fish is on and the reel is up above the rod, you reel in by turning the handle toward you, in the natural way, although when you're casting, the reel is below the rod. There's a reason for this. Since you cast many many many times more often than you reel in a fish, but the strain on the rod is more prolonged when you're playing a fish than when you're making a cast, it tends to equalize the stresses on the two sides of your rod, if you do all your casting with the rod held one way and all your reeling with the rod held the other way. It's the best insurance you can carry against acquiring a "set" in the rod. Also there's an added safety factor. Since you are using lighter lines on the featherweight rods than you would be using on conventionally heavy tackle, you're much better off with the line rewound upon the reel rather than lying loose around you. Even the best lines tend, in the lighter weights, to snarl up into loops and knots more. readily than the heavier ones, and it's a hell of a way to lose a fish, as well as a hazard to the health of your first rod guide, to have one of those snarls jerked up onto the rod in the run of the fish. So, since you're going to be using the reel a lot more with the light rod, even in fishing for trout, it acquires first-line importance in the prospective inventory of your light tackle.

Most fly fishermen, in the past, had more rods of different sizes than reels. In light tackle, since you're going to be using an ultra-light rod for different kinds of fishing, you'll want different sizes of reels, to equip the same rod for different kinds of fish. The simplest way to do this, of course, is to get reels with extra spools, so you can carry the different sizes more handily than if you had to carry a separate whole reel for each different combination of line and backing. Good reels are expensive, especially in the light of the old-timer's attitude that for fly fishing just about any old reel will do. But even the best ones cost a lot less than comparable rods, so you can afford more reels than rods more readily than the reverse.

Besides, the money side of all this is something we really should have got out of the way in the last chapter, when we were attempting the checking-out process as a sort of prerequisite to this chapter. So let's consider, again, what the pursuit of a hobby means. It may be anything from collecting books or stamps or old coins to building scale models of one thing or another. Whatever it is, once the bug has bitten the hobbyist, it puts a whole new set of values on both the time and the money that he devotes to it. He's doing it only for the fun there is in it, ninety-nine cases out of a hundred, but he will take in stride hours and days and nights spent in work and study connected with it, and dollars out of pocket, either of which would have him yelling Uncle if he were compelled to the expenditure by anything other than his own awakened interest.

Work that's fun and fun that's work—they're all one if the desire is there that drives the man like one possessed. Remove the one element of fun, and the rest is only toil, sweat, and drudging. Then you get out of the classification of things a guy does because he wants to, into the dreary area of things we all do only because we can't get out of them. Most fun involves pursuits that aren't really necessary, which is probably a large part of their attraction. Certainly the fisherman, and undoubtedly the yachtsman and the hunter too, often finds himself in situations possessing the common denominator of "I wouldn't do this for a thousand dollars and here I am doing it for nothing." The craze for a hobby, the collecting bug, and the passionate pursuit of a sport are alike in that, once men get bitten by them, they find all their standards of value vastly altered. The same man who will scream blue murder at paying fifty dollars for a new lawn mower that he honestly doesn't want but knows he needs will blithely part with two to three times that much for a new fly rod that he needs somewhat less than a hole in the head, but wants like crazy. Both objects are manmade, but one fires the imagination as the other doesn't.

To get involved in this fishing only to the extent required by the absolute essential for its pursuit as a sport, you could be adequately equipped at an outlay of from $100 to $300. To indulge yourself to the hobby degree would probably involve from three to six times as much. Beyond that, when you get to the collector's level, it can easily run to the cost of a luxury car, a spread of say $6,000 to $16,000. We might confine ourselves to the first two levels, because by the time you've achieved the hobby stage, you wouldn't need any guidance or advice, from me or anybody else, to go on from there to the collector's stage.

It's easy to tell, quite apart from such a mundane consideration as keeping track of the money you've spent, when you've passed from the first stage, of equipping yourself adequately for the pursuit as a sport, to the second stage, the degree of addiction that gives you the status of hobbyist. It's like the study of a foreign language; you're a beginner until the first time you dream in it. That's the end of the beginning. You've reached it, in this fishing, when you find yourself counting tackle instead of sheep, nights when you're trying to get to sleep. The first time you start saying off your tackle inventory to yourself, that's the sign that your degree of interest has reached the hobby stage. Of course, there are guys who count women instead of sheep, and I've nothing against that except perhaps on the purely pragmatic ground that I wouldn't think it would be a particularly soporific thing to do. But it is comforting to reflect that this hobby, even if pursued to the collection level, can't possibly be as expensive as women, or horses, or backing plays, or even starting magazines, except that all of those are subject to Morgan's Law on yacht ownership, in that if you have to consider how much they cost, you know you can't afford them.

What do you get, within the limits indicated for the first two degrees of involvement, and where do you get it? If you're going to try this out for the minimum investment, which is $100, you start by sending the first dollar to Norm Thompson, 1805 N. W. Thurman, Portland, 97209, for a copy of *Norm Thompson's Angler's Guide*. This makes sense for three reasons: first, because you need something in the way of a book that will show you how to tie your tippets on, and attach your leader to your line, and give you the diagrams of various casts, including the double-line haul, and you won't find one for a dollar anywhere else; second, because it is also a catalogue of the widest selection of the right fly-fishing tackle offered by any single retailer anywhere; and third, while it won't tell everything you need to know ultimately, or offer you every item in the field of light tackle that you might eventually want, it won't tell you anything you'll ever have to unlearn, nor will it offer you, at any price, anything you'll ever feel you've outgrown, or regret and want to discard. So spending the first dollar this way is almost tantamount to getting an insurance policy, for a one-dollar premium, against spending that first hundred dollars foolishly.

Norm Thompson handles fly-fishing tackle exclusively and

they carry all the best items, including Hardy reels, lines, and rods, as well as rods by H. L. Leonard, Charles Ritz (Pezon & Michel), Orvis, Thomas, Winston, Horgard of Norway, and Phillipson; lines by Scientific Anglers and Cortland; and flies by Cooper, Don Gapen, Dan Bailey, Wayne Buszek, Ramona Bressler, Dick Alf, and Jack Dennis, Jr. About the only thing you could ask for that they don't stock is a Paul Young rod or a Payne, and the former omission is due only to the fact that they couldn't get the necessary quantity production after Paul Young's death. As for a Payne rod, you can always get that, along with other things you'll be wanting, from Abercrombie & Fitch, when you reach the hobby stage.

Right now the problem is how to sail past that embarrassment of riches to select an adequate outfit for $100, if only to prove that it can be done. It isn't easy, but here's how I'd do it: Saving the delights of bamboo for later, I'd start with their Phillipson Uniglas Midge Fly Rod outfit, comprised of a true midge at 6 feet and 1¾ ounces that is the nearest thing to bamboo to date, fitted with a Pflueger Medalist 1494 reel, and a white, floating, torpedo-tapered nylon HCF line and fifty yards of backing, four Gladding tapered knotless leaders with 5X and 6X tippets, and eighteen midge flies on 16 and 18 hooks, three each of Adams, Blue Dun, and Royal Coachman. These components list at an aggregate of $65 but are offered in combination at $49.50, so counting the dollar spent for the copy of *Norm Thompson's Angler's Guide*, there's another $49.50 left to spend. I'd order an extra spool for the reel at $3.25, and on it I'd put a Cortland sink-tip torpedo taper nylon-dacron HDF line at $12.50, and 150 yards of 15 lb. test braided nylon backing line, and I'd also order an extra 100 yards of the backing, making $7.50 worth at $1.50 per 50 yards. Three thick butt knotted tapered nylon 1X leaders at $2.00 would complete this part of the order, adding $25.25 to the $49.50 already earmarked for the midge rod outfit and the dollar for the *Angler's Guide*, and leaving me $24.75 to spend for flies.

I'd spend it on an assortment of 9 Muddler Minnows, including two weighted ones, sizes 4 to 10, at $4.50; the Al McClane assortment of eight dry flies, comprised of Adams, Light Cahill, brown bivisible, and Quack Royal Coachman (hair wing), each pattern in sizes 12 and 14, at $3.50; an assortment of six Cooper Nymphs, consisting of one each, size 10, of Stone Fly Creeper, March Brown Creeper, Little May Creeper, Dark Hendrickson, Light Cahill, and Grub, at $3.00; and an assortment of eight Wooly Worms, sizes 6 and 8, at $2.50. This would give me a selection of thirty-one flies, from 4 to 14, to supplement the eighteen flies on sizes 16 and 18 already included with the midge rod outfit.

Then I'd order two Tenite unbreakable-plastic compart-mented fly boxes at $1.55 each, to fit in the two lower pockets of a Tac-L-Apron at $6.95, in the center of the three upper pockets of which I'd carry the extra spool for the reel, putting three spools of platyl in 4X, 5X, and 6X—which I'd also order, at 35 cents each—in one of the other upper pockets, leaving me the third for cigarettes and lighter.

Totaling up, I'd realize—boing!—that I was now a nickel over the $100 limit that was set beforehand. And although that first $100 went awfully fast, still it was very well spent. It achieved only an austerity level of outfitting, true; but the proportions allocated to flies, leaders, lines, reels, and rod are about right for a proper balance of spending as you go on acquiring more tackle. Meanwhile, although this outfit would not make any of the boys at Keener's Pool on the Beaverkill turn enviously green when they saw it, you would get fish with it, just about any time when you or anybody else were destined to get any, and none of it would be in any way substandard.

You'd take the rod out on the lawn, cast as far as you could with it, and then, allowing about ten feet more for future possible improvement in your casting, cut the line off at that point. That is, in addition to the forty-five feet or so of line that you've laid out, just to pull out another ten feet, and then cut the line off at the reel. Add backing, so that on each spool you have 150 yards, which will fill up the reel, leaving just enough room for your truncated line and your leader. Put the thick butt 9-foot leader on each line, and extend it by about four to five feet, cannibalizing the other leaders to add a quick taper down to the size where you can have the last thirty inches or so as your tippet of 4X for the larger wooly worms and muddlers, 5X for the nymphs and the size 12 dry flies, and 6X for the 14, 16, and 18 sizes. In general, casting your leader by hand will best determine when a leader is balanced to suit you best, but you ought to try to get accustomed to maintaining a total length of leader that is from 2½ to 3 times the length of your rod, in other words, from 15 to 18 feet for a 6-foot rod. There's no sense in casting a longer leader than you can manage to turn over cleanly in the air and lay down on the water without "bird-nesting," so you may have to start out with a total leader length of around ten feet and just try to master longer lengths as quickly as you can. With the assortment of leaders and tippets indicated, you can experiment with practice until you find you are managing the desired length.

For about $200 you could make the rod a Hardy Midge, 6 feet at 1⅞ ounces, for $67.50, with a Hardy L. R. H. Lightweight reel at $27, and two extra spools at $11 each, with a number 2 Corona silk line (equivalent to IEI) at $19.50 for the third spool, using the white floater and the sink tip for the other two spools, as in the first outfit. You would be adding approximately $80 to the rod, reel, and line elements, but of course you would be getting a third spool and line and backing. You would have to add another $5 for a line dryer, as you should never leave a silk line on a reel wet, so that's an additional $85. The other $15 or so would get you a wider assortment of flies, as follows: six Lee Wulff flies, one each of Grisly, White, and Royal Wulff in size 10 and 12, for $2.50; ten assorted Dick Alf flies, from size 8 to 16, including bivisibles and variants and a semi-streamer wet fly, at $5.00; an assortment of six "old faithful" dry flies, size 12 and 14, consisting of Light and Dark Cahill and Quill Gordon, at $3.35; and an assortment of six streamerettes, the small streamers worked out by Sam Slaymaker II and John Wise, Jr., comprising Gray Ghost, Little Rainbow, Black Nosed Dace, Summer Gold, Edson Tiger Dark, and White Cargo, all size 10, at $5.00, for an added total of $15.85. That would make a beautiful outfit, including as it does both the Hardy reel and the Hardy Corona silk line, a sweet combination. As for the rod, Hardy's version of the Midge, while running three inches shorter and an eighth of an ounce heavier than the classic original by Paul Young, is the closest thing to it, in its action, its combination of suppleness and backbone, and its versatile adaptability to different line and leader set-ups, from the most delicate trout to intermediate salmon, that I have yet found.

Still within the range of choice offered by Norm Thompson, for between $250 and $300, you could get a 6-foot Winston, a hollow-built bamboo rod of tremendous power, weighing almost 2 ounces, for $100. Or for $135 you could get the Leonard Baby Catskill 6-foot rod, weighing between 1½ and 1¾ ounces, and including, unlike any of the three previously mentioned, an extra tip. And, still within the $300 limit, you could add the rest of the Norm Thompson fly assortment to round out your "get-started" outfit.

Actually, once you get started, you'll branch out quickly to a point where you won't be getting all you want from any one supplier, and you'll want a half dozen catalogues, at least, from which to order. There will be certain things that only this one offers, and certain others that only that one does. But by way of getting started, and particularly if you want to limit your initial tackle investment to under $300, you couldn't get off to a better or safer start than by making your initial selection from the *Norm Thompson Angler's Guide*, both in rods and in fly assortments. The assortments are a good way to start because they enable you to find out quickly which types and patterns of flies work particularly well for you. You won't be burdened with a lot on hand of the ones that don't, and you will soon be getting quantities of those that develop into your favorites. I buy my Hewitt nymphs and my "bicuspids," the Cahill bivisible spider, from

William Mills & Son, Inc., 21 Park Place, New York, by
lots of six and seven dozen, leading my wife, who apparently
confuses the place with the Mills Hotel, to think it's some
kind of bargain basement. It's anything but, which she would
soon realize if she saw the bills, but for once I was smart
enough to arrange to have them sent to the office instead of
home.

Mills is the oldest American establishment dealing in fishing tackle exclusively, and looks it. The store front has
obviously had no attention, beyond painting, in a dark shutter green, since 1875. That was when the female line of
succession in the family of the original founders of 1822,
T. & J. Bate, brought the name of Mills on to the establishment's shingle for the first time, William Mills having been
the son-in-law of Thomas H. Bate. His son, in turn, combined
the two names as Thomas Bate Mills. Until very recently
their catalogue looked as old-fashioned as their storefront and
fixtures, but within the last couple of years it has taken on
a new look, and has added attractions like articles by such
okay modernists as Ernie Schwiebert and Ray Ovington. Up
until the late fifties it grudgingly acknowledged the existence
of such a newfangled thing as nylon by referring to it as
"imitation gut," and it still proudly features gut leaders,
stained according to Mr. Hewitt's patent, and gut tippets
down to .004, which is 8X by genuine gut measure. Until
very recently it also gave prominent display to snelled flies,
which is about like featuring Congress gaiters.

But although you have to know your way around in select-
ing from all the clutter of the outmoded and the extraneous,
such as bait and salt-water items, to say nothing of a host of

spinning and casting lures, some gems are to be found only at Mills, and they are to be cherished. Mills has, for instance, the very best wading shoes of anybody anywhere, made all over of chrome leather (and not just the vamps of leather and the rest of canvas, which are subject to mildew and giving out at the creases, like everybody else's), and you can order them either with felt or hobnailed soles and heels, or (which I prefer) with felt soles and hobnailed heels. They are imported from England and, as usual with English shoes, although they cost about twice as much, they are actually cheaper because they wear about five times as long. The other unique Mills item is their fishing shirt which is marvelous for warm weather when you don't want to be encumbered with a vest or a Tac-L-Pak. It has three breast pockets and a rod-holding strap in front, a big bellows pocket opening on both sides in back, for storing your rain shirt, lunch, etc., and pockets in each sleeve above the elbow. It's around $15 and the shoes are around $30. Mills also carries, for around $15 a Leonard bamboo wading staff, which is the cheapest way there is of attaining that heady point when you can claim to have some H. L. Leonard item among your angling impedimenta. They feature, of course, all the Leonard rods, since they long ago took over the original Leonard firm. The range includes A. H. E. Wood's "greased line" rods from 10½ to 13 feet and 10 to 14½ ounces (Mr. Wood was such a bear of a man he could handle them with one hand), and goes on all the way up to rods for Norway and Sweden to 14 feet long and weighing 23 to 25 ounces. One other long-exclusive Mills distinction, although—as of early 1965—due soon to be shared with Abercrombie & Fitch, is the Walker hand-made salmon reel, featuring a wonderfully smooth progressive brake (like a fifteen-speed gearbox on a truck), made by Arthur L. Walker and his son Archie, at Hempstead, Long Island.

Other "must" catalogues are those of Charles F. Orvis Co., Manchester, Vermont; Abercrombie & Fitch, at Madison Avenue and 45th Street, "where the blazed trail crosses the boulevard," in New York (and Chicago, San Francisco, Colorado Springs, Short Hills, Hyannis, Bay Head, Southhampton, Palm Beach, and Sarasota—in other words, all over, man and boy, summer or winter, the greatest sporting-goods store in the world, with prices to match, but they do turn up with an occasional exclusive, made just for them, by somebody like Hardy, so you can't afford to be without their catalogue); and, of course, last though really foremost for this kind of fishing, Paul H. Young Co., 23800 West Eight Mile Road, Detroit, Michigan. The only reason for mentioning them last is that a new catalogue hasn't been issued since Paul's death, and there's always the chance that they might have run out of them entirely by the time you write for one. The situation is further complicated by the fact that their wonderful woman fly-tyer, whom Paul had broken in over thirty years ago, at last report had left. She was a genius. Once she tied three dozen flies for me while I waited, and I didn't have to wait long, in the course of a quick call I paid Martha Marie and Jack when I was between other appointments in Detroit on business. So even if you manage to lay hands on a Young catalogue, I can only hope that by the time you do, they will be in a position to supply all the items that it lists, because some of them really are indispensable.

The Orvis catalogue was for many years the best of all, until Norm Thompson came along, and it's still the best free catalogue to be had. Their range of selections for this kind of fishing is splendid, and while Orvis rods are featured by both Abercrombie & Fitch and Norm Thompson, neither of them stocks such superb Orvis specialties as their *one-piece* Superfine rod, 6 feet long and weighing in at 1⅞ ounces, a gorgeous stick and "all wood" because it has no ferrule. It sells for $110 and while it's a damned nuisance to transport, every time you go fishing, unless you have some place where you can leave your tackle all season long, it's almost worth the extra bother, because it's such a joy to use. In recent seasons, when what I first thought was a grilse turned out to be a salmon, I've caught myself indulging in such a faithless and unworthy thought as being glad I had it on my Orvis Superfine instead of my old original Paul Young Midge. Orvis makes what they now call a Midge, too, although it is the equivalent of what in the Paul Young line is known as the Martha Marie, 7½ feet and 3⅝ ounces. If you're going that big, I'd rather have the Martha Marie, myself, in the featherweight version, with spaced skeleton cork grip, two-band reel seat and heat-treated aluminum ferrules, which brings its weight down to 3.05 ounces. But in addition to the full line of Hardy lightweight reels, ranging from the Flyweight at 2½ inch diameter and at 2⅜ ounces on up to the new St. Aidan at 3¾ inches and 6 ounces, and a superb selection of lines, Orvis has a better selection of flies than anybody else. They offer the best range of all types, that is, and in the 18 to 22 sizes the best of anybody except Paul Young. They carry Lew Oatman's Darters, Lee Wulff's Stone Fly as well as his original hair wing dry flies in both trout and salmon sizes, Jassids and midges, and also both Ed Koch's midge and terrestrial assortments.

Because Duckie Corkran of Orvis is a golf nut, whereas Peter Alport of Norm Thompson is a maniac for fly-fishing equipment only, the Orvis catalogue carries a lot of golf items, as well as pages devoted to decorative items and jewelry featuring fish and game-bird motifs. It is also replete with both spinning and salt-water tackle, whereas the Norm Thompson catalogue sticks strictly to the subject at hand. Still, the Abercrombie & Fitch catalogue ranges even further afield, and in both instances you are not obliged to read those extraneous pages, although it is annoying to have to plow through so many of them on the lookout for things that do pertain to this kind of fishing.

One puzzlement is that since Garcia Corporation took over the J. W. Young English fly reels, Pridex, Beaudex and Landex, Orvis doesn't carry them any more; Abercrombie & Fitch does have them in stock, at least in their New York store, but doesn't feature them in their catalogue, so if you want one you'll probably have to check with Garcia Corporation, Alfred Avenue, Teaneck, New Jersey, to see where you can get it. For salmon the Landex has a wonderful feature, a free-stripping release that gives the fish line when you don't have sense enough to do so yourself. It has often saved me salmon I would have lost when they made unexpected runs just as I was busily reeling them in. Charlie Ritz hates them, and I will concede that he has a point, because they do have one unfortunate feature, in that the base bar is screwed, rather than riveted, to the spool case, with the unfortunate consequence that it is very likely to start to wiggle and wobble on your rod when a sufficiently vigorous salmon, or even grilse, becomes cantankerous. But nothing's perfect, and I treasure four Landexes, in three sizes, 3½, 3¾, and 4 inch diameters, and simply try to remember to carry a small screwdriver, to tighten up the bar every so often, whenever I'm using one of them. Rod varnish on the screws would help.

The Paul Young catalogue is, or maybe I should say was, since unfortunately there isn't a new one every season as with the others, an abiding joy, and I suppose if you can lay hands on one you ought to cherish it like a first folio. Paul's motto for it was "More Fishing—Less Fussing," and I never could see the sense of that: anybody who is willing to fool around with minute flies, gossamer tippets, and slender rods must be fuss-prone to begin with. Almost every page reflects Paul's personality, and about every tenth page there's some kind of crack about the ignorance or awkwardness or general ineptness of most people. Paul also went into more detail about the heat treatment and the protective coating of Bakelite and Zylol, and the mitering and tapering of the hexagonal sections of his rods, than the average casual user would care to try to follow. It is apparent throughout the catalogue, that Paul lived and dreamed fly rods for fifty years, and the descriptions of the characteristics of the different rods are positively loving. The Young featherweight rods range from the Midge at 6 feet 3 inches and 1¾ ounces and the Perfectionist at 7½ feet and 2½ ounces and the Driggs at 7 feet 2 inches and 2⅞ ounces to the Martha Marie, in its featherweight version, at 7½ feet and 3.05 ounces. They are all ridiculously underpriced, at $98 for the Midge, and $100 for each of the other three, as they are all full equals in every way, and in my own judgment superior to other custom-made bamboo rods priced as high as $159. But the price is more or less academic, since the big question is whether you can get delivery on them. The only way to know is to write Martha Marie or Jack Young, and offer to line up and take your turn.

The Young flies are probably as big a problem to obtain as the rods, but if you can get them they are worth waiting for. If you can't, I don't know how you're going to get along without some of them. For that matter, I don't know how I am either, because my own stock, while large, is certainly not inexhaustible, if I'm lucky enough to get to fish another three decades, until I'm ninety. The dry-fly special assortment, two dozen midges in all shades and types, from size 16 to 24, comes in a plastic box for about $10, as does the special nymph offer, an assortment of nymphs and small streamers for $3.50.

The Muddler Minnows and the Jassids you can get at Orvis or at Abercrombie, but where you're going to get some of the other Young flies I don't know, unless you tie them yourself, which maybe you can but I'm long since resigned to the fact that I can't. But the Strawman nymph, for instance, what to do about that? That was Paul's own creation, and although admittedly aided by a small Colorado spinner, it took the largest trout ever taken on the Letort—fifteen and one half pounds! And the Betsy Streamer! That's a simple enough fly, consisting merely of a peacock body and a white calf-tail hair wing, which can be fished both wet and dry, and comes in sizes 8, 10, 12, and 14. Somebody can probably make them up for you, but you at least ought to have one to copy from.

The Muddler Minnow can be fished much the same way, dry on the float down and then diving and bobbing on the retrieve. And its long shank hook has a virtue that I wouldn't have believed except for what happened to me on the Upper Beaverkill, when an eight-inch rainbow hit it and then was hit in turn by an eleven-incher. The second one just nudged the first one far enough along the long shank to hook himself too, so they both came in, probably less surprised than I was, looking like an animated cluster of bananas, two rainbows on one Muddler Minnow, truly one for the book. I'd often enough had "doubles" in Austria, when I'd skip two spiders on a bifurcated tippet, riding about twelve inches apart on the water, and get a couple of nice browns at once, but I'd never even heard tell of getting two trout on one fly until the Muddler showed it could be done.

Other Young flies that it's hard to imagine doing without are the Letort Beetle and the horse-hair midge nymph, both on sizes 18 and 20; the Green Worm Leaf Roller, on 12 and 14 hooks; the floating midges, or No-C-Ums, the floating midge bivisible, and the wonder wing midges, all size 20 and the daintiest dry flies imaginable; the midge nymphs, black, yellow, gray, and green, all size 20; and his nature nymphs, in assorted colors on size 16 hooks. One other unique Young item, and it may seem silly but Paul himself called it the most useful piece of fishing tackle in his catalogue—the Trik-Kutter tweezers and gut cutter, for 90 cents. But Hardy's scissor pliers, with tweezer tips, are perfectly all right, though at about three times that price; they are carried by Mills, Norm Thompson, and Orvis. So that's hardly the thing to mourn, though some of the flies certainly would be, if they should ever turn out to be no longer available.

It's worthwhile to shop the catalogues with an eye out for price differences, which seem to crop up frequently and unpredictably. In their 1965 catalogues, for instance, Orvis and Abercrombie were eye to eye and penny for penny on the prices of Orvis rods, but they veered apart on the Hardy Flyweight reel, for which Orvis asked $25.95 and Abercrombie $25.50. Norm Thompson asked $26.50. On the Featherweight, Orvis was $26.95 and Abercrombie was $26.75, but Norm Thompson was $27. On the L. R. H. Lightweight, Orvis wanted $27.95, against Abercrombie's $27.75, and Norm Thompson stood pat at, again, $27. On the Princess, Orvis went up to $29.95, Abercrombie passed, not even listing it, and Norm Thompson came in, not for the first time, with the low figure at $28. On the other hand, Abercrombie listed extra spools for all these models, at $12.75 each, regardless of their differences in size, whereas Norm Thompson offered extra spools for the Flyweight and the Featherweight at $10 each, and asked $11 each for the extra spools for the L. R. H. Lightweight and the Princess.

You will not look through any of those three catalogues, or the Mills catalogue either—whatever my wife may misapprehend about that one—in search of bargains. In fact, on these same four Hardy reels, Mills came between Abercrombie and Norm Thompson on the Flyweight at $26.75; upped all three of them over a dollar on the Featherweight, by asking $28.00 for it, though still shaded one dollar by Norm Thompson; topped everybody on the L. R. H. Lightweight by listing it at $29; and was high again on the Princess at $31.50. You will simply check them for the things they may have that are not offered elsewhere, and you may also check them, as we have just noted, to see if they vary on the items they all carry, and by how much.

Oddly enough, one way to get bargains which you might not expect to be worthwhile but is in my experience, is to buy direct from Hardy Brothers, figuring out the prices by agonizing arithmetic, reckoning the amount of the check to enclose by converting all their prices, first into shillings— say seventy shillings for something they've listed at three pounds ten—and then into dollars at the rate of fourteen cents per shilling. You pay the duty when the package is delivered (though that could be a nuisance if you don't have a metropolitan office address where they'll deliver a dutiable package, but have to go to your post office yourself), and find that with duty, postage and all, you've still come out some miles ahead, assuming that the order is a fairly big one. It's not quite as easy as it used to be, when you could deal direct with the factory at Alnwick. Now, and as of the last couple of years, you have to place your orders with the Pall Mall branch, across the way from St. James's Palace, and in consequence the service is neither as fast nor as exquisitely meticulous as it was. There are things to be said both for and against it. You won't get some of the very lightweight tackle items that they have made for Americans but presumably despair of ever selling to the English and hence don't even feature in their catalogue. On the other hand, you will find some things that are not carried over here at all, such as their number 1 Corona silk line, which mikes to IGI; their white and green Terylene lines, in the Filip

IEH forward taper, which are the British equivalent of Dacron, make a wonderful sinking line, and cast like bullets; or their smallest salmon flies in the standard patterns, sizes 10 and 12. And such things, if you go in for this in a way that is at all extensive, are worth almost any amount of trouble to get.

I got two things from them neither of which I thought I would get over here. One was their Lightweight reel. Not the new L. R. H. Lightweight, which everybody has, but their old Lightweight, which nobody here seems to carry. I also got some of their very high black-rubber Altona hip boots, with laced insteps and hobnailed soles and heels, which I thought were both practical and exotic. When I got them, all the way from England, I was startled to see that they carried an embossed rubber seal, just back of each ankle, with the legend "Made in Canada."

The first obstacle to get over, in dealing direct with Hardy, is to get their current catalogue and price list—the two are separate—and the quickest way is just to send them a letter requesting it and enclosing your check for two bucks, rather than exchanging letters to find out how much it is. Address: Hardy House, 61 Pall Mall, London S. W. 1, England. Their catalogue is called *Angler's Guide*, which is probably where Peter Alport got the idea, but the instructional articles are seldom changed, from one edition to the next; they still feature the same pieces, written by various Hardys over a generation ago, and unlike the *Norm Thompson Angler's Guide*, you won't get your money's worth, except perhaps in some nostaglic kicks, out of the illustrations and text of the angling features, apart from the merchandise itself.

There are other catalogues worth having, particularly as concerns the care of your tackle and your creature comforts while fishing or living in camp. In these catalogues you will find bargains, and in some you will find the same kind of crusty opinionated expression that crept into Paul Young's every so often. One of the best, in both respects, is that of L. L. Bean, Inc., Freeport, Maine. In fields where they overlap, however, Bean is outdone in both respects by Herter's, Inc., Waseca, Minnesota, which offers some bargains that seem beyond belief—flies for four and five cents apiece, nymphs for $1.38 *a dozen*, and streamers for under fifteen cents apiece—and invidious comparisons, in certain categories of merchandise, where Herter's say things about the kinds of things they don't carry—which must skirt the edges of commercial libel. Herter's catalogue costs a quarter. Going through it reminds me of a typical Wednesday with the boys upstairs at Manny Wolf's; you have to plough through deep drifts of guns and ammo and archery and all that, before you ever get to the fishing tackle. But then it must be seen to be believed.

Another Minnesota outfit has a catalogue worth having, and that's Gokey Co., St. Paul 1, Minnesota, the makers of the famous Botte Sauvage. It's particularly good on footwear and leather goods, and various wearables that are paradoxically elegant in the rough and ready category. Their selection of tackle is small but super-choice, with a preponderance of Orvis and Hardy items. One superb item they carry that I haven't found elsewhere is their three-quarter-length parka, which is a godsend to anybody who fishes in thigh boots in heavy rains.

One especial favorite of mine among the catalogues is an ugly duckling to look at, because it shouts its bargains so loudly it's hard to hear what they are. It looks like an army-surplus catalogue and in many instances actually does feature army surplus. But I treasure it. It's the catalogue of the Dave Cook Sporting Goods Co., Inc., 1601 Larimer St., Denver, Colorado 80201. In among pages of the most low-life fishing paraphernalia imaginable—stinky baits, and bloody scents, and gook that purports to be catnip to fish, all calculated to appeal to what Chetham called "idle pouching fellows"—you will come upon one gem of the purest ray serene, their unique, their invaluable, Zip leader straightener, a little arrow-shaped piece of pure India rubber. It comes six for 49 cents, and I buy them by the dozens, not to exaggerate and say by the gross, and give them away to everybody who will take one, because I know I'll never be rich enough to give away dimes. This, ah this, is the very thing that Al McClane told me, years ago, would matter more than any other, in bringing fish to my fly, and oh 'tis true. I buy other things along with them, because I'm ashamed to send orders all the way to Colorado for nothing but Zip leader straighteners, precious though they are to me, so I buy felt-soling kits from them, to keep my wading brogues and boots in a style to which no stream bottom ever lets them stay long accustomed, and reel oils and oilers, and Silicote pads and fly and line oils and pastes and dressings and such, to flesh the order up a little.

One other thing they have at Dave Cook's, and that's a retractable cord that pulls out of a button that fastens on your fishing shirt or vest. They mean it for a landing net, to let you reach out with the net to arm's length, and then have it snap back when you no longer need it. I don't use or want a net, but a thing like that is great to attach to the clippers or scissors or whatever you use to cut off flies and trim knots. There are lighter and smaller ones that work just as well and can usually be found at an optometrist's— intended for old ladies who want to pin their spectacles to their dresses. But if you can't find one of the small ones, then the larger net retriever of Dave Cook's is worth having. Checking this again, I find that while I had to get mine at an optometrist's, Mills has since begun to feature it in their catalogue, and at the same two bucks they charge for the net retriever at Dave Cook's.

One thing I can't find in any of the catalogues, and had a hard time tracking down for myself, is a micrometer. Without it, you're at the mercy of what have always been most inaccurate markings of sizes on leaders and fly lines; though they're better now than they were just a few years back, they are still far from reliable. You can't hope to make decent leaders if you can't gauge the various diameters accurately, and fly lines are more confused than ever, since they are now identified by weight rather than diameter. Without a micrometer you'll be absolutely in the dark as to the breadth of the tip and the belly and the running line of all your tapers. A good micrometer, which I've used now for well over a decade, is the Starrett 1010, made by the Starrett Instrument Company, Norwich, Connecticut. Even away back then it cost $30, so it's probably more now. But when you come back from trips, after getting it on the fritz from taking dirty spills, they're awfully nice about fixing it up again, and if you have sense enough to keep it dry it's a life-time tool. However, if you don't want to spring for that much money, you might try a gunsmith's micrometer, which you can get at Herter's for under $6, gauged from .o to 1.

Another catalogue whose selections more nearly resemble those of L. L. Bean than any other, but which still has an occasional unique item, is that of Corcoran Inc., Zero Canton Street, Stoughton, Massachusetts. Add that to the others already mentioned, and there won't be much going on in the way of new gadgetry and developments in gear that will take you by surprise.

Of course, the amount of money you can spend in this pursuit, once the hobby phase has pushed you on up into the status of a collector, is a caution. You won't be satisfied with one of those Hardy Lightweight reels, but inevitably will want a full run of them, just as you won't stop with one book if you start collecting an author, but will shoot for completeness. Even if you never reach that degree of addiction, you will still lay out astonishing totals if you allow your interest to go beyond pure trout equipment into the postgraduate stage represented by salmon tackle. A full run of sizes, in anything like adequate quantities of each, in just one pattern—say, Jock Scott—when filled out all the way in both standard and low water dressings can run you well over $100, and that's only one of at least two dozen you'll think you simply have to have. So if you lose a box of salmon flies, as I have twice, you'll be saying goodbye to the better part of $1,000 each time it happens.

That's probably one reason why your mind is apt to resemble a counting house, nights when you're lying in bed

wooing sleep. Telling off the weights and sizes of your various rod, reel, and line combinations, like the beads of a rosary, is a relatively simple exercise in mnemonics, but when you go on after that to spell out in your mind's eye the content, just by name of pattern alone, of each of your Wheatley fly boxes, the event takes on the proportions of a full-fledged decathlon, and it's next to impossible to finish before sleep calls the game on account of darkness. You start with the compartments on the left side, then go across the top row and the upper corner of the right side, then across the remaining three rows until you finish up in the lower right-hand corner, like this, for instance: lower left, Black Dose; upper left, Blue Charm and Silver Blue; across, Lady Amherst, Butcher, Durham Ranger; upper right, Logie and March Brown; across, Dusty Miller, Cosseboom and Green Highlander, Jock Scott; across, Mar Lodge, Mitchell and Night Hawk, Black Doctor, Blue Doctor, and Silver Doctor; across, Silver Gray, Thunder & Lightning, Silver Wilkinson; and lower right, Torrish and Hairy Mary. And you've said one box.

You may well have a dozen such boxes, to say nothing of your stock box, where you keep the reserves, to replenish the various compartments of the working boxes as their contents are depleted by fish, which is fairly seldom, or by rocks behind you that nick off your hooks just back of the barb, which is maddeningly frequent. And the stock box alone runs around $50. That's just the austerity model, in plain baked enamel with aluminum clip trays. A fancy one, in leather, which holds only 240 flies, or about forty percent fewer flies than the plain one, runs nearly $60. And the pocket-size Wheatley compartmented boxes, in the size you need for salmon flies, run about $12 each.

Suggesting that as a soporific device you will attend sleep by mentally enumerating the items of your tackle, "and count, and touch, and turn them o'er," as the poet said, may seem fatuous. I think of the man in Bermuda, years ago, who got booked into a $100 a day suite, in the days when suites just didn't cost $100 a day. He said he never slept a wink, hearing those hundred dollars ticking off like the meter in a taxi. Still, he did let them talk him into taking that suite. And you might let yourself get talked into worse things than becoming a tackle collector.

21 · The Well-Tempered Angler

The last point of all the inward gifts that doth belong to an
angler, is memory. . . .   The Arte of Angling, 1577

Reflection is the broad deep and quiet pool into which the
stream of an angler's thought opens out from time to time.
               A. A. Lucas, in
               Fishing and Thinking, 1959

You DON'T THINK you're thinking, at the time. You actually
try to be as nonthinking, as instinctive and intuitive, as the
trout or salmon that is your partner of the instant. That's why,

both before and after I read Walton, I felt that "the contemplative man's recreation" was a ludicrous misnomer for this kind of fishing. And yet the fair rewards, the things that are left with you afterward, are of sweetly silent thought all compact. So the thinking must be retroactive. Maybe angling is not, as old Izaak said, like mathematics. Maybe it's more like sex—and I'm not thinking of that vulgar definition of sex as "the most fun you can have without laughing." What I am thinking of is that couple of lines of Houseman:

> The night my father got me
> His mind was not on me.

For fishing seems to me to be divided, like sex, into three most unequal parts, the two larger of which, by far, are anticipation and recollection, and in between, by far the smallest of the three, actual performance.

Maybe Izaak was more of a humbug than I've been willing to concede. Even his kind of fishing, in his time, couldn't have been that idyllic. And I can't honestly believe that in the course of its literal practice he noticed, as he would have us believe, all those lovely sights and sounds and lyric elements that caused Andrew Lang to say that *The Compleat Angler* is "a book to be marked with flowers, marsh marigolds and fritillaries and petals of the yellow iris, for the whole provokes us to content . . ." and to apostrophize him with:

> Ah, Father Izaak, teach us thy content
> When time brings many a sorrow back again.

I can see that the effect of it, on a reader of subtle sensitivity, could warrant such rapt ecstatic reaction, but something at the back of my mind was bothering me vaguely even as, earlier on, I quoted one of its most beautiful lines. I have since happened upon the line, in a poem by Sir John Suckling published in 1638, fifteen years before the first edition of *The Compleat Angler:*

A silver stream ran softly gliding by.

Can the echo of that line in Walton be pure happenstance? Well, yes, I suppose it can, given the difference in mind and imagination between an Izaak Walton and a Sir John Suckling.

That Walton knew the line seems probable, but that he consciously stole it seems unlikely. I think rather that the alchemy of memory and reflection transformed Suckling's line in Walton's mind, to make it come out naturally the way he, quite possibly all unconsciously, paraphrased it as: "These silent silver streams which we now see glide so quietly by us." I'm thinking of what Aldous Huxley did, quite unconsciously I'm sure, to a line of Hemingway's which he quoted without looking it up—in other words, quoted it as he remembered it. He was referring to a line in *A Farewell to Arms* and was making the point that Hemingway's clipped and disciplinedly sparse and meager style was by no means as simple as it seemed but was replete with deliberately poetic elements, and he cited that line about "the bitter nailholes of Mantegna's Christs." I thought, at the time, "My God, that sounds like something out of Walter Pater," and made a mental note to look up the line at the next opportunity. I didn't find it, but I found the elements of it, as they had been reassembled into that "one line of Hemingway," as later transformed by Huxley's memory and reflection.

It was a patch of dialogue between Catherine Barkley and Lieutenant Henry. They were discussing painters, and when they came to Mantegna, she said: "Very bitter." And he said: "Very bitter. Full of nailholes."

It's this kind of almost submerged thinking that we do, I am sure, whenever we fish and think, as we concentrate on the business at hand, of reading the water—and at the same time trying to keep our balance in it while wading—and changing the flies and tying the knots—that we're not thinking. Well, we are and we aren't. We certainly aren't consciously thinking about thinking. But probably every one of those familiar motions of fishing that we go through in the course of what becomes an almost intuitive routine of reflex reactions to the fishing situation of the given moment, every one of those motions is linked to a vast number of memories and reflections, as complex and complicated as a giant switchboard. I know, for instance, that I never pinch the barb off the hook of my fly with the squeeze of my pliers that I don't see Louie Renault, standing across from me on the other side of his pond in Stamford, saying: "I cannot hold ziss fish, because I lost ze barber off ze hook of my *Vivif*," and that memory invariably triggers a whole related set of reflections, so that as much as ten minutes later, whatever may have occurred in the interim in terms of fish and fishing, I am still thinking about Louie, remembering other funny mixups that occurred in consequence of his fractured English, remembering how Gene Tunney called him "the most uninhibited man I've ever known." And after a dozen other recollections, I would wind up, perhaps, with that of Louie's great idea for a soft drink concession at the 1939 World's Fair: how he dreamed up the great new drink, made of watermelon juice and cola syrup, and the marvelous slogan he thought up to go with it: "Why be melancholy? Drink Melon-cola." And I burst out laughing every time, so that anybody watching me at my fishing would be convinced I had gone out of my mind.

As indeed I have, as indeed we all do, because each of us acquires, in the course of time, some set of memories and reflections that embellish, like a cadenza, almost every different action as we go endlessly over and over again through the set routines of our fishing. This is the tempering of the angler's mind. And it is these things, and not what goes into our notebooks or our angler's log or is mounted on our office walls or in our photograph albums, that constitute the fairest rewards of all our angling. I never lower my rod tip at the leap of a jumping fish without thinking, or even saying, "Take it easy," and there always flashes then, on my memory's screen as if on cue, the picture of three of us in a boat on Pistakee Bay, almost forty years ago, the one time Dave Smart ever came along on one of those Saturday mornings when Ed Loebe and I used to play hookey from our work to go fishing. Dave had never fished in his life, but he became curious as to why it took us away so many Saturday mornings, and wanted to see for himself. He soon saw that we were going about it all wrong, that we were much too tense and trying too hard. In golfing terms, as he put it, we were "pressing." "Take it easy," he said, "here, like this, now just lemme show you," and as he hooked a bass—which neither of us had yet been able to do but he did with a maddening display of beginner's luck—he sat down in the middle seat of the boat, propped his rod up between his knees, set a cigarette in a holder at a jaunty angle in the corner of his mouth, poured himself a cup of coffee from the Thermos, began elaborately stirring it while puffing away serenely, obviously enjoying the sensation of feeling us seething, and said: "See, take it easy, like this—" as the bass jumped, showering him with spray, and fell, not in the boat but right alongside it, giving Dave a good splashing, and having shaken the plug, was suddenly free and away.

I never tie on a white maribou streamer, size 12, without reliving the scene one Sunday morning up at A. F. Wechslers', the place that used to belong to old Colonel Ambrose Monell, the crony of Hewitt and La Branche, on Eden Brook near St. Joseph, New York. It was six o'clock in the morning of July 13, 1958, and although I was tiptoeing, Jane heard me.

"What do you think you're doing?"

"I've got a date with a big brown."

"You're crazy."

"I know it. But I saw him last night and I threw the book at him. Now I just remembered that I didn't try a white maribou on him."

"I hope you fall in."

"I'll be right back."

"Oh, don't hurry. Honestly."

He took it at 6:10 and on my Midge, with 5X leader, it was 6:24 before I dared beach him, and as I did the white maribou dropped out of his mouth on the bank. It was the first fish I had kept in a long time. He was a big old brown, deep-bodied as a bass, so that although he measured only 20⅛ inches he weighed 4¼ pounds. He was the only fish I have ever had mounted, and I probably wouldn't have mounted him, but Jane had him mounted for me. I only wanted to trace his outline in the book they've kept up there, which goes back to Colonel Monell's day. In all that time, back to before the First World War, except for a six-pound pickerel that General Walter Bedell Smith took out of the lake, he was the biggest fish ever put in the book.

I lost a bigger one than that, on that same size white maribou, just at dusk one Friday night in the Buttonwoods Pool at Henryville, on the Paradise branch of the Brodheads. I couldn't even be sure he was a brown, though it's hard to think of anything else he might be there, but the one glimpse of him I had in the half-light made him seem the size of a large grilse. Again it was a 5X tippet, but the way he snapped it off it might as well have been 10X. That's another of those storied waters, "haunted by old legends," and the Zieglers who own Henryville Lodge—she was a Henry—can show you a deed to the place dating back to 1811. If you're looking to find waters to fish where you can have the feeling that you're standing in a stream that is steeped in tradition, in surroundings that are wreathed with the laurel of past fishing glories, you could go a lot farther and do worse. In a sense it's "made" fishing, as almost all of the fishing we get today must be, but you can feel a little set up every time you tie into one of the big ones. Alvin Ziegler keeps them in his ponds, where, before he turns them loose in the stream, they're fished over for a year by the tourists fishing by the pound; and if you can raise one of over sixteen inches, in any of the pools such as Pine Tree, or the Twins, or the Slide, you can honestly feel that you have emerged from the tyro's cocoon as an angler. When you come into the Lodge for meals, which in April and May are served in the little room that becomes a card room later on in the season, you come into the easy casual company of real anglers, with whom you can loaf and invite your soul. By mid-June the whole character of the place changes, and the big dining porches are opened up and everywhere it's chock a block with jumping teenagers and the blare and din of rock and roll—just another Pocono resort. But before that, when there are still roaring fires in the oxenample fireplaces, and the dawns are still frosty, and nobody is stirring on the stream but the wise old-timers like Ed Schlechter and Darlington Culp, who have fished it for years, Henryville is a place to cherish.

Outside of Suffolk Lodge out at Brookhaven, and Kahil's Rainbow Lodge up at Mt. Tremper on the Esopus, it's hard to think of another, except of course for private places, like Blooming Grove, near Hawley, Pennsylvania, which Charles Hallock was hailing in print as long ago as 1873, and the Tuscarora Club, near Margaretville, New York, and the Brooklyn Fly Fishers, on the Beaverkill. But you go to those places only as the guest of a member, and in consequence you feel that, whatever the sport, you must fish with a standing broad grin.

So it's better to fish almost anywhere that you've fished before, enough that you have at least begun to know it a little, than to be taken for first-time fishing even where it's certified marvelous. Even so, the very act of fishing comes to be rewarding in and of itself, whether you catch fish or not. That isn't true of fishing on a lawn, of course. Somehow you must have water to stand in or beside, and it helps enormously to know that it has, or at least has had, fish in it. So far gone you will never be that you can enjoy yourself fully, with your

tiny flies and fine tippets and small light rod, even where
there isn't the outside chance of ever having your preoccupa-
tion intruded upon by a fish. But how big or how many soon
begins to be the least important aspect of your total pleasure
in the exercise of your acquired skill.

Even Dr. Johnson, who has ever since been railed at by so
many angling authors for once having made that rude remark
about "a worm at one end and a fool at the other," could
see that there was something in this sport, and I've often
wondered whether it was from ignorance or from anger that
so much contumely has been heaped upon him in so many
subsequent books on fishing. In fairness, the complete quota-
tion, though it comes to that in the end, starts out quite
otherwise, as what he said reads, in full: "Fly-fishing may be a
very pleasant amusement; but angling, or float-fishing, I can
only compare to a stick and a string, with a worm at one end
and a fool at the other." Maybe it was his pejorative use of
the word "angling" that first got their dander up, because
some anglers have tried to establish a class distinction between
angling, as the diversion of gentlefolk, and fishing, as a common pursuit and including within the term its practice as a
livelihood.

I don't hold with the feeling that angling is too good for the
common people, and use the terms for the most part as if
they were interchangeable. I notice that both Lee Wulff and
Al McClane, while they might admit to being anglers, still
always refer to it as "going fishing," and if they aren't gentle-
men I have no way of telling who is. I like to talk about it,
and like Major Hills I love to read about it, and I'm pleased
to think of it, perhaps selfishly, as a means to attaining old

age gracefully, echoing the sentiment expressed by George Smith in *The Gentleman Angler* in 1726:

> Then you who would be honest,
> And to Old Age attain,
> Forsake the City and the Town
> And fill the Angler's Train.

So now I live in a house by the side of a river, and hope I'm none the less a friend of man. There are trout there, by the grace of the state of New Jersey, and to me, as it did to old Dr. Masaryk, that makes it beautiful. I don't walk a dog, but of an evening I'm likely to take a rod out for an airing instead, maybe my Midge or the Superfine one piece, although more often if I'm heading for the more overgrown spots it's a bantam rod, of four feet four inches in length and one ounce in weight, because it's a small river. My apparel is plain and comely, as adjured by Gervase Markham in *Country Content-ments* as long ago as 1614, and "of a dark colour, as Russet, Tawny, or such-like," lest I scare away the trouts.

I still get my fly hung up in the trees, for a disgraceful percentage of the occasions when the opportunity for such impediment presents itself, and always will, wherever I fish, except in Iceland, where there are a lot of rocks to do an even greater disservice on the back cast. I fish an eighteen-foot leader tapered to 7X (.0039) and sometimes even finer, down to .0031, and get feeling very chesty about it, which all too often amounts to a clear and present indication that the next cast will be inexplicably dumped or jarred or suddenly windswept into an unholy mess, resulting in a tangle so complicated that I will have to cut off the last five feet or so,

and tie it afresh. It is at such moments that I wonder if Dr.
Johnson wasn't being even more sardonic in his reference to
this as a very pleasant amusement than he was in the part
about the stick and the fool.

But I know one place, even in my narrow stream, where beneath an overhanging tree it's deep enough that now and
then, when the light is right, I can see "where the grey trout
glide silently by" and no matter how often I see it, there's an
equal thrill in the sight every time. I dream of a house on a
headland, where looking one way you gaze up a gleaming
river and looking the other you see the shining sea, and of
fishing in the estuary for sea-run brookies as long as your arm.
But I know it's a dream, because in all such places I have so
far seen, the estuary is a stinking mess of gook.

I have a new Bogdan reel, with a two-to-one retrieve, big
enough to accommodate a Cortland rocket taper sink-tip
HCF and two hundred yards of backing, yet small enough to
make a lovely mount on a stout little stick like the Superfine.
It's the first American reel I've added to my collection since
the acquisition, eight years ago, of a pair of prized antiques, a
Conroy and a vom Hofe, each about sixty years old, and
each smaller than the Hardy Flyweight, which were given me
by a friend of my wife's, who had them from her grand-
father. I think of wielding that Bogdan with the Superfine,
and I cry for stronger salmon and for stouter grilse, sure that I
have the combination that is the midget giant killer of all
time. But I cry quietly, beating my chest like a subdued Tarzan
who must yell in a whisper, because now and for some time
I've been doing all my serious fishing (I don't count evenings
airing my rod on the Saddle River) in a room in the New

York Public Library, where I dare not disturb my fellows. For the tempering of an angler, I know of no better place, for with very little paraphrase you could say of it what was said of another fishing spot: "It is rich in memories of Walton and Cotton; it is a dream of peace," and they bring you your books by the deskside.

Actually, though being well read must be a part of the process, an angler is tempered chiefly by practice and experience, by learning and attempting to reach the successively higher goals of his sport, and thus acquiring, through any amount of disappointment and frustration, the satisfaction of knowing that he is doing the simplest thing in the hardest way possible. Then, be he never so churlish, short in his patience, hateful to his kids, mean to his mother, no matter what—as an angler, at least and at last, he is well-tempered.

So saying, I will arise and go now, giving you the fair warning of that long-lost little book, *The Arte of Angling*: "Wel, if you hie you not apace, I will be at the River before you." May we be well-met there, and fish together well and long, until at last we can intone in unison with Andrew Lang:

> Girdling the grey domain of Death
> The spectral fishes come and go;
> The ghosts of trout flit to and fro.
> Persephone, fulfill my wish,
> And grant that in the shades below
> My ghost may land the ghosts of fish!

A Selective Bibliography

OF BOOKS MENTIONED, QUOTED,

OR OTHERWISE RECOMMENDED

NOTE: Dates are not necessarily of first editions but, where possible, of latest or most generally available editions or reprints.

Adamson, W. A.: *Lake and Loch Fishing*. London: A & C Black; 1961.

Alexander, Col. Sir James Edward, ed.: *Salmon Fishing in Canada by a Resident* (Rev. Wm. Agar Adamson). London: Longman, Green, Longman, and Roberts; 1860.

Angler's Guide to Ireland. Issued by Bord Failte Eirann (Irish Tourist Board), 33 E. 50 St., New York, New York (14 Upper O'Connell St., Dublin).

Three Anglers: *How to Catch Trout*. Edinburgh: David Douglas; 1910.

Annual British Fishing Guide: *Where to Fish*. Published by *The Field*, Harmsworth Press, London.

Atherton, John: *The Fly and the Fish*. New York: The Macmillan Co.; 1951.

Austin, A. B., ed.: *An Angler's Anthology*. London: Country Life, Ltd.; 1930. New York: Charles Scribner's Sons; 1930.

Bates, Joseph D., Jr.: *Trout Waters and How to Fish Them*. Boston: Little Brown and Co.; 1950.

Bentley, Gerald Eades, ed.: *The Arte of Angling, 1577*. Introduction by Carl Otto v. Kienbusch. Princeton, N. J.: Princeton University Press; 1958.

Bergman, Ray: *Trout*. New York: Alfred A. Knopf; 1952.

Blades, William F.: *Fishing Flies and Fly Tying*. Harrisburg, Pa.: The Stackpole Co.; 1962.

Boulenger, E. G.: *British Angler's Natural History*. London: Collins; 1947.

Bradford, Charles Barker: *The Brook Trout and the Determined Angler*. Richmond Hill, N. Y.: The E. P. Grow Publishing Co.; 1900.

Brooks, Joe: *Greatest Fishing*. Harrisburg, Pa.: The Stackpole Co.; 1957.

———: *The Complete Book of Fly Fishing*. New York: A. S. Barnes and Co.; 1958.

Burns, Eugene: *Advanced Fly Fishing*. Harrisburg, Pa.: The Stackpole Co.; 1953.

Burns, Eugene, ed.: *An Angler's Anthology*. Harrisburg, Pa.: The Stackpole Co.; 1952.

Calderwood, W. L.: *The Life of the Salmon* (with reference more especially to the fish in Scotland). London: Edward Arnold & Co.; 1907.

———: *Salmon and Sea Trout*. London: Edward Arnold & Co.; 1930.

Carhart, Arthur H.: *Fresh Water Fishing*. New York: A. S. Barnes and Co.; 1949.

Chalmers, Patrick: *The Angler's England*. Philadelphia: J. B. Lippincott Co.; 1938.

Chaytor, A. H.: *Letters to a Salmon Fisher's Sons*. London: John Murray; 1910.

Cholmondeley-Pennell, H.: *Fishing (Salmon and Trout)*. London: Longmans, Green and Co.; 1895.

Connett, Eugene V.: *Any Luck?* London: Hutchinson & Co.; 1935.

———: *My Friend the Trout*. New York: D. Van Nostrand Co.; 1961.

Crowe, John: *The Book of Trout Lore*. New York: A. S. Barnes and Co.; 1947.

Davy, Sir Humphrey: *Salmonia or Days of Fly Fishing*. Boston: Roberts Brothers; 1870.

Dawson, Major Kenneth ("West Country"): *Casts from a Salmon Reel*. London: Herbert Jenkins Ltd.; n.d. (1947).

D(ennys), J(ohn): *The Secrets of Angling*, 1613. A reprint, with introduction by Thomas Westwood. London: W. Satchell & Co.; 1883.

Deren, Jim: *Family Circle's Guide to Trout Flies and How to Tie Them*. New York: A. S. Barnes and Co.; 1954.

Dewar, George A. B.: *South Country Trout Streams*. London: Lawrence and Bullen Ltd.; 1899.

Bibliography

————: *Life and Sport in Hampshire*. London: Longmans, Green and Co.; 1908.

Dickie, John M., ed.: *Great Angling Stories*. London: W & R Chambers; 1947.

Doucette, Earle: *The Fisherman's Guide to Maine*. New York: Random House; n.d (1957).

Dubois, Donald: *The Fisherman's Handbook of Trout Flies*. New York: A. S. Barnes and Co.; 1960.

Dunne, J. W.: *Sunshine and the Dry Fly*. London: A. & C. Black; 1924.

Edwards, Capt. T. L., and Turner, Eric Horsfall: *The Angler's Cast*. London: Herbert Jenkins; 1960.

"Ephemera" (Edward Fitzgibbon): *The Book of the Salmon*. London: Longman, Brown, Green, and Longman; 1850.

Fennelly, John F.: *Steelhead Paradise*. Vancouver, B. C.: Mitchell Press; 1963.

Flick, Art: *Streamside Guide to Naturals and their Imitations*. New York: G. P. Putnam's Sons; 1947.

Fox, Charles K.: *This Wonderful World of Trout*. Carlisle, Pa.: Foxcrest; 1963.

Francis, Francis: *A Book on Angling*. London: Herbert Jenkins Ltd.; 1920.

Garrow-Green, G.: *Trout Fishing in Brooks*. New York: E. P. Dutton; n.d. (1910).

Gingrich, Arnold, ed.: *The Gordon Garland*. New York: Theodore Gordon Flyfishers; 1965.

Goodspeed, Charles E., ed.: *A Treasury of Fishing Stories*. New York: A. S. Barnes and Co.; 1960.

Gordon, Sid: *How to Fish from Top to Bottom*. Harrisburg, Pa.: The Stackpole Co.; 1955.

Grey, Sir Edward: *Fly Fishing*. London: J. M. Dent and Co.; 1899.

Grove, Alvin R., Jr.: *The Lure and the Lore of Trout Fishing*. Harrisburg, Pa.: The Stackpole Co.; 1951.

Haig-Brown, Roderick: *Fisherman's Winter*. New York: William Morrow and Co.; 1954.

————: *Fisherman's Fall*. New York: William Morrow and Co.; 1964.

————: *A Primer of Fly-fishing*. New York: William Morrow and Co.: 1964.

Hall, John Inglis: *How to Fish a Highland Stream* (The Truim). London: G. P. Putnam's Sons; 1960.

Hallock, Charles: *The Fishing Tourist*. New York: Harper & Brothers; 1873.

Hamilton, Edward: *Recollections of Fly Fishing for Salmon, Trout, and Grayling*. New York: Orange Judd Company; 1885.

Hardy, House of: *Angler's Guide and Catalogue* (annual). Issued by Hardy Brothers (Alnwick) Ltd., 61 Pall Mall, London.

Harris, J. R.: *An Angler's Entomology*. Woodstock, Vt.: The Countryman Press; n.d. (1954).

Hewitt, Edward Ringwood: *Secrets of the Salmon*. New York: Charles Scribner's Sons; 1922.

————: *Handbook of Fly Fishing*. New York: Marchbanks Press; 1933.

————: *Handbook of Stream Improvement*. New York: Marchbanks Press; 1934.

————: *Nymph Fly Fishing*. New York: Marchbanks Press; 1934.

————: *A Trout and Salmon Fisherman for Seventy-five Years*. New York: Charles Scribner's Sons; 1950.

Hills, John Waller: *A History of Fly Fishing for Trout*. New York: Frederick A. Stokes Co.: 1921.

Holland, Dan: *Trout Fishing*. New York: Thomas Y. Crowell Co.; 1949.

Hutton, John E.: *Trout and Salmon Fishing*. Boston: Little, Brown and Co.; 1949.

Jennings, Preston J.: *A Book of Trout Flies*. New York: Crown Publishers; n.d. (1935).

Jones, J. W.: *The Salmon*. London: Collins; 1959. New York: Harper & Brothers; 1959.

Knight, John Alden: *Modern Fly Casting*. New York: G. P. Putnam's Sons; 1942.

———— and Richard Alden: *The Complete Book of Fly Casting*. New York: G. P. Putnam's Sons; 1963.

Koller, Lawrence R.: *The Complete Book of Fresh Water Fishing*. New York: The Bobbs-Merrill Co.; 1954.

————: *Taking Larger Trout*. Boston: Little, Brown and Co.; 1950.

La Branche, George M. L.: *The Dry Fly and Fast Water* and *The Salmon and the Dry Fly*. New York: Charles Scribner's Sons; 1951.

Lamb, Dana S.: *On Trout Streams and Salmon Rivers*. Barre, Mass.; Barre Publishers; 1963.

Bibliography

————: *Bright Salmon and Brown Trout.* Barre, Mass.: Barre Publishers; 1964.

Le Danois, Dr. Edouard: *Fishes of the World.* Woodstock, Vt.: The Countryman Press; n.d.

Leonard, J. Edson: *Flies, A Dictionary of 2200 Patterns.* New York: A. S. Barnes and Co.; 1950.

Luce, A. A.: *Fishing and Thinking.* London: Hodder and Stoughton; 1959.

McClane, A. J.: *The Practical Fly Fisherman.* New York: Prentice-Hall; 1953.

————, ed.: *The American Angler.* New York: Henry Holt and Co.; 1954.

————, ed.: *McClane's Standard Fishing Encyclopedia.* New York: Holt, Rinehart and Winston; 1965.

McCormick, Robert C.: *The Angler's Almanac.* New York: Harper & Brothers; 1955.

McDonald, John: *The Origins of Angling* (and a new printing of *The Treatise of Fishing with an Angle,* attributed to Dame Juliana Berners). New York: Doubleday and Co.; 1963.

McDonald, John, ed.: *The Complete Fly Fisherman* (The Notes and Letters of Theodore Gordon). New York: Charles Scribner's Sons; 1947.

Macdougall, Arthur R., Jr.: *The Trout Fisherman's Bedside Book.* New York: Simon and Schuster; 1963.

McNally, Tom, ed.: *Fisherman's Digest* (annual). Issued by The Gun Digest Company, Chicago 24, Ill.

Marbury, Mary Orvis: *Favorite Flies and Their Histories.* Boston: Charles T. Brantford Co.; 1955.

Marinaro, Vincent: *A Modern Dry-Fly Code.* New York: G. P. Putnam's Sons; 1950.

Markham, Gervase: *The Pleasures of Princes,* together with Robert Venables's *The Experienced Angler.* London: The Cresset Press Ltd.; 1927.

Marston, R. B.: *Walton and Some Earlier Writers on Fish and Fishing.* London: Elliot Stock; 1903.

Michael, William W.: *Dry-Fly Trout Fishing.* New York: McGraw Hill Book Co.; 1951.

Mottram, James Cecil: *Fly-fishing: Some New Arts & Mysteries.* London: The Field Press., Ltd.; n.d. (1915).

Ovington, Ray: *How to Take Trout on Wet Flies and Nymphs*. Boston: Little, Brown and Company; 1952.

Platts, W. Carter: *Modern Trout Fishing*. London: Adam & Charles Black; 1961.

Prime, W. C.: *I Go A-Fishing*. New York: Harper & Brothers, 1873.

Quick, Jim: *Trout Fishing and Trout Flies*. Woodstock, Vt.: The Countryman Press; 1957.

————: *Fishing the Nymph*. New York: The Ronald Press Co.; 1960.

Righyni, R. V.: *Salmon Taking Times*. London: Macdonald; 1965.

Ritz, Charles: *A Fly Fisher's Life*. New York: Holt, Rinehart and Winston; 1959.

Robb, James, LL.D.: *Notable Angling Literature*. London: Herbert Jenkins; n.d. (1945).

Rondelet, Guillaume: *L'Histoire Entière des Poissons*. Lyons, 1558.

Salmon, Richard: *Fly Fishing for Trout*. Greenberg, New York, 1952.

Sandeman, Fraser: *By Hook and By Crook*. London: Henry Southeran & Co.; 1894.

Scharff, Robert, ed.: *Esquire's Book of Fishing*. New York: Harper & Row; 1963.

Scholes, David: *The Way of an Angler*. Brisbane, Queensland, Australia: Jacaranda Press; 1963.

Schwiebert, Ernest G., Jr.: *Matching the Hatch*. New York: The Macmillan Co.; 1955.

"Scott, Jock" (D. G. H. Rudd): *Greased Line Fishing for Salmon* (compiled from the papers of the late A. H. E. Wood). Philadelphia: J. B. Lippincott Co.; 1935.

Scrope, William: *Days and Nights of Salmon Fishing in the Tweed*. London: Edward Arnold; 1898.

Shaw, Helen: *Fly-Tying*. New York: The Ronald Press Co.; 1963.

Skues, G. E. M.: *Side-Lines, Side-Lights & Reflections*. London: Seeley, Service & Co.; 1932.

————: *Minor Tactics of the Chalk Stream*. London: Adam & Charles Black; 1910.

————: *Nymph Fishing for Chalk Stream Trout*. London: Adam & Charles Black; 1939.

Smedley, Harold Hinsdill: *Fly Patterns and Their Origins*. Muskegon, Mich.: Westshore Publications; 1950.

Sparrow, Walter Shaw: *Angling in British Art*. London: John Lane, The Bodley Head Ltd.; 1923.

Bibliography

Steel, Frank R.: *Fly Fishing.* Chicago: Paul, Richmond & Co.; 1946.

Stefansson, Vilhjalmur: *Iceland, The First American Republic.* New York: Doubleday, Doran & Co.; 1939.

Stewart, Maj. Gen. R. N.: *Rivers of Iceland.* Issued by the Iceland Tourist Bureau, Reykjavik, Iceland, 1950.

Stewart, W. C.: *The Practical Angler or The Art of Trout-Fishing More Particularly Applied to Clear Water.* Edinburgh: Adam & Charles Black; 1883.

Taverner, Eric: *Fly-Tying for Trout.* London: Seeley, Service & Co.: n.d.

——:*Trout Fishing from All Angles.* Philadelphia: J. B. Lippincott Co.; n.d. (1933).

——: *Salmon Fishing.* London: Seeley, Service & Co.: n.d. (1935).

Thompson, Norm: *Angler's Guide for Fly Fishermen* (annual). Issued by Norm Thompson, 1805 N. W. Thurman, Portland, Ore.

Traver, Robert (John Voelker): *Anatomy of a Fisherman.* New York: McGraw-Hill Book Co.; 1964.

——: *Trout Madness.* New York: St. Martin's Press; 1960.

Turing, H. D.: *Trout Fishing.* London: Adam & Charles Black; 1943.

Van Fleet, Clark C.: *Steelhead to a Fly.* Boston: Little Brown and Co.; 1954.

Venables, Bernard: *Fishing.* London: B. T. Batsford; 1953. New York: British Book Centre; 1953.

——: *The Angler's Companion.* London: George Allen & Unwin Ltd.; 1958. (Distributed by Macmillan in the United States)

Veniard, John: *Fly Dresser's Guide.* Thornton Heath, England: E. Veniard; n.d. (1952).

Waddington, Richard: *Salmon Fishing: Philosophy and Practice.* London: Faber and Faber; 1959.

Walton, Izaak, and Cotton, Charles: *The Compleat Angler.* London, 1676 et seq.

Walton, Izaak: *The Lives of Dr. John Donne, Sir Henry Wotton, Mr. Richard Hooker, Mr. George Herbert and Dr. Robert Sanderson.* London: Henry Washbourne; 1838.

Williams, A. Courtney: *Trout Flies.* London: A. & C. Black; 1932.

Wulff, Lee: *New Handbook of Freshwater Fishing.* Philadelphia: J. B. Lippincott Co.; 1951.

——: *The Atlantic Salmon.* New York: A. S. Barnes and Co.; 1958.

Yarrell, William: *A History of British Fishes,* 2 volumes. London: John van Vorst; 1836.

A List of Pertinent Addresses

Abercrombie & Fitch Company
Madison Avenue at 45th Street
New York, New York 10017
Catalogue

Air Canada
680 Fifth Avenue
New York, New York
Fishing in Gander vicinity
Dan De Guerre, public relations office

Alaska Sleeping Bag Company
334 N.W. 11th Street
Portland 9, Oregon
Catalogue

Angler's Roost
405 Lexington Avenue
New York, New York

Angler's Cove
478 Third Avenue
New York, New York
Bob Zwirz

Arsenault, J. C.
P.O. Box 1
Atholville
New Brunswick, Canada
Salmon flies, particularly hair-wing

Ashford Castle Hotel
Cong
County Mayo, Ireland
Prop.: Noel Huggard
Fishing on loughs Corrib, Inagh, and Derryclare

Atlantic Salmon Association
1559 McGregor Street
Montreal 25
Quebec, Canada
Annual membership fee, $10, includes subscription to *Atlantic Salmon Journal*

Austrian Fishing Association
Elizabethstrasse 22
Vienna I, Austria
Rods in Lower Austria (Vienna vicinity)

Austrian State Tourist Dept.
444 Madison Avenue
New York, New York 10022
Guidebook *Fishing in Austria*

Ballynahinch Castle Hotel
Ballinafad
County Galway, Ireland
Fishing on Ballynahinch River and Lough

A List of Pertinent Addresses

Bauer, Eddie
 417 East Pine at Summit
 Seattle 22, Washington
  Catalogue

L. L. Bean, Inc.
 283 Main Street
 Freeport, Maine 04032
  Catalogue

Birnam Hotel
 Near Dunkeld
 Perthshire, Scotland
  Fishing on the Tay River

Boyd's Fishing Lodge
 Blackville
 New Brunswick, Canada
  Fishing on Southwest Mira-
  michi River. *Address* Tom
  Boyd, Golf Club Road, Fred-
  ericton, New Brunswick,
  Canada

British Book Centre, Inc.
 122 E. 55 Street
 New York, New York
  Books and periodicals

British Travel Association
 680 Fifth Avenue
 New York, New York
  *Fishing in Britain and North-
  ern Ireland.* Lists and brochures

Brown, Billy
 Chaplin Road
 Newcastle
 New Brunswick, Canada
  Salmon flies, particularly
  hair-wing and small sizes

Butler Arms Hotel
 Waterville
 County Kerry, Ireland
  Fishing on Currane River
  and Lough

Campbell Fishing Camps
 Upper Blackville
 Northumberland County
 New Brunswick, Canada
  Fishing on Southwest Mira-
  michi and Cains rivers. *Ad-
  dress* Herman H. Campbell

Cappoquin Estate Company
 Cappoquin
 County Waterford, Ireland
  Rods on Blackwater River
  (Fermoy, Mallow, Millstreet
  vicinities)

Carrick-on-Suir & District A.A.
 P. J. O' Sullivan
 Park View
 Carrick-on-Suir, Ireland
  Rods on river Suir in Car-
  rick vicinity

Chalets Castor
 St. René-Goupil
 Matane
 Quebec, Canada
  Rods on the Matane River.
  Address Emilien Côté

Clonmel and District A.A.
 J. Kavanagh
 Sports Tackle
 Westgate
 Clonmel, Ireland
  Rods on river Suir in Clon-
  mel vicinity

Clonmel and District A.C.
   M.O'Sullivan
   5 O'Rahilly Avenue
   Clonmel, Ireland
      Rods on river Suir in Clon-
      mel vicinity

Conservationist, The
   Official publication of New
   York State
   Conservation Department
   State Campus
   Albany, New York
      Bimonthly, annual subscrip-
      tion $2

Consolidated Paper Corp., Ltd.
   Anticosti Division
   1643 Sun Life Building
   Montreal
   Quebec, Canada
      Rods on six salmon rivers of
      Anticosti Island. Address
      D. J. Wallace

Corcoran, Inc.
   Zero Canton Street
   Stoughton, Massachusetts
   Catalogue

Craigellachie Hotel
   Banffshire, Scotland
   Prop.: D. W. Carmichael
      Fishing on river Spey in mid-
      dle reaches

CREEL: A Fishing Magazine
   Paulton House
   8, Shepherdess Walk
   London, N. 1, England
      Annual subscription 42 shil-
      lings (including postage in
      British Isles); overseas, $7.75.
      All subscribers are eligible for
      membership of the CREEL
      International Fishing Club

Cristiansen, Anton
   Angling Consultant
   Box 154, Myrvoll Station
   Oslo, Norway
      Rods on various Norwegian
      rivers

Crossroads of Sport
   5 E. 47 Street
   New York, New York
      Sporting books

Dave Cook Sporting Goods Co.,
Inc.
   1601 Larimer Street
   Denver, Colorado 80201
   Catalogue

Doak, Wallace
   Doaktown
   New Brunswick, Canada
      Salmon flies and tackle

Dromoland Castle Hotel
   Newmarket-on-Fergus
   County Clare, Ireland
      Fishing on Shannon, Fergus,
      and Rine rivers

Dschulnigg, Helmut
Salzburg, Austria
 Rods on Austrian and Bavarian rivers

Dubé, Jean Paul
c/o Hotel Restigouche
Matapaedia
Quebec, Canada
 Rods on Matapaedia River

Dunraven Arms Hotel
Adare
County Limerick, Ireland
 Rods on Maigue River

Field, The
England's Country Newspaper
8, Stratton Street
Piccadilly, W. 1
London, England
 Weekly, annual subscription
 £6/6; U.S. and Canada,
 $19.50

Field & Stream
383 Madison Avenue
New York, New York 10013
 Published monthly; annual
 subscription U.S. and Canada, $4; other countries $6

Foran, Gerald W.
R. R. No. 2
Red Bank
Northumberland County
New Brunswick, Canada
 Fishing on Little Southwest
 Miramichi River

Garcia Corporation
329 Alfred Avenue
Teaneck, New Jersey
 Catalogue (J. W. Young
 English Fly Reels)

Gelot
12 Place Vendôme
Paris, France
 Fishing hats

George Hotel
Hatherleigh
Devon, England
 Fishing in Torridge River

Gillespie, Maxwell
Blackville
New Brunswick, Canada
 Guide for Renous and Southwest Miramichi rivers

Gokey Co.
Saint Paul 1, Minn.
 Catalogue

Griff Inns
Boiestown
Northumberland County
New Brunswick, Canada
 Fishing on Southwest Miramichi River. *Address* Clayton Stewart

Half Moon Inn
Sheepwash
Devon, England
 Fishing on Torridge River. *Address* Wing Commander Inniss for brochure

Hallam, E. Chalmers
Angling Books
Earlswood
Egmont Drive
Ringwood
Hampshire, England
Lists

Hammond, Horace B.
13 Cathedral Street
Dublin, Ireland
Rods on Blackwater River in
Fermoy vicinity

Hardy Bros. (Alnwick) Ltd.
Hardy House
61 Pall Mall
London, S. W. 1, England
Catalogue and Angler's
Guide

Henryville Lodge
Henryville, Pennsylvania
Props.: Alvin and Eleanor
Ziegler
Lodging and rod fee

Herter's Inc.
R. R. 1
Waseca, Minnesota
Catalogue, 25 cents

Hillhouse
11 New Bond Street
London, England
Fishing hats

Icelandic Airlines, Inc. (Loftleidir)
15 W. 47 Street
New York, New York
Fishing arrangements for
groups (4 or more)

Irish International Airlines (Aer
Lingus)
572 Fifth Avenue
New York, New York
Arranges 7-day all-expense
Irish fishing trips. Address
airline or your travel agent
for current details

Irish Tourist Board
(Bord Failte Eirann)
Ireland House
33 E. 50 Street
New York, New York
Angler's Guide to Ireland.
Lists and brochures

Johnson, Herbert
38 New Bond Street
London, England
Fishing hats

Kahil's Rainbow Lodge
Mt. Tremper, New York
Props.: Dick and Blanche
Kahil
Lodging (fishing public)

Lake Hotel
Llangammarch Wells
Breconshire, Wales
Fishing on the Wye River

Lismore Estates Company
  Lismore
  County Waterford, Ireland
    Rods on Blackwater River in
    Lismore vicinity

Martin, S. H.
  Portmahon House
  Rialto
  Dublin, Ireland
    Rods on Blackwater River
    between Lismore and Bally-
    duff

McChrystal, Gen. Arthur
  Bristol Hotel
  Salzburg, Austria
    Rods on River Traun

Matamec Salmon Club
  P. O. Box 248
  Sept-Iles
  County Duplessis
  Quebec, Canada
    Rods on Moise River. *Ad-
    dress* W.-E. Gallienne

Mills, William & Son, Inc.
  21 Park Place
  New York, New York 10008
    Catalogue

Norm Thompson
  1805 N. W. Thurman
  Portland, Oregon 97209
    Catalogue and Angler's
    Guide, $1

Norwegian National Travel Office
  Norway House
  290 Madison Avenue
  New York, New York 10017
    Folders and guide, *Angling in
    Norway*

Olson, Olaf
  Laerdal, Norway
    Salmon flies and rods on
    Laerdal River

Orvis, Charles F. Company
  Manchester, Vermont
    Catalogue

Palace Hotel
  Grantown-on-Spey, Scotland
    Fishing on the Spey River
    and nearby lochs

Pennsylvania Angler, The
  Published monthly by the
  Pennsylvania Fish Commission
  South Office Building
  Harrisburg, Pennsylvania
    25 cents a copy, $2 yearly,
    three years $5

Poplar Camps
  Penniac
  York County
  New Brunswick, Canada
    Fishing on Cains River. *Ad-
    dress* Wendell V. Allen

Restigouche Reserve Salmon Water
Dept. of Lands and Mines
Frederickton
New Brunswick, Canada
Daily rods on Restigouche River. Apply Deputy Minister

River Ilen Angling Club
P. Armitage
Skibbereen
County Cork, Ireland
Rods on River Ilen

Rowland, Elmer E.
446 Park Avenue
Paterson, New Jersey
Taxidermist

Roy System Shoe Repair
26 Broadway
Denver, Colorado
Re-felting waders with aluminum rivets imbedded in woven felt.

Russ Fisher
Taxidermist
The Deer Skin Shop
Route 69
Flemington, New Jersey

Scottish Tourist Board
Room 23, 2 Rutland Place
Edinburgh, Scotland
List of fishing hotels and angling clubs

Shute, Frank
Shute & Company
566 Queen Street
Frederickton, New Brunswick
Limited number of rods in September on Southwest Miramichi

Sporting Book Service
Box 181
Rancocas, New Jersey
Lists

Starrett Instrument Co.
Norwich, Connecticut
Micrometer 1010

Steurer, Fritz
Rathausstrasse 5
Vienna I, Austria
Lists and folders

Suffolk Lodge Game Preserve
Brookhaven, New York
Prop.: Kenneth B. Hard
Lodging and rod fee

SUNNA Tourist Bureau
Bankastroeti 7
Reykjavik, Iceland
Package tours

The Sportsman's Vacation Guide
Recreation Associates
7 W. 44 Street
New York, New York 10036
Compiled, edited, and published by Robert O'Byrne.
Annual; $1.50

Theodore Gordon Flyfishers
24 E. 39 Street
New York, New York
    Non-profit organization de-
    voted to conservation; $10
    annual membership fee.

Thomas, Capt. Terry
c/o Milwards
Redditch, England
    Rods on salmon rivers of
    British Isles

Trout, Unlimited
900 Lapeer Avenue
Saginaw, Michigan
    National organization dedi-
    cated to the perpetuation of
    trout fishing. $10 annual
    membership fee includes
    subscription to bimonthly
    magazine *Trout*

Walker, Arthur L.
P.O. Box 249
Hempstead, New York
    Custom-made salmon and
    trout reels

Westwood, Frank
The Petersfield Bookshop
16a Chapel Street
Petersfield, Hants, England
    Lists

Where to Fish
8 Stratton Street
London, W. 1, England
    *Guide and Handbook to
    Fishing in Britain*, published
    by *The Field*. Annual giving
    details of 3,500 fishing sta-
    tions; illustrations, diagrams,
    detailed map: 25 shillings

Witherell, Mrs. Percy
Gilks P.O.
Northumberland County
New Brunswick, Canada
    Fishing at Blissfield on
    Southwest Miramichi River

Paul H. Young Company
23800 W. 8 Mile Road
Southfield, Michigan 48075
    Catalogue

Index

Abercrombie & Fitch, 63, 76, 135, 164, 283, 289, 290, 291, 292, 294, 296, 324

Adams fly, 283, 284

Adamson, W. A., 204, 205, 206, 216, 217, 264, 317

Alexandra fly, 47

Alport, Peter, 292, 298

Angler's Companion, The, 181, 184, 193, 323

Angler's Guide (Hardy), 298, 320, 328; *see also* Hardy Bros. (Alnwick) Ltd.

Angler's Guide (Norm Thompson), 113, 282, 283, 284, 287, 298, 323, 329; *see also* Norm Thompson

angling, compared to golf, 42, 140, 309

angling literature, 5, 6, 65, 74, 221-252; discursiveness of, 65, 234; duplication and repetition in, 234, 239, 240; short course in, 234-52; Big Ten classics, 233, 236, 237

angling scholar, aid in becoming, 234, 235, 236

Arte of Angling, The, 228–31, 233, 276, 305, 316, 317

Atlantic Salmon, The, 113, 203, 207, 208, 209, 213, 238, 249, 250, 323

Baby Catskill rods (Leonard), 104, 111, 287

backing, 176, 197, 198, 199, 205, 216, 217, 278, 279, 283, 285, 286, 315

bamboo, 31, 106, 107, 109, 175, 212, 283, 287, 289

bantam rods, 34, 104, 110, 314

barbs, off hooks, 33, 48, 303, 308

barracuda, 24, 25

bass, 10, 11, 29, 30, 80, 101, 153, 211, 212, 218, 309, 310

Beaudex reel (J. W. Young), 220, 292

Beaverkill River, N. Y., 8, 56, 118, 122, 125, 128, 141, 189, 261, 285, 295, 312

Berners, Dame Juliana, 75, 221, 228, 232, 233, 234, 236, 238, 240, 242, 247, 252, 321

Betsy streamer, 40, 142, 144, 145, 146, 147, 148, 149, 294

bibliography: of angling, 232, 234, 235; of ichthyology, 232

"big bait, big fish" premise, 36, 68

Black Ant fly, 135

Black Doctor fly, 160, 188, 303

Black Dose fly, 191, 199, 303

Blue Charm fly, 160, 199, 249, 303

Blue Doctor fly, 303

Blue Dun fly, 94, 283

bluegills, 11, 12, 153

Blue Spider fly, 142, 143, 144

boat fishing, 26, 29, 35, 69–70, 132-3, 175, 177

Bogdan reel, 315

Boswell: to A. H. E. Wood ("Jock Scott"), 249, 252; to Capt. Marryat (Halford), 246, 252; to Dame Juliana (John McDonald), 252; to Theodore Gordon (John McDonald), 252

Bowlker, Charles, 131, 236, 244

Britain and British, 159, 160, 194, 195, 196, 204, 207, 209, 217

British tackle, 36, 47, 48, 159, 204, 209, 217, 249, 297, 298

brook trout, 13, 14, 65, 87, 150

brown trout, 14, 15, 65, 68, 77, 80, 83, 86, 87, 128, 130, 145, 146, 150, 189, 310, 311
bucktail flies, 51, 56, 142, 200
Butcher fly, 303

Caddis grub, 142
Cahill bivisible spider fly, 56, 122, 128, 141, 142, 143, 144, 147, 287
Cahill Dark, fly, 68, 83
Cahill Light, fly, 68, 82, 83, 85, 86, 142, 284, 286
cannibal trout, 59, 95
casting, see fly-casting
Catskills, 76, 77, 121, 267
chalk streams, 8, 62, 190
changing flies, 122, 266, 308
char, 9, 159
Charles, anglers named, 131, 132
Cinnamon Ant fly, 135
coarse fish, 192
Coiner, Charles, 129–30, 131, 132
collecting and fishing, 273, 274, 277, 302
color-sensitivity of fish, 88, 89
Compleat Angler, The, 5, 221–32, 233, 237, 306, 307, 323; editions of, 226–7
Conrad fly, 199
Conroy reel, 315
Cooper nymphs, 283, 284
Cosseboom fly, 303
Cotton, Charles, 110, 131, 222–3, 225, 227, 229, 231, 232, 233, 237, 316, 323
couples, fishing, 67
"creating a hatch," 249, 265
creel, 51, 140, 274
cutthroat trout, 15

deep-sea fishing, 20, 26, 27
Deren, Jimmy, 83, 84, 318
Deutsch, Hermann, 268
distance, casting, 37, 41, 204, 216
double-line haul, 41, 111, 112–17, 212, 214, 215, 266, 282
"doubles," 56, 295

downstream fishing, 40, 64, 81, 90, 94, 96, 146, 147, 148
drag, 38, 270
dream river, 154, 155
drinking 164, 165, 167
dry flies, sizes 20 & 22, 35, 37, 142, 147, 160, 270, 271, 294, 295
dunkings and spills, 69, 80–1, 120, 164; see also mistakes
Durham Ranger fly, 303
Dusty Miller fly, 303

Edwards, Capt. Tommy, 117, 207, 319
England, 61, 137, 180–93, 224, 241, 246, 289, 297–8
Esopus creek, N. Y., 8, 11, 75–91, 98, 141, 143, 147, 189, 312
exasperations of trout fishing, 43, 46, 67, 68, 69, 74, 75, 193, 246, 270–1, 280, 314, 315; see also mistakes, dunkings
extra spools, 279, 283, 284, 286, 296; see also reel spools
extra tip, 287

Fairy reel (Mills), 111
felt-soling kits, 300
Field & Stream, 37, 113, 120, 121, 126, 140, 255, 259, 260, 261, 327
fish, as partners, 72, 269, 272, 305
fishing: by the pound, 30, 32, 33, 62, 151, 311; collecting and, 273, 277, 302; competition in, 21, 67, 70, 151, 208, 209, 241, 268; hobbies and, 273, 280; of the absurd, 10; shirt, 289
fishing fine, 31–41, 110, 111, 240, 251, 269–71; rewards of, 41, 42, 140, 306, 316
Fitzgerald, F. Scott, 23, 101, 259
fly: assortments, 287; boxes, 18, 121, 175, 244, 284, 303, 304
fly-casting: new style of, 41, 110, 111, 112–17, 204, 211–15, 218; orthodox, 31, 32, 114, 116, 117, 136, 214, 215
Flyfisher's Life, A, 121, 238, 251, 322
fly rod, 30, 31, 32, 33, 34, 35, 47, 61,

80, 81, 103–11, 112, 114, 159, 160,
199, 202, 204, 206, 207, 208, 209,
210, 211, 212, 213, 214, 215, 216,
218, 219, 277, 278, 279, 281, 283,
285, 286, 287, 289, 291; *see also*
Bantam rod, Midge rod, light tackle
forefinger grip on rod, 115, 214
Fox, Charles K., 131, 133–5, 137, 138,
216, 238, 251, 319
France and French, 62, 88, 136, 137,
230, 265
Francis, Francis, 237, 239, 242, 245,
251, 319
fulcrum, of the fly-cast, 114

gaff, ix, x, 175, 176
Gingrich, Jane Kendall, 26, 43, 70,
101, 106, 109, 119, 121, 136, 137,
154, 163, 164, 165, 167, 168, 175,
176, 187, 210, 310, 315; *see also*
Mason, Jane Kendall
Gingrich, Michael (my son, the fly-
fisher), 48–56, 57
Gordon, Theodore, 71, 76, 93, 246,
252, 321
grayling, 4, 5, 9, 13, 15, 138, 190, 191,
192
greasing the line, 145, 146, 249
Green Highlander fly, 198, 303
Green Worm (Leaf Roller) fly, 295
Grey Ghost streamer, 66
Grey, Sir Edward (Lord Grey of Fal-
loden), 190, 237, 239, 246, 247, 319
Groth, John, 82, 259
Grove, Alvin R., Jr., 134, 238, 251, 319

hair wing flies, 199, 294
Hairy Mary fly, 260, 303
Halford, Frederic M., 133, 237, 245,
246, 251, 252
Hardy Bros. (Alnwick) Ltd., 22, 23,
35, 47, 104, 107, 158, 213, 219, 220,
275, 283, 286, 291, 295, 296, 297–8,
302, 315, 320, 328
Hardy Corona silk line, 36, 286, 297
Hardy Lightweight reels, 296, 297,
298, 302, 315

Hardy L.R.H. Lightweight reel, 217,
286, 296, 298
Hemingway, Ernest, 20–7, 30, 33, 101,
265, 307
Henshall, Dr. James Alexander, 218
Hewitt, E. R., 28, 42, 71, 75, 90,
92–102, 133, 140, 142, 147, 149,
208, 209, 215, 216, 219, 237, 239,
249, 250, 251, 263, 267, 273, 288,
310, 320
"high-speed high-line" casting, 136,
214
Hills, Major John Waller, 235, 239,
242, 244, 245, 313, 320
hip boots, 64, 69, 158, 298
hobbies and fishing, 273, 280
horsing in, of fish, x, 24, 50, 52, 158,
210
"hung up," 68, 69, 314

index finger on rod, 115, 214

Jassid fly, 135, 142, 294
Jeannie fly, 18
Jennings, Preston, 85–91, 320
"Jock Scott" (Donald G. H. Rudd),
207, 249, 252, 322
Jock Scott fly, 198, 199, 260, 303
Johnson, Dr. Samuel, 223, 313, 315

Kerlee, Charles, 92–5, 97, 99, 131, 132,
133
Kerlee, Vivian, 92, 93, 97, 132
Kienbusch, Carl Otto von, 229, 231,
317
knot(s): nail, 126; wedge, 125; leader,
125, 126

La Branche, George M. L., 133, 215,
237, 249, 250, 251, 273, 310, 320
Lady Amherst fly, 303
Landex reel (J. W. Young), 176, 292,
293
landing net, 39, 198, 274, 300, 301
Lang, Andrew, 221, 224, 231, 238,
239, 306, 316
leader(s), 31, 36, 47, 48, 51, 89, 90,

111, 120, 123, 124, 125, 145, 146,
158, 176, 208, 209, 216, 217, 218,
263, 270, 271, 273, 274, 283, 284,
285, 286, 300, 310, 311, 314; casting
the, 123, 285; length of, 123, 124,
285, 314; straighteners, 37, 123, 243,
300; *see also* tippets
left hand: in casting, 113, 114, 116,
117, 204, 212; in reeling, 278
Leonard, H. L. rods, 104, 283, 287,
289
Letort Beetle, 135, 142, 144, 295
light tackle, 6, 11, 34–42, 103, 104,
105, 112, 114, 123, 124, 133, 135,
159, 160, 175, 199, 200, 204–20,
250, 263, 269–72, 279, 282, 283,
285, 286, 287, 291, 314; *see also*
Bantam rod, Midge rod, tippets
line dressing, 145, 146, 270, 300
line dryer, 286
lines, 36, 41, 43, 111, 116, 117, 145,
146, 197, 199, 208, 277, 278, 279,
283, 284, 286, 297, 298; *see also*
leaders, tippets
"locators," 40, 143
Logie fly, 303
longevity of anglers, 239, 273, 314

McClane, A. J., 37, 41, 70, 71, 84, 99,
108, 110, 112, 113, 115, 118–28,
133, 154, 155, 164, 165, 168, 191,
206, 211, 214, 250, 251, 261, 267,
268, 284, 300, 313, 321
McDonald, John, 236, 238, 252, 261,
321
March Brown fly, 249, 303
Maribou, white streamer, 142, 310, 311
Marinaro, Vincent, 133, 134, 238, 251
Markham, Gervase, 228, 233, 243, 244,
314, 321
marlin, 21, 22, 26
Mar Lodge fly, 176, 303
Marryat, Capt. G. S., 133, 246, 252
Marston, R. B., 226, 235, 321
Martha Marie rod (Paul Young), 291,
293
Mason, Jane Kendall, 21, 22, 23, 26

Mickey Finn streamer, 51, 142
micrometer, 301–2, 330
midge flies, 34, 35, 36, 37, 38, 111,
117, 123, 134, 135, 142, 150, 160
260, 270, 271, 273, 283, 292, 294,
295, 313
Midge rod (Paul Young), 11, 12, 35,
97, 103–8, 110–11, 117, 132, 133,
135, 146, 205, 211, 212, 213, 217,
218, 291, 293, 310
midge rods, 34, 35, 104, 105, 117, 207,
264, 278, 279, 283, 286, 287, 291.
midnight sun, 156, 166
Mills, Wm. & Son, Inc., N. Y., 104,
111, 216, 288–9, 295, 296, 301,
329; *see also* Leonard, H. L. rods
minutae, 135, 142, 251, 271, 293, 294,
295
Miramichi River, New Brunswick, 99,
127, 130, 132, 133, 258, 267, 325,
327, 331
mistakes, 67, 68, 69, 70, 80, 120, 271,
314
Mitchell fly, 303
Montana nymph, 142
Mottram, James Cecil, 215, 322
Muddler Minnow fly, 284, 294, 295
muskellunge, 29, 30, 67

naturalist–anglers, 133, 134, 245
net, landing, 39, 198, 274, 300, 301
Neversink River, N.Y., 71, 92, 93–9,
102, 131, 132, 133, 153
Neversink Skater, *see* spider
Newman, Ellis, 94, 113, 115, 118, 212
Night Hawk fly, 303
Norm Thompson, 282–7, 291, 292,
295, 296, 323, 329; *see also* Angler's
Guide (Norm Thompson)
nymphs, 14, 40, 75, 85, 86, 87, 88, 89,
90, 94, 96, 105, 111, 142, 144, 147,
149, 250, 270, 284, 287, 294, 295

Orvis, Chas. F. Co., 104, 105, 107,
135, 214, 218, 283, 290, 291–2, 294,
295, 296, 329; *see also* Superfine rod
outfit, 282, 283, 284

Index

Parmachene Belle fly, 51, 68, 142
Parmachene Belle streamer, 13
partners, 72, 269, 305
Payne rods, 104, 105, 283
Perfectionist rod (Paul Young), 108, 293
Pezon et Michel (Charles Ritz) rods, 107, 213, 283
Pink Lady fly, 17, 143
point system of scoring, 149, 150
Practical Fly Fisherman, The, 41, 113, 238, 250, 251, 321
Prefontaine fly, 219
price differences, 296

Quack Royal Coachman fly, 40, 99, 142, 284
Quill Gordon fly, 286

rainbow trout, 14, 38, 54, 65, 67, 68, 80, 87, 96, 99, 123, 150, 295
rainwear, 162, 299
Ratface McDougall fly, 142, 260
reel(s), 93, 94, 110, 111, 176, 210, 220, 243, 277, 278, 279, 283, 285, 286, 290, 291, 292, 293, 315; mounting of, 278-9
reel above rod, playing fish, 278-9
reel below rod, casting, 278-9
reel spools, 279, 283, 284, 285, 286, 296; *see also* extra spools
release, of fish, x, 39, 42, 48, 49, 65, 77, 122, 140, 141, 189, 206, 219, 269, 272
Renault, Juliette K., 153, 154
Renault, Louis, 153, 154, 211, 308
retrieve, 40, 68, 90, 145, 146, 147, 148, 278, 315
revival, of fish, 39, 206
rhythm, 113, 116, 212, 266
Ritz, Charles, 46, 60, 67, 70, 108, 121, 131, 135-8, 200, 213, 214, 238, 251, 267, 283, 322
Robb, James, 235, 243, 322
rocks, 157, 159, 162, 186, 206, 217, 267, 303, 314,
rod-set, insurance against, 279

rod tip, 146, 198, 211, 213, 309
Royal Coachman fly, 86, 87, 88, 89, 283
Rudd, Donald G. H. ("Jock Scott"), 207, 237, 249, 252, 322

salmon: average, 158, 159, 161, 176, 177, 178, 186, 197; beaching of, x, 158, 198, 199; contrasted to brown trout, 16, 130; effect of sunshine, 157, 178; jumps, 18, 19, 138, 218; literature, 18, 207, 247, 248, 249, 250; non-taking jumps, 188; par for playing, x, 201, 206, 219; the *persona* of, 16; photographing jumps, 138, 218; record, 158, 161, 176, 177, 178; taking times 197
salmon flies, 17, 18, 117, 160, 188, 191, 198, 199, 200, 219, 220, 302, 303, 304
Schwiebert, Ernest G., 133, 144, 238, 251, 258, 288, 322
scoring, systems of, 149-50, 151; score-card, 142
Scrope, William, ix, 8, 237, 239, 247-248, 249, 263, 265, 322
sea lice, 176, 188
sea trout, 9, 159, 160, 161, 168, 190, 191, 192, 193, 205
"set" in rods, insurance against, 279
Shaw, Helen, 238, 252, 259, 260, 322
Silver Blue fly, 200, 249, 303
Silver Doctor fly, 160, 199, 200, 303
Silver Grey fly, 200, 303
Silver Rat fly, 198
Silver Wilkinson fly, 160, 200, 303
sink-tip line, 283, 315
Skues, G. E. M., 3, 14, 221, 237, 247, 273, 322
snobbery and the dry fly, 245, 246, 247, 254; salmon versus trout, 189, 218; trout versus grayling, 189, 192
"solitaire" in fishing, 139
spider, fishing the, 17, 56, 122, 128, 142, 143, 144, 147, 148, 149, 150, 200, 250, 270, 287
spills and dunkings, 69, 80-1, 120, 164

spinning, 41, 61, 133, 254, 274, 289, 292
Stewart, W. C., 237, 242, 244, 245, 246, 323
strain, on rod and leader, 208, 209, 210, 211, 212, 213, 215, 218, 278
Strawman nymph, 105, 294
stream fishing, 6, 11, 27, 65, 67–9, 70, 71, 75, 93, 140–9, 233, 311, 314
streamers, 13, 40, 56, 66, 120, 121, 142, 145, 200, 211, 286, 294, 310
sunshine and salmon, 157, 178
Superfine rod (Orvis), 107, 218, 291, 314, 315
Supervisor streamer, 142, 145

tailer, x, 219
tarpon, 132, 218, 220
tempering of an angler, 309, 316
terrestrials, 134
thinking, role in fishing, 74, 273, 302, 303, 305, 306, 308, 309
Thor sea trout fly, 160
Thunder & Lightning fly, 191, 303
tiger trout, hybrid of brook and brown, 13, 120, 121
tippets, 36, 37, 38, 39, 40, 74, 80, 89, 90, 91, 111, 120, 146, 175, 176, 200, 270, 283, 284, 285, 288, 293, 295, 310, 311, 314; see also leaders
tipping, of guides, 201
Torrish fly, 303
Treatysse of Fysshynge with an Angle, 152, 228, 232, 233, 234, 236, 238, 240, 242, 247, 252, 321
trees, 157, 158, 167, 178, 314, 315
trout, see brook, brown, rainbow, tiger; see also grayling and cutthroat trout
Turner, E. Horsfall, 117, 319
20/20 angling, 15, 34–43, 123, 218, 270, 271

underwear, cashmere, 164; ski, 162, 164

upstream fishing, 38, 40, 41, 94, 96, 147, 148, 244

Venables, Bernard, 181, 184–6, 187, 188, 193, 195, 323
Vom Hofe reel, 315
von Kienbusch, Carl Otto, see Kienbusch

waders, 47, 64, 69, 82, 119, 158, 162, 206
wading, wet, 47
wading shoes, 289
wading staff, 275 289
Walton, Izaak, 221–31, 232, 233, 234, 237, 239, 241, 242, 247, 248, 273, 306, 307, 316, 323; plagiarism charges against, 221, 228–31, 306, 307
wedge knot, 125
Whiskers fly, 17, 219
White Wulff fly, 17, 160, 286
wind, 157, 158, 162, 213, 214, 314
Winston rods, 104, 283, 287
women, fishing with, 67–71, 202
Wood, A. H. E., 237, 249, 289, 322
Wooly Worm fly, 284
Wulff, Lee, 35, 113, 133, 138, 203–20, 238, 249, 257, 258, 267, 286, 313, 323

Young, J. W. fly reels, 292–93
Young, Jack, 106, 290, 294
Young, Martha Marie, 290, 294
Young, Paul, 35, 97, 103–11, 117, 133, 144, 147, 210, 212, 215, 218, 283, 287, 290, 291, 293–6, 299, 331; see also Midge rod, Martha Marie rod, Perfectionist rod
Young, Paul, Jr., 105, 106

Zen, 268, 272
Zern, Ed, 255, 258, 262

A NOTE ABOUT THE AUTHOR

ARNOLD GINGRICH, founding editor of *Esquire* in 1933 and publisher of that magazine since 1952, was born in Grand Rapids, Michigan, and was graduated from the University of Michigan in 1925. Although his reputation as editor, publisher, novelist, and essayist is a distinguished one, he is known among his angling friends as an ardent fly fisherman and as a proponent and enthusiastic practitioner of "midge" fly fishing, the art of taking big trout and salmon with short, super-light rods. Mr. Gingrich, a collector of fine rods and fly tackle, is also a collector of angling literature, and his own book reflects the great angler-writer tradition begun by Izaak Walton.

A NOTE ON THE TYPE

THIS BOOK is set in *Electra*, a Linotype face designed by W. A. DWIGGINS. This face cannot be classified as either modern or old-style. It is not based on any historical model, nor does it echo any particular period or style. It avoids the extreme contrasts between thick and thin elements that mark most modern faces, and attempts to give a feeling of fluidity, power, and speed.

W. A. Dwiggins (1880-1956) was born in Martinsville, Ohio, and studied art in Chicago. In 1904 he moved to Hingham, Massachusetts, where he built a solid reputation as a designer of advertisements and as a calligrapher. He began an association with the Merganthaler Linotype Company in 1929, and over the next twenty-seven years designed a number of book types for that firm. Of especial interest are the Metro series, Electra, Caledonia, Eldorado, and Falcon. In 1930, Dwiggins first became interested in marionettes, and through the years made many important contributions to the art of puppetry and the design of marionettes.

Binding based on designs by W. A. Dwiggins